D0216398

THE CHANGING CONTRACT ACROSS GENERATIONS

SOCIAL INSTITUTIONS AND SOCIAL CHANGE
An Aldine de Gruyter Series of Texts and Monographs
EDITED BY
Michael Useem • James D. Wright

Larry Barnett, **Legal Construct, Social Concept: A Macrosociological Perspective on Law**

Vern L. Bengtson and W. Andrew Achenbaum, **The Changing Contract Across Generations**

Remi Clignet, **Death, Deeds, and Descendants: Inheritance in Modern America**

Mary Ellen Colten and Susan Gore (eds.), **Adolescent Stress: Causes and Consequences**

Rand D. Conger and Glen H. Elder, Jr., **Families in a Changing Society: Hard Times in Rural America**

Joel A. Devine and James D. Wright, **The Greatest of Evils: Urban Poverty and the American Underclass**

G. William Domhoff, **The Power Elite and the State: How Policy is Made in America**

Paula S. England, **Comparable Worth: Theories and Evidence**

Paula S. England, **Theory on Gender/Feminism on Theory**

George Farkas, Robert P. Grobe, and Daniel Sheehan, **Human Capital or Cultural Capital?**

F. G. Gosling (ed.), **Risk and Responsibility**

Richard F. Hamilton and James D. Wright, **The State of the Masses**

Gary Kleck, **Point Blank: Guns and Violence in America**

David Knoke, **Organizing for Collective Action: The Political Economies of Associations**

Dean Knudsen and JoAnn L. Miller (eds.), **Abused and Battered: Social and Legal Responses to Family Violence**

Theodore R. Marmor, **The Politics of Medicare** (*Second Edition*)

Clark McPhail, **The Myth of the Madding Crowd**

Clark McPhail, **Acting Together: The Organization of Crowds**

John Mirowsky and Catherine E. Ross, **Social Causes of Psychological Distress**

Steven L. Nock, **The Costs of Privacy: Surveillance and Reputation in America**

Talcott Parsons on National Socialism (*Edited and with an Introduction by Uta Gerhardt*)

Carolyn C. and Robert Perrucci, Dena B. and Harry R. Targ, **Plant Closings: International Context and Social Costs**

Robert Perrucci and Harry R. Potter (eds.), **Networks of Power: Organizational Actors at the National, Corporate, and Community Levels**

James T. Richardson, Joel Best, and David G. Bromley (eds.), **The Satanism Scare**

Alice S. Rossi and Peter H. Rossi, **Of Human Bonding: Parent-Child Relations Across the Life Course**

David G. Smith, **Paying for Medicare: The Politics of Reform**

Martin King Whyte, **Dating, Mating, and Marriage**

James D. Wright, **Address Unknown: The Homeless in America**

James D. Wright and Peter H. Rossi, **Armed and Considered Dangerous: A Survey of Felons and Their Firearms**

James D. Wright, Peter H. Rossi, and Kathleen Daly, **Under the Gun: Weapons, Crime, and Violence in America**

Mary Zey, **Banking on Fraud: Drexel, Junk Bonds, and Buyouts**

THE CHANGING CONTRACT
ACROSS GENERATIONS

Vern L. Bengtson and W. Andrew Achenbaum

EDITORS

ALDINE DE GRUYTER
New York

About the Editors

Vern L. Bengtson is AARP/University Professor of Gerontology and Sociology at the University of Southern California, and Past President of the Gerontological Society of America. His publications include *The Social Psychology of Aging; Youth, Generations, and Social Change; Grandparenthood; The Measurement of Intergenerational Relations; Emergent Theories of Aging,* and *The Course of Later Life.*

W. Andrew Achenbaum is professor of history at the University of Michigan, Ann Arbor, and is Deputy Director of its Institute of Gerontology. His research focuses on the history of the elderly in the United States. He currently is completing a book on the history of gerontology. Among his numerous publications are *Images of Old Age in America; 1790 to the Present* and *Social Security: Visions and Revisions.*

ALDINE DE GRUYTER
A division of Walter de Gruyter, Inc.
200 Saw Mill River Road
Hawthorne, New York 10532

This publication is printed on acid-free paper

Library of Congress Cataloging-in-Publication
The Changing contract across generations / edited by Vern L. Bengtson and W. Andrew Achenbaum.
    p. cm. — (Social institutions and social change)
    Includes bibliographical references and index.
    ISBN 0-202-30459-0. — ISBN 0-202-30460-4 (pbk.)
    1. Youth—Attitudes—Cross-cultural studies. 2. Aged—Attitudes—Cross-cultural studies. 3. Conflict of generations—Cross-cultural studies. I. Bengtson, Vern L. II. Achenbaum, W. Andrew.
III. Series.
HQ796.C4515   1993
305.2—dc20   92-39624
                                           CIP

Manufactured in the United States of America

10 9 8 7 6 5 4 3 2 1

To the memory of Lawrence Cremin, Ph.D.
1929–1991
Scholar, Teacher, Policymaker, Friend
Director, the Spencer Foundation
who funded the conference on which this volume is based

Contents

Preface

This volume presents commentaries by a multidisciplinary group of social scientists about new developments in basic human relations: bonds
between generations and age groups, and the implicit "contract" among
them concerning solidarity, support, and succession across the adult life
cycle. The purpose of this volume is to examine whether the age-old
expectations and obligations among and between age groups may today
be changing, in light of profound demographic shifts and public policy
alterations reflecting population aging.

That problems about the *contract across generations* are not new is
suggested from even a cursory examination of Hebrew scripture, Greco-
Roman literature, classical Eastern and Western myths, and 1960s rock-
and-roll lyrics. Absalom, the heir apparent, rebels against his father,
King David, and is killed. Oedipus slays his father, sleeps with his
mother, and is forever cursed. Godfather Zeus eats his offspring.
Parent-child conflicts have been a perennial theme in Western literature.

However, something new seems to have happened in the latter decades of the 20th century. Traditional problems of generational relations
have been altered by phenomena of worldwide population aging—in
which average life expectancy has almost doubled in the Western world
during the past century, and the "normal" balance of generational support has tilted toward the upper end of the life cycle. As children become contemporaries of their parents, issues of filial responsibility are
bound to be renegotiated. Societies rightly accustomed to investing in
the future through their children now worry about the mounting costs
of *eldercare*.

In consequence there has arisen a debate within the last decade concerning "generational equity" and "justice between generations"—issues which would have appeared quite foreign to early 20th century
politicians and policymakers. Once accused of viewing all older people
as marginal and poor, journalists now exaggerate elders' power in the
voting booth and chide them as "greedy geezers." A new class warfare,
they claim, has emerged—with classes defined along age or generational
lines.

Origins of this Volume

These pages reflect multidisciplinary perspectives on emerging issues of generational and age group relationships from an international group of scholars. Two organizations provided the impetus for this debate, and for the collection of scholarly papers which is published here.

The first was the Gerontological Society of America. The GSA organizes its annual scientific meetings around a theme, chosen by the incoming president, reflecting a current scientific issue of importance to the multidisciplinary community of gerontologists. This theme characteristically reflects the longstanding scientific focus of the president's research activities. The GSA President also has the responsibility to develop a midyear symposium to focus on the topic from specialists' perspectives. Upon his election as President in 1989 Vern Bengtson, a sociologist and gerontologist who has been conducting research on generational relationships for the past two decades, selected as the theme for the 1990 annual meeting *Generations: Continuities, Conflicts, and Reciprocities*. He chose a related theme for the midyear Presidential Symposium, organized for February 1991: *The New Contract Between Generations: Social Science Perspectives on Cohorts in the 21st Century*.

The second organization supporting this venture was the Spencer Foundation, which has long been interested in educational and developmental issues that are relevant to contemporary society. In October of 1989 the late President of the Spencer Foundation, Dr. Lawrence Cremin, convened in Chicago a conference of social and behavioral scientists interested in gerontology to consider "life span education" issues. James E. Birren chaired this meeting. One of the themes that emerged was the importance of the changing relationships between age groups during the 20th century, alterations created by unprecedented population aging.

The Spencer Foundation encouraged development of dialogue around this emerging theme, so Bengtson wrote Lawrence Cremin about supporting an expanded conference in conjunction with the GSA's midyear Presidential Symposium. Cremin pledged the Spencer Foundation's support, and the planning for this volume began.

Support for the conference also came from the Andrus Gerontology Center of the University of Southern California, through funding provided by Dean Edward Schneider, and from the American Association of Retired Persons, through its support for the newly established AARP/University Chair in Gerontology at the University of Southern California. None of these organizations, it should be noted, is responsible for the opinions expressed by authors or participants in the conference.

Participants and Discussants

Those invited to contribute to the conference and to this volume represent some of the most prominent social scientists who have written recently on the topic of generational and cohort relations. They were chosen to represent the spectrum of social science disciplines and specialties currently researching changing age group relations: anthropology, economics, gerontology, history, policy analysis, sociology, and social psychology.

Authors prepared drafts of chapters for discussion and criticism prior to the conference, which was held at the University of Southern California in February 1991. Discussion at the conference resulted in substantial revision of first drafts—to a degree unusual in our experience as editors.

Each chapter was critiqued by two or three discussants, who also served as an editorial panel for the volume. Much of the unity of the resulting chapters is due to their comments and suggestions, and for this they deserve considerable thanks. The discussants were:

Dr. Carlfred Broderick, Professor of Sociology at the University of Southern California and Director of the Marriage and Family Therapy Training Program

Mr. Jack Cornman, Executive Director of the Gerontological Society of America (now Executive Director of the American Anthropological Association)

Dr. Rose Gibson, Faculty Associate at the Institute for Social Research and Professor, School of Social Work, University of Michigan

Dr. Mark Hayward, Associate Professor of Gerontology and Sociology, University of Southern California (now Associate Professor of Sociology and Assistant Director of The Gerontology Center, Pennsylvania State University)

Dr. Tom Hickey, Professor of Public Health at the University of Michigan and past President of the Gerontological Society of America

Dr. Jill Quadagno, the Mildred and Claude Pepper Chair of Gerontology and Professor, Department of Sociology, Florida State University

Dr. Judith Treas, Chair of the Department of Sociology at the University of California, Irvine

Dr. Lillian Troll, Professor of Human Development at the University of California, San Francisco

Organization of the Volume

Edited volumes are notoriously uneven. In our experience some contributors obviously are brighter than the editors; others never quite get the point of the title. Ultimately, it is the responsibility of the editors to try to impose some coherence on a volume, if a sense of uniformity and unity of purpose does not emerge naturally in the editorial course of critiques of first drafts and subsequent revisions. In this volume, the editors, themselves prodded by several authors, did try to nurture closure on possible strategies for linking macro- and microlevel issues involved in the *changing contract* across age groups. The brief introductions that head each part of the volume were written using the themes set forth in Chapter 1 and restated in Chapter 13. Even so, discerning readers will notice that not all authors share the distinction drawn between a *generation* and a *cohort* that Bengtson attempts in Chapter 1 and the Rileys advanced early in the conference. These pages bristle—ever so politely—with disagreements over what past trends about age group relations portend for our future selves.

Because of the diversity of approaches taken in these chapters, and because so many conceptual and methodological issues remain unresolved, the editors have organized this volume to reflect the different points of view, rather than to try to synthesize them. In Part I, the conference organizer and senior editor, Vern Bengtson, presents the central issues as he summarized them in his conference keynote paper, an elaboration of his presidential address to the Gerontological Society of America in 1990. Co-editor Andrew Achenbaum has amplified them and placed them in a comparative-historical framework. Against this framework of nomographic and idiosyncratic historical factors, the chapters in Part II provide greater understanding of the importance of sociotemporal contexts in shaping *generational contracts*, real or implied. The three chapters in Part III delve into conflict as they turn the argument on its head and show unexpected opportunities for generational consensus. The pair of chapters in Part IV deal with familial networks, typically the mainspring of generational relations, as an institution in sociohistorical contexts that are malleable. In Part V, macrosocial institutional politics and policy implications are reflected in commentaries that seek to recast the current debates.

Readers should not expect a "party line" to emerge from these pages, but they should appreciate the extent to which various authors tried to take account of their colleagues' differing perspectives on critical issues. By and large these essays seek to recast basic issues of age group responsibilities and expectations in ways that might more fruitfully inspire creative scholarship and fresh thinking about generational politics in an aging society.

Acknowledgments

There are many individuals who should be thanked for their contributions to this volume. First and foremost is Pauline Robinson, until recently UPS Professor of Gerontology at the University of Southern California, who has served as managing editor of the volume and whose contributions are reflected on every page.

Thanks go to Linda Hall, Administrative Coordinator in the Andrus Gerontology Center of the University of Southern California, who planned the GSA Presidential Mid-Year Symposium, managed the manuscript preparation, and saw to the countless exchanges between authors and editors that resulted in this volume. Her contributions are also reflected in every page (and reference) of this volume.

Acknowledgments are due to Christopher Hilgeman, Technical Assistant in the Andrus Gerontology Center, who took care of the financial arrangements of the conference and volume and provided the graphics for the publication; and to Jodi Catherine Kraus, who assisted in the manuscript processing of each chapter's several drafts.

Thanks to past presidents of the Gerontological Society (James Birren, Barbara Silverstone, Dick Adelman, and Jack Rowe) who encouraged the development of the conference and lobbied for support from the Gerontological Society; and to Leonard Cain, Professor of Sociology at Portland State University, who provided valuable comments on the first draft of the manuscript.

Finally, we want to acknowledge our debt to Dr. Larry Cremin, late President of the Spencer Foundation, beloved Professor and President of Columbia University's Teachers' College, and an internationally recognized scholar in educational policy. Dr. Cremin's untimely death occurred four months after the conclusion of the conference he enabled. This volume is dedicated to his memory, in recognition of his many contributions to the study of the life course and lifelong learning.

Vern L. Bengtson
W. Andrew Achenbaum

Foreword

Policymakers and journalists in this country frequently comment that an aging society may bring with it age polarization or age divisiveness. The issue is often posed in terms of intergenerational conflict, reminiscent of the ways in which the so-called *generation gap* was described during the 1960s. At that time, the gap was said to be between college age students and their parents, but a number of studies showed that college students, in truth, shared the social and political views of their parents more often than not.

Today, many American observers are expressing concern about so-called conflict between workers (roughly aged 25 to 50) and retirees (roughly aged 60 and over). Now, as in the 1960s, the conflict may be more mirage than reality.

The aging society faces real problems of resource scarcity and resource distribution that are complicated by demographic changes in the population. But is it true that different age groups perceive the solutions to those problems quite differently? The available research evidence says "not so."

The adhesives between generations in the family appear to be as strong today as they were in earlier periods, and it may be that people's views of their family generational relations are projected onto their societal views of age groups, for there is little evidence of a politics of age developing in this country, nor of an "old-age bloc." These facts are probably reflections of another fact: that older persons, like younger, are very heterogeneous in social, political, ethnic, and economic terms.

In this volume, a wide array of issues and points of view are presented, as well as disagreements among authors. One example is whether the term *generation* or *age group* should be used. The very title of this book is itself controversial—has there been, indeed, a "contract" between generations at the societal level? Or is this only a metaphor that arises from the presumed contract between younger and older members within families? Either way, what is the true nature of that contract?

The problem of words becomes even greater when the question of "equity" arises. Whether the term to be used is generations or age groups, how is equity to be assessed? And when should it be assessed?

At a given point in historical time? Or, in the longer context of the life cycle, when successive cohorts reach their old age?

To suggest that we are presently caught up in words that may not reflect the realities is only to acknowledge that we are in a new field of inquiry, a field that brings together social scientists and policymakers. As one of the authors points out, it will take time to make clear the meaning of the term *generation*, just as, earlier, it took us a long time to make clear the meaning of the term *social class*. And it will take time to frame the issues more clearly than at present.

This volume is a step in the right direction. The editors have selected a first-rate group of contributors, all of them articulate; have let them speak for themselves; and have not attempted to push for agreements. The book therefore makes an important contribution by illustrating the complexities that face us, and some of the unreconciled differences, in our attempts to understand the relations between young and old in a rapidly changing society.

Bernice L. Neugarten

PART I

Conceptual and Contextual Issues in the Current "Generational" Debate

The chapters in this section set the stage for the forthcoming debate among social scientists and policymakers concerning age group responsibilities and rights in an increasingly aging society. The intent of these two chapters is to describe some parameters of past, contemporary, and future problems concerning age group and generational relations.

In Chapter 1, Vern Bengtson argues that something indeed is changing in the understanding of obligations and rights across age groups and generations. He analyzes the "traditional contract" concerning aging and succession within social groups, and documents the apparent changes in these norms. Based on these changes he predicts more age group conflicts in the 21st century; but at the same time, he notes greater potential for generational solidarity among individuals from differing birth cohorts who are aging together during ever-longer periods of time.

In Chapter 2, Andrew Achenbaum asserts the importance of historical context in analyzing the "problem of generations." He argues that generational relations most resemble a negotiation—or more precisely, a series of negotiations—in particular historical contexts. He presents three quite different case studies that reflect this negotiation: the American "revolutionary generation"; the generational theory reflected differently by Matthew and Luke in their accounts about Jesus in the New Testament; and the generational/class politics that are emerging in caring for Vietnam veterans. His analysis of these case studies is based on the trenchant observations of Karl Mannheim (1928/1952), the classical sociological theorist concerned with the succession of generations and consequent social change. He concludes with comments about the future of age group relations in the context of past negotiations.

1

Is the "Contract Across Generations" Changing? Effects of Population Aging on Obligations and Expectations Across Age Groups

Vern L. Bengtson

My concern in this chapter is with the obligations and expectations across groups who differ in age, and whether they may be changing in some unique ways as the result of population aging in the late 20th century.

The phrase chosen as the title of this volume—*The Changing Contract Across Generations*—may be misleading, since it implies at least three things about relations across age groups that may or may not exist:

1. Is it a *contract*, this complex set of expectations and obligations underlying relations between generations and between age groups that we find in contemporary societies? Certainly not in the legal definition of what is involved in a contract: a set of formal agreements binding parties within a specific exchange. However, in terms of the sociologist's concept of social norms, involving the unwritten informal expectations and obligations that create solidarity or conflict, and the negotiation of these in everyday life—yes, I think it may be called a *contract*.

2. Is it *changing*, this situation of relations and expectations among age groups? I think so; but historians and anthropologists may find more continuity than change in their assessment of what has been happening between age groups at the close of the 20th century.

3. What about the term *generations*, so frequently and casually employed in both mass media and scholarly writing? What is meant by the

term? We will be focusing on *groups defined by age* as units of social organization. But *which* are the social groups involved: the demographers' and economists' macrosocial categories based on year of birth (*age cohorts*)? Or the sociologists' and anthropologists' microsocial *generations within family lineages*? Or the European social historians' concept of *historical generations*, which refers to age cohorts (usually youth) who emerge as self-defined groups to become agents of change and forerunners of social innovation?

These semantic and conceptual distinctions are important. They relate directly to analysis of the new social problem that is the focus of this chapter. That new social problem, which has emerged during the last decades of the 20th century in industrialized societies, is the changing demographics of generational succession and expectations. The central argument I will be making can be summarized as follows:

1. We have reached a cultural watershed concerning the implicit understanding of rights and obligations between age groups and generations in human societies. Never before have so many elders lived so long; never before have so relatively fewer members of younger age groups lined up behind them in the succession of generations.
2. In consequence we are faced with new and historically unique dilemmas of family life and social policy agendas regarding the expectable life course and the succession of age groups. These dilemmas are reflected in emerging questions about social welfare, both private and public, directed to age groups, as well as in more general issues of conflict and solidarity between them. Can we afford an aging society? Can we afford to grow old in the 21st century?

The generational/age group dilemma we face can be traced to two significant changes during the 20th century: (1) the effects of worldwide population aging—the result of steadily increasing longevity and steadily decreasing fertility over the 20th century; and (2) the confusions and conflicts that have arisen in cultural values concerning aging, succession, productivity, and families. One possible consequence of these changes is that conflict between age groups in the 21st century may be considerably greater than conflicts experienced in previous historical eras. The second possible consequence, paradoxically, is the potential for greater solidarity between adult generations within the family, and possibly across age groups in the broader society, than has been experienced in the previous 500 generations of human recorded history.

What is the *contract across generations and age groups*? Put most simply, it is a set of shared expectations and obligations—what sociologists term

Table 1. The "Contract Across Generations" and Levels of Social Structure

Problem	Microsocial Mechanisms	Macrosocial Mechanisms
Biosocial generation and socialization	Family socialization	Public education
Gerosocial succession	Family sponsorship and aid (financial, emotional)	Public transfers; retirement
Geriatric dependencies	Family caregiving	Public support (Social Security and Medicare)

norms—regarding the aging of individuals and the succession of generations, through time and within social structures. There are three clusters of these expectations and obligations, and each has parallel mechanisms at the micro-and macrolevels of social structure (see Table 1). One set of expectations and obligations concerns biosocial generation and socialization: that the first will succor and bring up the second, who then will produce a third generation. A second set of expectations and obligations involves *gerosocial succession:* that the second generation will have sufficient resources to bring up the third, an expectation that in the past has most often been predicated on the retirement or death of the first generation—usually in their fifth or sixth decade of life. A third set of norms involves *geriatric dependencies:* that the first generation will be honored and helped during their decline—and death—by their descendants, the second or third generation.

This is the traditional image of the cycle of generations, at least from the standpoint of Western societies; this is the historical expectation regarding the normative contract of generations. In terms of the traditional life span of humans, the temporal boundary of this contract is 70 years, the biblical threescore and ten, with most of the first generation having died somewhat earlier than this.

But the traditional contract across generations and age groups, whether implicit or formal, has been altered by at least three factors: (a) demographic trends such as population aging; (b) the simultaneous political and economic trends of state-sponsored public welfare provisions during the 20th century; and (c) at the more personal level, changes in family structures (which have gone from an age pyramid to a beanpole in shape), with their attendant changes in demands and resources available to the family. Each of these factors has, in multiple ways, altered normative life course concerns for the average citizen of a Western industrial society, and also for public policy priorities regarding responsibilities toward aging citizens. Each has created changes in the generational/age group contract at both micro- and macrosocial levels of structure.

Therefore, the focus of this chapter will be on four issues:

1.   What is the traditional "problem of generations" in human societies, and how does this relate to conflicts and solidarities between emerging age groups today?

2.   What are some major concerns about age cohorts, and the implicit social contract between them, that have emerged at the macrosocial level in the last decades of the twentieth century?

3.   What are some concerns about generational relations in the family—the microsocial level—in contemporary Western societies?

4.   What do all of these concerns suggest about the future of the implicit "contract of generations"? Will there be more or less conflict in the 21st century?

Perspectives on Age Groups, Aging, and Social Change

First, what is the "traditional" problem of generations and age groups in human social structures? And what is new about it, in the contemporary context of worldwide population aging and social change?

Relations between age groups, and between generations within the family, have been the source of both profound solidarity and serious conflict throughout human history. In Western literature, there are the biblical stories of Job and his irreligious sons, the revolt of the young leaders in Jeremiah's time, and the problems of King David and his rebellious son Absalom. There is also the saga of the unfortunate Oedipus, killing his father unawares and forever cursed as the result; and the mistaken confidence of King Lear in his offspring. Such examples from Western literature (and there are similar accounts in the Eastern tradition; see Kelley, in press) suggest how tenuous the contract between family generations can be, and how severe the results of generational conflict can become. The problem of generations and aging, and the resulting difficulties of generational/age group succession, support, stability, and change, have represented one of the enduring human dilemmas throughout history.

Continuity, Change, and Adaptivity

The recurring problem of generations and age groups in human society boils down to this: the challenge of *ensuring group continuity over time, as well as adaptability and innovation in the face of time-related changes.*

First, how will the human group maintain enough *continuity of social order* over time, in the face of continual changes in its membership that reflect the life cycle of individual members—birth, aging, and generational succession? Second, how will the group foster *adaptivity to changing social and environmental circumstances*? Third, how will the group deal with differences or conflicts that arise between generations and between age groups, in pursuing a balance between continuity and innovation? (The term *group* here is used in its broadest sociological sense, as it applies to individual family units, to communities, or to larger social systems reflected in societal institutions and cultures.)

This challenge for human groups—to find the most desirable balance between continuity with the past and adaptability to a changing future environment—must occur in the context of changes in the nature and composition of the group, of which generational turnover is the most obvious, and in the context of changes in environmental circumstance, of which material needs are the most pressing. Moreover, this balancing of continuity and change with generational succession and the transfer of responsibility must be achieved without serious conflicts that would disrupt the group.

Conflicts and Solidarity

At the microsocial family level, conflicts within generational lineages are certainly not new—they are, in fact, the material for much of Western literature and drama (from Sophocles' *Oedipus Rex* to American television's *Falcon Crest*). Here the problems of generational succession—power and autonomy, as well as solidarity and affirmation—are portrayed in what passes as entertainment. Being a parent is a precarious enterprise, because children often seem to shun generational continuity in the service of their own autonomy and identity. Being a child is often a burden, since filial expectations may be unrealistic or onerous. Such is the plot line of much intergenerational family drama, along with the equally strong forces of intergenerational solidarity, reflecting affect, association, consensus, and exchanges between generations (see Rossi, Chapter 10, Riley & Riley, Chapter 9, and Foner, Chapter 6, in this volume).

At the macrosocial level, conflict versus solidarity between age groups is also reflected in history, though the evidence here is more ambiguous. Why do occasional societywide conflicts of "generations" (age groups) emerge at some periods of history, but not others? This question was the focus of Karl Mannheim's (1928/1952) seminal analysis of the problem of generations, and has been recently addressed by psychologists, sociologists, and historians (Hagestad, 1990; Simonton, 1984).

The answers seem to lie in the interaction of four factors: (a) a particular birth cohort with particular characteristics (for example, a larger size than preceding cohorts); (b) their growing up or coming to a turning point in life span development (for example, youth attaining maturity, or elders becoming aged); at the same time that there are (c) political or social events that are of traumatic historical significance (for example, the Vietnam War); and that produce (d) an awareness by significant members of the birth cohort that they are specially influenced by the historical event(s) (for example, the Vietnam War produced protests by youth across America). This set of events is what happened among American and European youth in the protests of the 1960s (see Bengtson, 1989), and the result was highly publicized conflict between age groups in Western society. This is what may also occur in elements of tomorrow's older age cohorts: We may see a revolution of the elderly in the next three or four decades, reflecting a truly *new problem of generations and age groups* in industrialized societies.

The New Problem of Age Groups and "Generations"

In the latter decades of the 20th century some new wrinkles seem to have been added to the age-old problem of generations. Judging from recent mass media accounts in the United States and Europe, the major protagonists of today's and tomorrow's "generation gap" are not limited to youth and the middle-aged—the classical case of "generational" confrontation, exemplified most recently in the revolt of the young during the 1960s. Rather, the focus has shifted to the oldest age group. The debate has begun to center on the economic, moral, and social obligations of the middle-aged and young to an ever-growing group of elderly; and, in turn, on the elders' obligations to those younger than themselves in our increasingly aging societies.

The rhetoric of this new confrontation between age groups has already become harsh. In 1988, the United States business magazine *Forbes* titled its cover story, "Cry, Baby: The Greedy Geezers Are Taking Your Inheritance." Its message: "Simply put, in economic terms we are consuming our children . . . The old are getting richer at the expense of the young" (Chakravarty, 1988, p. 222). A year later a cover story in *Der Spiegel*, the largest circulation German-language weekly publication, was titled "The Struggle of Generations: Young Against Old." It gives the opinion that there will be "battles without any mercy," and goes on to say, "Unique in the history of mankind . . . neither the state nor the communities are equipped for this clash: the power of the aged against the claims of the young" ("Kampf der Generationen," 1989). And political issues of elections reflect the continuing debate; for example, the *Washington Post* ran a front-page article under the heading, "Older Voters Drive Budget: Generational Divide Marks Benefits Battle" (1990).

It seems to me that the *new problem of generations and age groups*, like the old one, is rooted in issues of succession and power/autonomy expectations and resources. But what is new are two issues that make the problem different, in the latter years of the 20th century, from other periods of human experience:

1. Because of the phenomenon of population aging, especially notable in industrialized nations, and because of the life cycle position of the population members who are the target of potential conflict, the "generation gap" has moved up a generation. It is no longer youth versus elders, but rather elders versus middle-aged and youth.

2. The focus of the problem has shifted from *generations* to *age groups*, that is from family-based age conflicts to society-based age conflicts, and this has created an increase in the magnitude and complexity of the issues involved.

Population aging and resulting problems in age group interactions. Three recent trends have contributed to the problems of population aging and make the new concerns about relations between age groups especially salient for the 1990s and beyond. First, there have been dramatic *increases in life expectancy* during the 20th century, such that almost one in five citizens of many industrial societies are now above the age of 60, and great-grandparenthood has emerged as a common family structure in some populations.

Second, there have been *decreases in fertility*, with one result being fewer workers per pensioner than ever before (along with fewer second- and third-generation family members to care for dependent elders).

Third, there have been increased *policy concerns about welfare costs and public expenditures* targeted for various age groups, especially for the elderly as contrasted with the young. These reflect broader debates over basic cultural values: issues of individualism versus collectivism; issues of equity versus entitlement; issues of filial piety versus needs of a younger generation. These policy concerns have resulted in growing debates over "generational equity" in macrolevel public policy discussions (Achenbaum, 1989b; Bengtson, Marti, & Roberts, 1991; Binstock, in press; Kingson, Hirshorn, & Cornman, 1986; Quadagno, 1990; Thomson, 1989, and Chapter 11 in this volume; Walker, 1990a, and Chapter 7 in this volume). But at the microsocial level of families, as is increasingly reflected in the mass media, anxieties are expressed over providing care for the elderly and reciprocities between generations in kinship relations.

From generations to age groups. Certainly as social scientists we should be precise about our terminology and concepts, but the term *generation* is being used in the literature in multiple ways, with the meaning frequently ambiguous and dependent on the context in which a particular writer employs it.

The several meanings of *generation* can be seen in recently published works by scholars. Kotlikoff (1992) titles his volume *Generational Accounting;* what he appears to mean by generation is a group of individuals who have in common nothing more or less than birth in a particular year or interval. Strauss and Howe (1991) based their *Generations: The History of America's Future, 1984–2069* on the concept of a "cohort group . . . whose boundaries are fixed by peer personality" (p. 60).

On the other hand, Russell (1982), in *The Baby Boom Generation and the Economy,* refers to those born between 1946 and 1964 as a *generation.* This encompasses an 18-year span of births, and the defining characteristic of the generation appears to be shared membership in a period of higher American fertility than occurred prior to 1946 or after 1964—ignoring the vast diversity in other demographic characteristics of those born during this time, or the fact that some "Baby Boomers" have children who, by this definition, are also members of the "Baby Boom Generation." Russell's concept is in contrast to the focus by family scholars, such as Hill (1970), who in *Family Development in Three Generations* uses *generation* to refer solely to family position in the sequence of biosocial ranked descent.

And then there is the tradition of European social theorists, following Mannheim's (1928/1952) "The Problem of Generations," who have discussed subsets of birth cohorts as they have influenced social change via self-defined awareness of "generational uniqueness."

These conceptual confusions will continue to disable productive discussion and empirical assessment of issues of justice between "generations" unless we answer the question, *Which* generations? It appears to me that four forms of age groupings must be distinguished in discourse and analysis. Table 2 summarizes the distinction between the popular terms and the social scientific terms reflecting the contexts in which the term generation is used (see the more complete discussion of the problem of generational concepts in Bengtson, Cutler, Mangen, & Marshall, 1985).

I believe we should use the term *cohort* or *age group* to refer to those individuals who have been born at roughly the same point in chronological time and who therefore experience specific environmental or historical events at a common point in their individual life course. And

Table 2. Which Generations? The Four Principal Terms Used in Social and Policy Analysis Today

Popular term	More precise terminology	Operationalization	Level of analysis
1. Generation	Age cohort	5- or 10-year birth group	Macrosocial level
2. Generation	Kinship lineage descent	Social/biological succession	Microsocial level
3. Generation	Historical generation: age cohort subgroup (elites)	Social movement led by cohort subgroup	Macrosocial level
4. Generation	Age group	Multiyear cohort	Macrosocial level

we should use the term *generation* primarily to reflect ranked-descent ordering of individuals within families.

The third usage of the term *generation*—reflecting age cohorts who share some elements of *identity* or group consciousness because they share some common experiences in history, and who become part of *social movements* based on age—is more difficult to define. There are important precedents in social theory for this usage; it is, for example, what Mannheim (1928/1952) had in mind when he defined "the problem of generations," and indeed this is the meaning used by many European social scientists. But this definition is difficult to operationalize, and may lend even more confusion to the debate. Thus I would recommend against using *generation* in this more ambiguous sense.

The fourth usage, generation as *age group*, is the most generic. Often *age group* and *age cohort* are used synonymously; sometimes it is used to mean *historical generation;* occasionally to mean *family generations.* I will use it to mean *age cohort.*

My comments about the need for conceptual clarity—one of the first requirements of scientific discourse, it should be noted—are in fact a reflection of a major change in the traditional "problem of generations" during only the past few decades of human experience, and this in the context of the new phenomena of population aging.

What I am arguing is this: Issues of family-based, microlevel generational obligations and exchanges have remained relatively similar over time; while issues of macrolevel, age group reciprocities and equities are new, and have come to be preeminent in domestic social policy and economic discussions in contemporary nation-states. This is indeed a new development in human experience, and I will comment on its implications next.

The Macrosocial Level: New Concerns About Age Groups
and Their Relations in the Broader Society

There are, of course, *inequalities* between age groups in the distribution of wealth and in access to wages. In nearly every occupation young workers start on the bottom rung and, with increasing seniority, achieve higher earnings. By virtue of a lifetime of capital accumulation, older married couples typically control more resources than younger married couples. But does this constitute *inequity*? When do economic inequalities between age groups become injustices?

Inequalities and Inequities Between Age Groups

In the mid-1980s a political issue emerged in several Western industrialized nations that illustrates the new debate regarding the "contract across generations." The issue concerns potential inequities between age groups in the distribution of economic advantage, and the desirability of redrafting public policy legislation to produce more "equity" among age groups. The issue has arisen out of profound demographic changes, which involve the aging of societies, and concerns by the "baby boom" cohorts that they will not receive the same level of benefits when they retire that today's aged received.

The most visible proponents of the "generational equity" concerns have so far been found in the United States, where the Americans for Generational Equity (AGE) organization was founded in 1984 to be "the lobby for the future, pledged to advocate policies that obey Thomas Jefferson's exhortation that each generation should leave the following one at least as well off as it was" (Durenberger, 1989, p. 5). In other nations with a much more explicit welfare state orientation, such as New Zealand and Great Britain, similar concerns have been voiced; Thomson (1988) argues that "the inability or unwillingness to operate intergenerational exchanges fairly is now revealed on such scale as to seriously endanger the continued consensus for collective welfare programmes" (p. 128).

The basic argument made by "generational equity" advocates can be summarized as follows: (a) In recent years there has been a growth of public resources directed toward elderly members of the population resulting from legislation to counter previous levels of poverty among the aged, and because of effective political lobbying. (b) This has led to substantial improvement in the economic status of the elderly and in their access to health care. (c) The elderly are becoming better off as a group than the nonaged population, especially children; and the proportion of federal funds directed to the oldest age group is increasing every year. (d) At the same time the flow of resources to children and other dependent populations has decreased, proportionally. (e) Thus, to continue the flow of federal resources to the elderly is inequitable, and will be the source of intergenerational conflict. Former Colorado governor Richard Lamm has written: "We have turned the Biblical account of the prodigal son on its head. Now we are faced with the prodigal father" (1985, p. 87).

Responses to the "Generational Equity" Position

Each of the arguments listed above is open to debate (see Kingson et al., 1986). Four assumptions are particularly questionable: (a) There can be no increase in federal support for the young except by decreasing benefits to the elderly; (b) the majority of older people are well-off, and thus undeserving of any public assistance; (c) the elders are "debtors" rather than donors in transfers across age groups; and (d) issues of equity are most crucial at one point in time, viewed as cross-sectional, rather than life course or longitudinal over time.

In addition, there is some basic confusion in conceptualization and data in this policy debate (Bengtson et al., 1991): (a) What the "generational equity" advocates draw attention to are actually *cohort inequalities*, real or presumed, in terms of public support; (b) these allegations are not supported by fiscal data, if we include state and community funding; (c) what the AGE position ignores are the life course reciprocities between cohorts over historical periods; and (d) these advocates ignore the distinction between family and society, and the vast transfer of private resources between generations in the family sector over time. In fact, recent nationwide survey data suggest that no age group is perceived as receiving an inequitable amount of government benefits, and that most people do not feel that programs that provide benefits are too costly (Bengtson & Murray, in press).

That this debate over life course distribution of resources has emerged today is an example of how contemporary the problem of generational succession is, and how new the issues reflecting on the aging of populations are. We will see many more policy arguments about redressing presumed inequalities across age groups in the future.

The Microsocial Level: New Concerns About Generational
Relations in the Family

Demographic changes in family structure have taken place over the course of the 20th century (e.g., the three- and four-generation family has replaced the two-generation family of a century ago); as a result many aspects of intergenerational structure and relations have changed. As Bengtson (1989), Hagestad (1987), Riley (1985), and Rossi and Rossi (1990) have documented, however, there is still much generational continuity through family transmission and solidarity processes.

What are the problems in family generational relations that have emerged in the last three decades of the 20th century? These are concerns that, whether actual or perceived, real or invented, have come into popular awareness through mass media attention, across the world, and that have set the stage for the new agenda of age group and generational relations in the 21st century.

*The Narrowing Demographic Pyramid and the
"Shrinking" Western Family*

Historically unique demographic trends in mortality and fertility rates have created dramatic changes in the age structure of industrialized societies. These trends have special relevance to intergenerational interaction at the microlevel of the family and to age group interaction at the macrolevel of industrialized societies.

For example, in the United States life expectancy has almost doubled in the past 150 years, while fertility rates have been reduced by over one half in the last century (Bengtson, 1990). At the same time, the population of those 65 and over is expected to grow more than four times as fast as the rest of the population from 1985 through 2050; and the 85+ population will grow even faster (Siegel & Taeuber, 1986).

Such marked changes in mortality have resulted in ever larger numbers of elderly who are living past the age of retirement, and ever larger numbers of "frail elderly" who require assistance in the activities of daily living, while at the same time changes in fertility have resulted in ever smaller cohorts of youth and middle-aged workers in the population.

At the family level these demographic changes have produced similarly dramatic changes in kinship structures and intergenerational relations. This has led to concerns about the "shrinking" family and, in the context of high divorce rates, about the "demise of the family" as a functional unit in postmodern societies.

It is more correct, however, to acknowledge the increasing heterogeneity and diversity of intergenerational family patterns at the end of the 20th century (Bengtson, Rosenthal, & Burton, 1990). This increasing diversity reflects five trends, each of which suggests that family structures and interactions are rapidly changing (in the Western world, at least).

First, there has been an emergence of *multigeneration kinship patterns* quite different in structure from those existing earlier (Crimmins, 1985). One pattern has been termed the *beanpole* family structure (Bengtson et al., 1990); more generations are in existence at any given point in time, while there are fewer members within each generation. During the 20th century, the demographic structure of many family lineages has gone from a pyramid shape—for example, 1 living grandparent, 4 or 5 adult children, 20 or so grandchildren—to that of a tall, narrow beanpole or flagpole: a verticalized family containing a great-grandmother, her daughter and son-in-law, their two children and spouses, and four great-grandchildren, for example. What this means in broader terms is suggested by the following statistic from the United States: For American women born in the 1930s who celebrate their 60th birthday in the 1990s, almost one in three will have a mother who is still living (Bengtson et al., 1990).

Second, greater longevity implies that family members will spend *more time occupying intergenerational family roles* than ever before. For example, members of cohorts born in 1960 and 1980 will spend more years both as parents and as children of aging parents than any earlier cohort in history, due to extensions in longevity (Watkins, Menken, & Bongaarts, 1987). In the 21st century, for the first time in history, many children will grow to maturity not only with grandparents still alive, but also with great-grandparents present in the family structure.

The emergence of four- and even five-generation families in 21st century societies suggests complexities of lineage relationships with implications for self-conceptions, roles, and social support. Consider, for example, the consequences of "early grandmotherhood" and the intergenerational structure and dynamics of five-generation families. Burton and Bengtson (1985) report a study of South Central Los Angeles women, some of whom became grandmothers as young as age 27 when their teenage daughters gave birth to a grandchild. For these women, the asynchrony between lineage generational placement (becoming a grandmother) and chronological age (less than 35 years) represented a major source of frustration regarding self-identity and satisfactions.

In many of these families early pregnancy (at 11 to 14 years) had occurred as a pattern across several generations, leading to an age-condensed family structure in which the age distance between generations could be just 15 years. In one six-generation family in the study, the 91-year-old great-great-grandmother was living alone, while the young mother and infant were living with the 29-year-old grandmother. In this lineage, four of the five generations of women were between 11 and 14 years of age when they gave birth to their firstborn. Most of the young grandmothers in the study refused to take on the role of surrogate parent to their grandchild, so the burden of care for the new child was pushed up the generational ladder to the great-grandmother in the lineage.

Third, another intergenerational pattern, more typical in Europe than the beanpole pattern, is what has been termed the *"age-gapped" intergenerational structure;* it is a result of delayed childbearing. Whereas teenage pregnancy creates multiple generations with very little age distance between tiers and unclear generation boundaries, delayed childbearing has the opposite effect. When women postpone giving birth until their mid-to-late 30s, particularly over two or more generations, a family structure with large age gaps is created.

These gaps have implications for intergenerational relationships: (a) Parents and grandparents who enter their roles much later in life may not experience their statuses for as long a period of time as their younger counterparts in other families. (b) The greater age distance between generations may create strains in the development of bonds across the life course, particularly since it may result in women simultaneously experiencing child-rearing problems with their adolescent children and caregiving demands from their aging parents (Rossi & Rossi, 1991). (c) The later in life that one has a child, the fewer children one can have, and the potential caregiver pool for aging parents is even smaller than in the beanpole family structure.

A fourth pattern emerging at the end of the 20th century is *voluntary childlessness*. Childlessness creates the shortest and narrowest generational age structure. Intergenerational bonds and options for receiving care within the family become quite limited for older childless adults. Often, the childless elderly establish bonds with extended or fictive kin. Building such connections, however, may become more difficult as the frequency of kin concomitantly declines with fertility.

A fifth demographic trend that has created diversity in intergenerational family life is the record-high *rate of divorce* among their young-adult and middle-aged offspring. When the children of elderly parents divorce, there is a marked effect on the intergenerational family life of the aged (Hagestad, 1987). The parents of the adult child who does not receive custody of his or her children are faced with the possibility of less active involvement in the lives of their grandchildren. Moreover, the elderly parents may be forced to restrict important relationships with their former daughter- or son-in-law and their in-law family. If divorce is followed by remarriage, elderly parents are faced with a complex reconstitution of the intergenerational family, and even further complexity emerges when remarriage involves integration of stepchildren into the kinship structure, as in the *steprelation* family.

In short, what has occurred in the later decades of the 20th century in

Western industrialized nations has not been the shrinkage or demise of family structures; rather there has occurred increasing heterogeneity and diversity of kinship structures and functions in ways uncommon to 19th-century family life. The beanpole, age-gapped, and steprelation intergenerational structures reflect the growing variations in kinship forms as we approach the 21st century; they also reflect a new generational contract for families in the next century.

Family Intergenerational Solidarity

One of the concerns about generational relations that emerged in the early 1960s was the specter of "the decline of the family" and its corollary, "the abandonment of elder family members." In the popular press and on television, much concern was voiced about the disintegration of traditional family forms (especially in the United States) and the inability of families to deal with problems of dependent elders. At the same time it was suggested that nursing homes had become "warehouses" for dependent family elders, who sat in wheelchairs and waited for family members who never visited. Jacques Barzun (1961) called this "the crowning insult of industrialization . . . that those elders who created their children's prosperity should now be abandoned by them as relics of an earlier era" (p. 234).

But these reports of the 1960s and 1970s seem now to have been quite stereotypic, and without foundation in fact. Shanas (1979) has called the "abandoned elders" stereotype "a hydra-headed myth: no sooner is one rumor lopped off by factual data, than another springs out to public awareness" (p. 3). For the fact is that many studies have shown the strength of families as functioning social support units, with frequent and regular intergenerational contact and assistance (see Rossi & Rossi, 1990). Far from being abandoned by family, it seems clear that the typical older person in industrialized societies is in close contact with kin, has warm relationships with them, and is both a giver and receiver of support and assistance (see Bengtson et al., 1990).

I will summarize some interactional outcomes (both positive and negative) of the emergent multigenerational "vertical" family structures, and I will illustrate them with case examples from a longitudinal study of three-generation families at the University of Southern California (USC) that began in 1971 (see Bengtson et al., 1991). These cases demonstrate some of the diversity in interactional consequences of the increasingly multigenerational kinship network.

On the one hand are possibilities for *enhanced social solidarity* across generations, reflecting many more years of shared lives between generations in tomorrow's families. First, it has been argued that grandparents (and great-grandparents) serve as role models, maintaining ties to the past and the future that have identity functions for younger family members of all ages (Hagestad, 1987). One woman in the USC study commented: "What I have learned about maturity is from my grandmother. She is now 87; and I, at 41, want my old age to be like hers."

Second, the presence of family elders also augments *"kin-keeping" activities* and enhances ritual solidarity, even over long distances (Rosenthal, 1985). One man in the USC study said: "My mother, even at age 80, keeps the family together. All the generations enjoy getting together at her invitation."

Third, several generations of adults in one family represent a significant increment in the potential support available for dependent family members, whether young or old. While longer lives may mean longer periods of chronic illness, longer lives also mean greater collective family resources when support is needed—and with fewer children and grandchildren, compared to decades ago, to compete for these resources.

But, on the other hand, there is also the potential for *negative effects* on family solidarity from the longevity revolution. A significant minority of intergenerational relationships—perhaps 10%—in the USC study of generations were judged to be difficult or unrewarding.

First, there were indications of intergenerational conflict with difficulties extending over many years or decades of shared life. One woman said:

> My mother has always tried to run my life—control everything I did; control my children, telling me what not to do, and what to do with my children. . . . My mother still checks up on my children, asks them too many questions as she did me over the years, and my children object very much.

What is the age of this woman? She is 67; her mother is 93 (Richards, Bengtson, & Miller, 1989). Such negative relationships can become a lifelong theme; one man said, "I've had a lousy relationship with my father for the last 45 or 50 years . . . and it never will change."

Second, there were indications of guilt, as when the 57-year-old woman said, "I feel I can never do enough to please my mother, and my guilt has come to run my life."

Third, there were descriptions of lifelong dependency—alcohol or drug abuse, a life of crime, mental illness—that constituted the major agenda, usually tragic, of the parent-child relationship. In these and other ways (e.g., geographic distance, conflicts with other family members, taking sides over divorce) tensions between parents and children can be spread over even longer periods of time in the coming century than they have been in the past.

There are, then, both positive and negative implications from the elongation of aging for family relationships. These too are reflections of a new "contract of generations" emerging for the 21st century.

Family Caregiving of Dependent Elders

Another implication of the verticalized generational structure is the increased probability that family members will be involved in longer periods of caring for elders, due to increased longevity and chronic health disorders associated with aging. Elder caregiving has already become a normative life event of middle age—that is, a situation that the average person can expect to encounter—for the majority of North Americans (Brody, 1985). The "middle-generation squeeze," experienced by those caring for both dependent elderly and dependent children (and possibly grandchildren), will become a pattern for even more individuals in the next few decades. Also, greater numbers of elderly and their greater longevity will contribute to the rise of "two-generation geriatric" families with adult children over 60 caring for parents in their 80s and 90s.

The challenges and sacrifices of taking care of a demented or dependent elder are severe (Gatz, Bengtson, & Blum, 1990; Zarit, Anthony, & Boutselis, 1987). It has been described as "the 36-hour day" (Mace & Rabins, 1981). In one national study, primary caregiving activities occupied on the average four hours a day, and 24% of the adult children caregivers also had a child under 18 residing in their home, while one half were working (Stone, Cafferata, & Sangl, 1987). However, the rewards of caregiving must also be noted (Gatz et al., 1990). In the USC study, one woman noted the unexpected positive consequences of her mother's decline:

> After my mother developed Alzheimer's I became closer to her. At last I felt I could do something meaningful for her, something that approached what she had done for me over the years. Even when she failed to recognize me, I could still love her. (Richards et al., 1989 p. 354)

Future Prospects for Increased Solidarity or Conflict Between Age Groups

What, then, are the prospects for generational and age group relations in the future? Is there likely to be more, or less, generational and age group conflict in industrialized societies? Are future age groups likely to support each other? Will there be solidarity and will there be reciprocities?

I am steadfastly ambivalent in forecasting future developments in cross-age relations. It is difficult to predict the future, and sociologists have seldom been highly regarded as prophets. Moreover, events that occur in economic and sociopolitical areas—effects exogenous to the process of aging and succession—will determine much of the fate of generational and age group conflicts and solidarities in the future. Be that as it may, we can explore some reasons why conflict will be more likely in the next few decades, at least in some Western, industrialized societies, and reasons why it will be less likely.

The Prospects for Increased Age Group Conflict in the Future

First, let us list some reasons why there might be an *increase* in age group or generational conflict between now and 2020:

1. Increases in the dependency ratio.   The decline in fertility translates into fewer workers left to support aging retirees. Indeed, it has been estimated by Soldo (1981) that, while the ratio of "dependent" aged to the working-age population was 18 to 100 in 1980, by 2000 it will be 26 to 100, and by 2030 it may be 32 to 100. Thus there will be fewer and fewer workers per dependent—along with increased medical care expenditures for older people. Unless there are marked increases in productivity, or a real "Cold War peace dividend" that will spread across the industrial world in the next decade, it will be increasingly difficult to continue as is without setting limits on medical care for the elderly, or on pensions (Bengtson & Dannefer, 1987; Callahan, 1987).

2. Increased perceptions of "generational inequity".   This is a particularly likely scenario in the United States. If inflation continues to rise (especially in housing costs), the elderly are more and more likely to be perceived as "greedy geezers" in their mortgage-free houses. It will be increasingly argued that public support for the aged comes from funds that could be allocated to other segments of society, such as youth, and to affordable housing for young families. This is the "generational equity" scenario, as discussed above; Callahan (1987) goes along with this by calling for "voluntary restraints" on pension and health care expenditures by tomorrow's aged.

3. Increased "ageism".   There will probably be a continuation of negative stereotyping that sees the elderly as rigid, terribly old-fashioned, unable to cope, irrelevant, and worthless. As more of the elderly population of the future live past 85, and as more live with mental impairments like Alzheimer's disease and strokes, it could be that aging itself will be more negatively viewed. Moreover, if technological advances become even more a part of personal life, those who cannot or will not learn the new techniques involving man-machine interfaces (such as computerized home banking) may be left behind. On the other side of the coin, there may be even greater emphasis on the virtues of youth. With fertility low and children proportionately less common, youth will be valued even more highly and attention will be turned to the young at the expense of the old.

Prospects for Lesser Age Group Conflicts in the Future

But there are other reasons to suggest that there may be less intergenerational conflict in the 21st century, and that solidarity between generations at both the micro- and macrosocial levels may be high. (My projections of future conflict or solidarity between age groups are based on American and European trends, which may not characterize Asian or third-world societies.)

1. The cultural (or structural) lag hypothesis. We may be in a situation of temporary normlessness now with regard to the longevity revolution; our social structures and norms may not have caught up to changes in the population age structure (see Riley & Riley, Chapter 9 in this volume). This argument would suggest that, in another several decades, social structures and cultural values will have evolved to reflect our changing age composition, with the result that we will have created more and more effective mechanisms to deal with large numbers of aged people.

2. Norms of solidarity and support. Many studies have described significant intergenerational solidarity at the family level, with relations between generations solid and rewarding and with a great deal of mutual support taking place (Rossi & Rossi, 1990). This solidarity reflects norms of (a) filial piety, (b) reciprocity, (c) altruism, and (d) self-interest (individuals' expectations for their own future). Cannot similar arguments be advanced at the macrosocial level? Are there not social or cultural values of elder caring, reciprocity, and self-interest—all of which may dampen possible "generational inequity" conflicts between age groups? It can be argued that the welfare state is not likely to go back on the moral principles that have been in effect for so many decades now.

3. *Norms of reciprocity.*   While we have only begun to research them (see Rossi, Chapter 10 in this volume), life course and intergenerational norms of reciprocity are very high. That is, people believe in a cyclical process of being helped and helping throughout life; they believe this is "normal" and so do not resent it (much of the time). The "burdens" of caretaking for a child are taken for granted. So too are many of the burdens of elder caring. Family contact seems to have high value, especially in terms of generational relations—even in case of divorce, when in fact the intergenerational bonds often seem to become more intense.

4. *New roles for the aged.*   As suggested earlier, we may also see the development of collective change in the definition of what older people can and should contribute to society. For example, they may be seen as the resource for noneconomic capital—knowledge about relationships and history. They may be increasingly viewed as repositories of wisdom.

Conclusions: Prospects for a New Contract
Across Age Groups and Generations

What I have suggested is that the age-old "problem of generations" has indeed changed, in America and Europe at least, and that social scientists and policymakers should be addressing these changes. In the last decades of the 20th century, there is much evidence to suggest that we have reached a cultural watershed concerning the implicit contract between generations and between age groups in human society. Despite this, however, there are many indications of continuity in the contract, not only within the family but at the macrosocial level of age populations and policies as well. I have suggested five points in advancing the argument that the social contract across generations and age groups is indeed changing.

1.   Never before have so many individuals lived so long, and never have there been so relatively few members of younger generations to support them. In consequence we are faced with new and perhaps historically unique dilemmas of social organization regarding the normal life course and the succession of age groups. Implications of these dilemmas can be seen in emerging questions about social welfare, both private and public, regarding age groups, as well as in more general issues of conflict or solidarity between generations and age groups.

2. The causes of the generational/age group dilemma we face can be traced primarily to effects of worldwide population aging, namely increasing longevity and decreasing fertility, as well as to socioeconomic changes reflecting conflicts in cultural values concerning aging, succession, productivity, and families.

3. The contract across generations and age groups centers on expectations and obligations (what sociologists term norms) regarding the aging of individuals and the succession of generations, through time and within social structures. One set of expectations and obligations concerns biosocial generation and socialization: that the first generation will succor and bring up the second, who then will produce a third generation. A second set of expectations and obligations involves gerosocial succession: that the second generation will have resources to bring up the third. A third set of norms involves geriatric dependencies: the first generation will be honored and helped in their decline—and death—by their descendants.

4. But the *traditional* contract across generations and age groups, whether implicit or formal, has been altered by demographic trends such as population aging, and by the simultaneous political and moral trends of collective public welfare provisions, as well as by the more personal involvements of "beanpole" family structures with their attendant demands and resources. Each of these factors has, in multiple ways, caused an altering of normative life course concerns for the average citizen of a Western industrial society, and also an altering of public policy priorities regarding responsibilities toward aging citizens.

5. One consequence of these factors is that conflict between age groups in the 21st century may be considerably greater than conflicts experienced in previous historical eras. But, paradoxically, there is a potential for greater solidarity between adult generations and across age groups than has been experienced in other historical periods.

It seems clear that issues of age group conflicts are going to be more visible in the decades to come.

In the closing decades of the 20th century we seem to be seeing some new and societywide variations on the age-old contract of generations. Aging has been postponed, dependencies have been altered, and generational succession has been attenuated—with significant social consequences for the 21st century. We may have arrived at a historical watershed regarding the expectations and interactions between age groups; it is time for gerontologists, social scientists, and policymakers to take that watershed seriously.

2

Generational Relations in Historical Context

W. Andrew Achenbaum

Vern Bengtson opens this volume by declaring that he is "steadfastly ambivalent" in forecasting future developments in (inter)generational relations. Concerned with theoretical issues related to generational succession and age group conflicts, he acknowledges that all human societies must strike a balance between the ways they maintain continuities with the past and how they accommodate to changing circumstances. Based on cross-cultural and longitudinal evidence, Bengtson hypothesizes that a "new problem of generations" may be arising. Population aging and ageism, as well as the growing perception of age-based inequities, are affecting how generational succession is being *negotiated*. Bengtson's hypothesis rests on earlier analyses: "[E]ach interacting generation will change, develop, or be socialized anew in the ongoing process of negotiating generational emergence" (Bengtson, 1989, p. 39; see also Bengtson, Marti, & Roberts, 1991), articulating a different "developmental stake" than prevailed at the turn of the century (Bengtson & Kuypers, 1971).

Much more work has to be done, however, in stipulating key elements in the *process* of negotiating generational emergence. Bengtson stresses shifts in demography, rhetoric, orientations, resources, expectations, and power (1990, p. 4). Yet do these factors *really* make the dynamics of generational succession new? Is he correct in assuming that they interact in ways that have created an unprecedented historical situation? Or might there be a predictable sequence and periodicity in events that affect changes in generational relations? How much has the pattern of generational succession itself altered throughout history? No definitive answers are available.

According to Alexis deTocqueville, a transformation in generational succession occurred long ago in the United States: "Even if a few conventions are accepted by one generation, it does not follow that the next will observe them too, for in a democracy each generation is a new people" (1969, p. 473). *Democracy in America* abounds in images of atomistic individuals consumed with their own busyness: "Those who have gone before are easily forgotten, and no one gives a thought to those who will follow. All a man's interests are limited to those near himself" (p. 507). To deTocqueville, the novelty of generational succession in the United States experience lies in its very pervasiveness:

> They clutch everything but hold nothing fast, and so lose grip as they hurry after some new delight. An American will build a house in which to pass his old age and sell it before the roof is on. . . . At first there is something astonishing in this spectacle of so many lucky men restless in the midst of abundance. But it is a spectacle as old as the world; all that is new is to see a whole people performing it. (p. 536)

If the attenuation of generational relations occurred in Jacksonian America, what can be "new" about the way emergent generations will negotiate the future?

Bengtson might reply that, with advances in adult longevity, successive generations no longer reach key points in their negotiation on a predictable schedule. Analyzing the rhythms of generational succession has attracted attention since at least Auguste Comte and John Stuart Mill. Jose Ortega y Gasset believed that "an historic generation lives fifteen years of gestation and fifteen years of creation" (1958, p. 60). F. Scott Fitzgerald defined a generation "as that revolt against fathers which seems to occur about three times a century" (quoted in Longman, 1987b, p. 2). Two of our greatest historians, Henry Adams and Arthur Meier Schlesinger, Sr., detected cycles in American politics every 12 and 16.5 years, respectively, which signaled that a new generation had come of age. Yet few still claim that generational sequences can be mathematically fixed. As A.M. Schlesinger, Jr. puts it, "Because the cycle is not a pendulum swinging between fixed points but a spiral, it admits novelty and therefore escapes determinism (and confounds prophecy)" (1986, p. 31). So is it a "shock of recognition," not necessarily linked to what Strauss and Howe (1991) characterize as a "social moment," which galvanizes members of some, but not all, cohorts into action?

"Whether a new *generation style* emerges every year, every thirty, every hundred years, or whether it emerges rhythmically at all de-

pends entirely on the trigger action of the social and cultural process,"
Karl Mannheim observed in his 1928 article, "The Problem of Generations" (1928/1952, p. 310). Mannheim's essay fittingly serves as the *clas-
sicus locus* for ideas about generational succession that I wish to pur-
sue. Mannheim did not consider it axiomatic that people born during
a certain period of time invariably constitute a generation. *"A generation as an actuality"* emerges "only where a concrete bond is created
between members of a generation by their being exposed to the social
and intellectual symptoms of a process of dynamic destabilization"
(p. 303).

Unfortunately, Mannheim never really explicates the relationship between what he calls "the trigger action" and what he refers to as "the
process of dynamic destabilization." Nor does he offer examples of how
different cohorts react to and interact within the same historical stimu-
lus. "'The Problem of Generations,'" in Edward Shils's opinion, remained "very general and vague and was never assimilated into this
sociology of knowledge" (1968, p. 559). Nevertheless, subsequent analysts elaborated on Mannheim's theme. Lewis Feuer claimed that "social
generations follow upon each other more rapidly in critical times than in
others" (1969, p. 26). Others have pointed out that age cohorts tend to
differentiate from the rest of society in persistent opposition to dominant values or customs: "In such a case differences that begin as political
or ideological may end as generational" (Spitzer, 1973, p. 1362). Foner
(1974) reported examples of the converse. It is not enough, however, to
identify the "trigger" that sets generational succession into motion. Analysts must identify when (and how) cohorts make strategic choices in
negotiations that effect a (new) contract among generations (Fisher &
Ury, 1983).

It is at this juncture that an empirical, historical approach becomes a
useful contribution to theory building. Taking cues from Mannheim, I
propose that generational relations in historical context resemble a negotiation—or more precisely, a series of negotiations. Because analogies
accentuate the idiosyncratic as well as the nomothetic features found in
any sequence of historical contexts and temporal patterns (Achenbaum,
1989a), I offer three very different case studies: whether relations among
this nation's Founding Fathers mellowed as they grew older, how two
Evangelists interpreted Jesus' genealogy, and why the Vietnam cohort
of United States veterans seem justified in claiming that they are not
getting their fair share under current Veterans Administration (VA) programs. These case studies illuminate in a general way likenesses and
differences (Neustadt & May, 1987) in the ways that different age groups
negotiate their place along a historical timeline in specific social contexts.
Ideally, they will sharpen our sense of the fluidity of continuities,

changes, and reciprocities in the process of negotiation between generations over time.

Did the American Revolutionary Generation
Share a Common Consciousness?

Within any generation there can exist a number of differentiated, antagonistic generation-units. Together they constitute an "actual" generation precisely because they are oriented toward each other, even though only in the sense of fighting one another. (Mannheim, 1928/1952, pp. 306–307)

Most of us remember the main events in United States history between 1765 and 1820. Roughly a third of the colonists remained loyal to the Crown; another third took up the revolutionary cause; the remainder hedged their bets until they could see whose troops were close by. The Continental Congress tried to bind the mutual interests of the 13 independent states through the Articles of Confederation (ratified in 1781), but its structure proved too decentralized, its authority too weak (lacking any specific judicial and executive authority), to meet basic needs during a protracted war and uneasy peace.

In 1787, a delegation charged with revising the Articles went beyond their mandate and drafted a new constitution. Those who supported the new document were called Federalists; those against, Anti-Federalists. The vote was close, and historians ever since have tried to discern patterns in people's preferences. Stanley Elkins and Eric McKitrick proposed that the Founding Fathers were "the young men of the Revolution": "the 'energy' principle may be more suggestive now, in reviewing the experience of founding, than the principle of political conservatism" (1962, p. 3).

Even after the new republic was created, divisions persisted. George Washington managed to stay above the fray, but partisan politics swirled around two strong personalities. Alexander Hamilton and his followers favored a powerful, central government supportive of mercantile interests; Thomas Jefferson and other planters advocated states' rights and agrarian virtues. When John Adams succeeded Washington, the Federalists won their only presidential election. From 1800 to 1825, the Virginia dynasty held sway, with each incumbent president succeeded in turn by one of his secretaries of state.

If this were a complete account of developments, the sequence of conflicts and mutual advantage in early United States history would seem to have little analogical value in challenging conventional wisdom concerning the dynamics of generational consciousness. But there is

more to the story. Mannheim's observation that a cohort group sometimes becomes an "actual generation" because of antipathies *within* its
ranks helps to explain the Founding Fathers' relations with successive
political factions.

For openers, it is debatable whether the "winners" were "the young
men of the Revolution." Historians have demolished the Elkins-Mc-
Kitrick thesis. The pair had simply taken nine Federalists and nine Anti-
Federalists, averaged their respective ages, and concluded that the
former were about a decade younger than the latter. Had they drawn a
different "sample," they could have shown that the Anti-Federalists
were 14 years younger. Had they done a more comprehensive analysis,
they would have detected no significant age differences at all (Fischer,
1970; Main, 1974). Furthermore, while the second generation of Federalists shared their elders' conviction that "men of talents should give,
not receive direction from the multitude" (Fischer, 1965, p. 29), they
adopted the political techniques of their rivals, the Jeffersonian Democrats. The heirs of the Federalist tradition aligned with the old school,
but they borrowed heavily from the new style of politics. Generational
adaptation sometimes is necessary to conserve values and to elaborate
norms of the elders.

Perhaps a more revealing way to observe how the revolutionary leaders negotiated their political thoughts and actions with advancing years
is to examine the correspondence of Thomas Jefferson. In 1791, he felt
obliged to apologize to John Adams, when some of their disputes were
publicized in the press:

> That you and I differ in our ideas of the best form of government, is well
> known to us both; but we have differed as friends should do, respecting
> the purity of each other's motives, and confining our difference of opinion
> to private conversation. (quoted in Koch & Peden, 1944, p. 507)

Twenty years later, at age 69, he reconciled again with Adams, then 76.
Jefferson attributed their past rivalry to human nature: "Men have differed in opinion, and been divided into parties by their opinions, from
the first origin of societies. . . . They denote the temper and constitution
of mind of different individuals" (quoted in Malone, 1981, p. 105). In old
age, Jefferson turned to members of his cohort who could sustain his
intellect and share remembrances of the "glorious achievements" of
their youth. Mutual pleasure took precedence over past partisanship.

Are we to infer generational relations invariably mellow in late life? If
so, then one might expect Jefferson's relationships with James Madison
to have been even more intimate than with Adams. Both were Virginia

intellectuals, and their homes were 30 miles apart. The pair had grown old fighting for big issues on the same side. Theirs was "a partnership of two philosophic statesmen, enduring with scarcely a ripple between them as long as they lived" (Peterson, 1970, p. 266). Yet their views of generational succession, radically different early in life, remained in opposition as they aged. In 1789, Jefferson declared:

> The earth belongs always to the living generations. They may manage it then, and what proceeds from it, as they please, during their usufruct. They are masters too of their own persons, and consequently may govern them as they please. . . . Every constitution then, and every law, naturally expires at the end of 19 years. If it be enforced longer, it is an act of force, and not of right. (quoted in Matthews, 1984, p. 23)

Jefferson repeated this theme in a letter to Samuel Kercheval in 1816:

> By the European tables of mortality, of the adults living at any one moment of time, a majority will be dead in about nineteen years. At the end of that period then, a new majority is come into place; or, in other words, a new generation. Each generation is as independent of the one preceding them, as that was of all which had gone before. (quoted in Koch & Peden, 1944, p. 675)

Just as he and his peers had enjoyed a "fresh start," so Jefferson believed that each generation had to begin anew. As he told his nephew Thomas Mann Randolph in 1787,

> Though we may say with confidence, that the worst of the American constitutions is better than the best which ever existed before, in any other country, and that they are wonderfully perfect for a first essay, yet every human essay must have its defects. It will remain, therefore, to those now coming on the stage of public affairs, to perfect what has been so well begun by those going off it. (quoted in Koch & Peden, 1944, pp. 424–425)

Jefferson spent much of his old age ensuring access to education through public schools and universities: Youth had to be prepared to make institutional reforms necessary in due course so that they, too, could advance societal progress.

Madison, in contrast, stressed the virtue of continuity. To Jefferson, in 1790, he wrote more in the tradition of Hume and Burke than of de-Tocqueville:

> There seems then to be a foundation in the nature of things, in the relation which one generation bears to another, for the *descent* of obligations from

one to another. Equity requires it . . . [and] mutual good is promoted by it. (quoted in McCoy, 1989, p. 58)

Unlike Jefferson, who viewed the Constitution ever ripe for improvement in light of advancing ideas about human nature, Madison feared that the universal truths embodied in the Constitution would be lost to the future if they were not preserved and cherished. He deemed it essential to cultivate its original meanings through generational continuity.

Not surprisingly, Jefferson and Madison had contrasting views of the future. In an 1816 letter to John Adams, Jefferson observed, "I like the dreams of the future better than the history of the past." At roughly the same age, Madison feared that the past was slipping away: "The infant periods of most nations are buried in silence, or veiled in fable, and perhaps the world may have lost but little which it need regret," he wrote in 1819. But "the origin and outset of the American Republic contains lessons of which posterity ought not to be deprived" (quoted in McCoy, 1989, p. 73). Madison believed that the Constitution provided the foundation for the American experiment. In this boundless land amidst all the bewildering changes, Madison sought ways to negotiate stability, whereas Jefferson encouraged reform, if not outright revolution.

Two points are to be underscored. First, note that deeply held *intra*generational differences existed in this period of revolutionary upheaval. Were Adams, Jefferson, and Madison simply bickering intellectuals, this case study would not be instructive. But these three men spoke for thousands of their peers, all of whom shared a common stake in ensuring the future well-being of their fragile new republic. Changes in focus and location, however, made some differences count for less, and others harder to reconcile. At successive stages in the maturation of an age cohort, disparate antagonisms manifest themselves.

Second, their differences in outlook and style notwithstanding, the Founding Fathers constituted an "actual generation," in Mannheim's sense of the term. They hoped that their successors would uphold their revolutionary ideals. Writing in 1847, Thoreau suggested that this did not happen: "I have lived some thirty years on this planet, and I have yet to hear the first syllable or even earnest advice from my seniors. They have told me nothing and probably cannot teach me anything" (quoted in Fischer, 1977, p. 113). Ironically, such an outcome might have been set in motion by the manner in which members of the revolutionary cohort negotiated their own way into power. "In establishing a republic, the Americans cut themselves off from the wisdom of the past and so, it seems, undermined the rank and respect that had traditionally been accorded the old," suggests historian Pauline Maier (1980, p. 293). Perhaps it was the legacy of the Founding Fathers that deTocqueville had in mind when he emphasized the atomistic nature of generational relations in America.

Establishing Generational Position:
The Jesus Movement's Place in the Bible

Any attempt to establish a direct identity or correlation between biological and cultural data leads to a *quid pro quo* which can only confuse the issue. (Mannheim, 1928/1952, pp. 306–307)

Biblical evidence amplifies Mannheim's insight that biological data must be differentiated from cultural factors in interpreting generational issues. A *generation*, as Vern Bengtson (Chapter 1 in this volume) and Matilda and John Riley (Chapter 9 in this volume) quite rightly point out, should be used precisely to refer to relations in a kinship context. *Intergenerational conflicts*, in contrast, typically encompass age categories (or strata) in society at a *given* period in historical time. Birth cohorts include sets of people moving through society *across* time (Riley & Riley, Chapter 9 in this volume). Perceptions of historical "reality," moreover, may be colored by a set of considerations that appear to have little to do with "actual" generational relations per se. Such is the theme of my second case study.

The first verse of the New Testament reads, "The book of the generation of Jesus Christ, the son of David, the son of Abraham" (Matt. 1:1). The Gospel according to Matthew was written for a predominantly Jewish audience, one accustomed to using genealogies to ground their relationship with God in historical context.

Hebrew genealogies settled questions of legitimacy concerning individual or group membership in a clan. They ensured the continuity of Israel's priesthood and revealed troubling features in Israelite and Levite marital patterns. The authors of 1 Chronicles (chaps. 2–9), drawing on biblical, military, folk, and cultic sources, seek to justify the prominence of the Davidic theocracy. Documenting generational succession thus served not only to establish degrees of kinship among the chosen but also to mark boundaries between Israelites and their neighbors.

Historical accuracy was not a hallmark of genealogies. The transmission of oral histories from one generation to the next led to considerable "generational fluidity" (Wilson, 1977). Sometimes the sequence was fabricated. No matter: Gaps in information had to be filled to give the appearance of continuity. Greek historians and other Near-Eastern chroniclers did the same thing. "The genealogical form can be said to have become one of the available forms of writing—and re-writing—history, and thus for expressing the nationalistic and religious hopes and beliefs of the people" (Johnson, 1969, p. 85).

In this context, any family tree that could trace Jesus' roots back to David and Abraham must have seemed comforting. Yet linguistic and conceptual ambiguities emerge in the very first verse of Matthew. The Greek word *genesis*, rendered "generation" in the King James Version, appears as "genealogy" in the Revised Standard Version, the Jerusalem Bible, and the Revised English Version, and as "a table of descent" in the New English Bible. Elsewhere Matthew uses other synonyms that are sometimes translated into English as "generation." Hence *genea* is translated "generations" to mean people with similar characteristics (Matt. 1:17, 17:17). A cognate, *gennema*, usually meaning "offspring," becomes more vividly expressed as "brood of vipers" (Matt. 3:7, 12:34, 23:33). Finally, *genos* captures in 1 Pet. 2:9 the sense of a people called to be a "holy race," which harks back to Ezra 2:59–67 and Exod. 19:6. That so many terms distinct in contemporary English can be interchangeably defined as "generation" by biblical scholars shows that "our" sense of what generational succession means may not be the same as the understanding shared by people more than two millennia ago.

Furthermore, Matthew's decision to end his genealogy with Abraham hardly would have allayed doubts about Jesus' standing among all traditional-minded Jews. Joshua's reference to Abraham's ancestry (Josh. 24:2) takes for granted that Israel's forebears worshipped pagan deities until Moses. Matthew appears to fuel Messianic speculation, rampant at the time. Claiming kinship with Isaac, Jacob, David, and Solomon seems calculated to strengthen claims of legitimacy by members of the Jesus movement. Yet each of these younger sons ultimately shunted his older brother(s) aside—hardly comforting to those eager to uphold the social order.

It is striking, moreover, that Matthew includes four women (Tamar, Rahab, Ruth, and Bathsheba) in his table of descent. "Safer" choices—Sarah, Rebekah, Leah, and Rachel—might have been made. Two, after all, were whores; one was an adulteress. None of the women would have been considered Israelites at the time the Gospel was composed. Their inclusion probably sets the stage for showing Jesus' concern for sinners and Gentiles. If so, Matthew's genealogy seems by design to anchor an ideological argument for authenticity far beyond its value in demonstrating a continuous line of succession from Abraham to Jesus. Matthew is setting forth a line of generational succession that reminds the people of Israel that their claims of exclusivity may contradict their covenant with God.

Luke, the other evangelist who recounts Jesus' genealogy, offers an alternative line of descent, which serves a different purpose—and not just because it is intended for a different audience. Matthew neatly divided Jesus' family tree into three units (from Abraham to David, from David to the Babylonian exile, and then to Jesus [Matt. 1:17]), each with 14 generations. That the number 14 happens to be loaded with symbolic connotations, because of its association with David's name (Argyle, 1963), fits Matthew's efforts to root Jesus' ministry in Hebrew traditions. Luke, who is thought to have written primarily for non-Jews, simply recites 72 names. Only 11 of them appear on Matthew's list!

Perhaps a more striking contrast is that Luke does not stop with Abraham, but goes all the way to "Adam, son of God" (Luke. 3:38). Like Paul, Luke envisions Jesus to be the second Adam, whose life will transform human experience. Whereas Matthew begins his Gospel with Jesus' genealogy, Luke places his genealogy immediately after Jesus is baptized (Tinsley, 1965). Unlike Matthew, who wants to demonstrate that Jesus works within Jewish traditions, Luke presents a radical alternative—spiritual rebirth—as an option open to all. Luke's terms are far more inclusive. Finally, it is worth noting that although both evangelists trace Jesus' lineage through Joseph, they do not get to King David the same way. Matthew follows the royal line through Solomon, whereas Luke's account goes through David's third son, Nathan.

For our purposes, the interesting question is *not* why leaders of the first generations of Christians tolerated such glaring discrepancies between the genealogies in Matthew and Luke. Few then and since have claimed that these passages should read literally. Paul's pastoral letters did not put much stock in them (1 Tim. 1:9; Titus. 3:9). And if the incongruities really had been irksome, there was ample time and opportunity to revise the Gospels before they became sacred texts. After all, neither Luke nor Matthew was written until at least five decades after Jesus was crucified. That differences of interpretation exist in the canon underlines the *intra*cohort diversity of opinion from the start. (Note the parallel with our first case study.) During the next four centuries, bishops and elders of the church tried to harmonize various renditions of relatively complete texts, and piece together fragments transcribed from oral histories or found in isolated communities (Lace, 1965). Hermeneutical efforts to recapture their original intent for modern readers remain far from completed, as the spate of new translations of the Bible indicates.

"Spatial and chronological relations within biblical texts," Edmund Leach declared, "always have symbolic significance whether or not they happen to correspond to reality as ordinarily understood" (1987, p. 581). Instead of reworking genealogies to make them seem more historically accurate, leaders of the Jesus movement, in a manner consonant with generations of Jews before them, sought to understand the bigger picture by presuming that the various pieces would somehow fit together in the future. The Bible's paradoxes, the parables, the poetic imagery made it both a source of dispute and a source of inspiration in negotiating developmental stakes among religious people.

Particularly after the destruction of the Temple in A.D. 70, conflicts arose over matters of doctrine, biblical texts, creeds, liturgy, apostolic succession, and mission (Meeks, 1983; Pelikan, 1971; Rowland, 1985). In this context, questions of generational succession shifted. The disciples had expected Jesus to come again soon, but as the Second Coming seemed less and less imminent, the task of institutionalizing community life became more pressing. No new "biological" evidence prompted revisionist interpretations. No one proposed a pruning of genealogical trees. But subsequent "cultural data" (in Mannheim's sense, 1928/1952) did reorder priorities as they wrestled with dissent, schism, and heresy from all quarters. The pluralist controversy embedded in matters of theology would rage for centuries thereafter, taking new form with each generation.

Generational/Class Politics in Caring for Aging Veterans

The real seat of the class ideology remains the class itself, with its own typical opportunities and handicaps. . . . Similarly, the real seat of new impulses remains the generation location (which will selectively encourage one form of experience and eliminate others), even when they may have been fostered by other age-groups. (Mannheim, 1928/1952, pp. 308–309)

No less than biblical scholars, students of American history invoke "pluralism" to take account of diverse racial, ethnic, class, and geographical variations shaping our nation's experiences. From a theoretical perspective, however, a major consideration must be whether *any* single factor—such as age or generation—can rightly describe and explain all the pertinent trends under investigation. "Discoverers often tend to be over-enthusiastic about phenomena they are the first to see," observed Mannheim in "The Problem of Generations" (1928/1952).

Theories of race, generation, "national spirit," economic determinism, etc., suffer from this one-sidedness, but it may be said to their credit that they bring at least one partial factor into sharp focus and also direct attention to the general problem of the structural factors shaping history. (p. 312)

Mannheim had ambivalent feelings about Marxist interpretations that restricted definitions of *social location* to issues of *class* (Longhurst, 1989). Similarly, those who treat the concept of *generational equity* in stark terms may miss the ways that the meanings and experiences of *cohorts* and *generations* can be transmogrified by shifting national priorities. Sometimes potential conflicts between two or more age groups are triggered (or defused) *by actions by people of different ages.* Reviewing recent developments in federal policymaking for aging veterans illustrates Mannheim's critical insight.

Committed in Abraham Lincoln's words "to care for him who shall have borne the battle and for his widow and his orphans," the United States government through its veterans' programs has long been a pacesetter in meeting some of the income security and health care needs of older Americans. The federal treasury paid out over $5.2 billion (not including the value of land bounties) between 1790 and 1917. It cost the North $4 billion to fight the Civil War; the price tag for pensions for Yankees and their widows exceeded $8 billion. Veterans' expenditures for the Spanish-American War ultimately cost more than eight times the military budget for that "splendid little war" (Glasson, 1918; Holmes, 1990; President's Commission on Veterans' Pensions, 1956). Designed as gratuities for sacrifices made, veterans' pensions served as a surrogate welfare program prior to the enactment of Social Security. In 1929, 82% of all beneficiaries of any public or private pension plan were receiving war-related survivor or disability pensions; 80% of all money distributed through pensions came from this single source (Achenbaum, 1978; in press).

The benefits enjoyed by World War II veterans have been quite generous. In 1943, Franklin Delano Roosevelt began legislative maneuvering for vocational rehabilitation programs, educational vouchers, and mustering-out pay benefits. Home mortgages and preferential treatment for public-sector employment quickly followed. Aiding veterans in this way was part of a larger strategy for promoting welfare and health care initiatives as well as for regulating the labor market.

> No status group of comparable size prospered as did veterans after the war. . . . It was a very middle-class program, all the more effective for the disguise it wore. And now, in the professional and managerial ranks, the veterans of World War II are represented out of proportion to their numbers. (Perrett, 1973, p. 342; see also Ross, 1969)

Having offered compensation when disabilities struck in midlife, the VA is now serving many of the World War II cohort in old age. The system's geriatric imperative seems demographically daunting. Three fourths of the men who had ever served in the armed forces since 1775 were alive on July 4, 1976. As of March 31, 1990, more than half of all United States veterans were 55 or older, and a quarter were at least 65 (Achenbaum, 1990; Damon, 1976).

Veterans of the Vietnam War have not been so fortunate. "The Vietnam war was a *generational* calamity," contends David Bonior, a Vietnam era veteran who is now a powerful congressman. "It has been calculated that there was a 'Vietnam generation' of draft-age men numbering 26,800,000, and it is probably fair to say that, one way or another, the war touched the lives of most of them" (Bonior, Champlin, & Kelly, 1984, p. 44). Even the government cedes as much: Its own studies document alcoholism, drug abuse, unemployment and underemployment, and psychological traumas. "Military duty in Vietnam had a negative effect upon post-military achievement" (U.S. Committee of Veterans' Affairs, 1981, p. 8).

Others add to the litany of complaints. Minority and lower-class veterans did not take advantage of the GI bill to the extent that previous cohorts of World War II and the Korean War did; benefits, in any case, were not as generous as other government tuition grants and student loan programs (Cohen, Segal, & Temme, 1986; Mattila, 1978). A decade before moviegoers got an insider's view of the Bronx VA ca. 1969 in *Born on the Fourth of July*, a Harris poll reported that 51% of all Vietnam era veterans gave the VA "an overall negative evaluation" (Rauch, 1981). There has been protracted litigation over whether tort law makes the United States government immune from claims of damages resulting from exposure to Agent Orange. That the government refuses to care for Vietnam veterans, even as the VA serves those veterans whose disability is attributable to cigarette smoking, hardly seems equitable (Jacobs & McNamara, 1986).

The disparity between the benefits received by World War II veterans and those who fought in Vietnam seems similar to David Thomson's description of cohort inequities in New Zealand:

> During their short lives the welfare states have seen the range and scale of their prizes and penalties alter so repeatedly and radically as to create persisting generations of "winners" and "losers"—successive cohorts of citizens who because of their varied birthdates are accumulating contrary experiences of what it means to live in a modern welfare state. (1989, p. 35; see also Chapter 11 in this volume)

The New Zealand and United States cases, however, differ in one important respect. Whereas the advantaged seem to get richer in the former instance, even aging American veterans are finding the VA system less responsive to their late-life vicissitudes than was true just a few years ago. The contract for those who "have borne the battle" is being redrafted.

Federal spending priorities and constraints have created a budget crisis for the nation's newest department, Veterans Affairs, thus adversely affecting the VA's ability to meet its geriatric mandate. Prior to a 1986 amendment, *every* veteran over 65 was eligible for care in VA facilities; now only those who meet income tests can enter. As it happens, roughly 75% of all older veterans still qualify for assistance. The catch is that there are not enough beds and geriatric units to serve all of the demand. VA nursing home capacity, for instance, would have to grow by 175% by 2010 to meet the projected need. Yet many VA officials fear that an "empty school syndrome" will beset the system in 15 years if it overbuilds now. Medical directors, dedicated to the acute-care model of hospital treatment that has dominated VA training and thinking since 1945, are loathe to reallocate funds to provide care and services for chronically ill elders (Demkovitch, 1984; Fackelmann, 1986; Sapolsky, 1977).

Despite badgering from outside experts, deft politicking within the department, and persistent congressional pressure, the VA seems unwilling and unable to reallocate funds for geriatrics to the extent that its current demographics and prior contributions to the field warrant. This may be a harbinger of things to come in United States policymaking, though as David Walker (Chapter 8 in this volume) as well as Fay Lomax Cook and Victor and Joanne Marshall (Chapter 7 in this volume) show us, perhaps not in all English-speaking nations. After all, the demise of the Medicare Catastrophic Act was due in part to a budget-neutral test on all new legislation imposed by federal lawmakers who could not afford any more red ink. There also was an unwillingness among relatively affluent senior citizens to pay for services they would probably not use due to their private-insurance coverage (Torres-Gil, 1990; Walker, 1990a). At the very least, both younger and older cohorts of veterans are "losers" nowadays in terms of what they might have expected.

Yet the World War II and Vietnam War cohorts are not the only groups of Americans with a stake in the VA. "Disgust with the V.A. is nationwide, and its expression is often visceral" (Klein, 1981, p. 22), but it is also the system many people turn to when they have no other choice. Veterans without health insurance are five times more likely to enter a VA center than those with insurance—regardless of age, income, or disability-connected status (Page, 1982). The VA's program for the homeless chronically mentally ill is one of the largest and most comprehensive in the nation (Gronvall, 1989). Many veterans dying of AIDS are entering VA facilities. Such data suggest that framing the VA's policy choices solely in terms of World War II and Vietnam War veterans misses those who served in the Korean War, or who gained eligibility in peacetime. (Note that my use of the term *cohort* here, unlike the first two case studies, refers to service, not birth year.) When no other alternative exists, many lower income Americans turn to the system. Roughly a third of all American families in 1977 benefited from VA programs (Cowan, 1988).

This case study reveals that rumblings of a class war lurk behind the cohort equity debate within the VA. Poor people have rarely done as well as the middle class in negotiating reforms of the American welfare state (Katz, 1986; Piven & Cloward, 1974). The vulnerability of the poor is becoming more apparent as cohorts of aging veterans, eligible for entitlements due to prior military service in different wars, find themselves denied access to health care. Institutional inertia, professional interests, messy politics, and competing national priorities suddenly have deflected generational negotiations in unexpected ways. Paradoxically, the injustice of current federal funding schemes highlights as it distorts the thrust of generational relations and inequities. Cohort interests are historically grounded in cultural norms. To suggest that the VA pits the needs of the young against the old misses Mannheim's point that not all generational issues deal primarily or exclusively with "age." This is why United States politics and policymaking regarding veterans make little sense to people in other countries.

How Historical Insights Might Shape Future Research on Generations

Historians typically choose not to make predictions about the future, but sometimes historical insights can suggest guidelines about future research on generations. Once again, Mannheim sets the theme:

> The *formal sociological* analysis of the generation phenomenon can be of help in so far as we may possibly learn from it what can and cannot be attributed to the generation factor as one of the factors impinging upon the social process. (1928/1952, p. 320; see also 1928/1956)

Any analysis of generational dynamics, succession(s), conflict(s), and negotiation(s) perforce must take the "lessons" of history seriously. Only by looking at transitions, turning points, variations, and contrarieties in the proximate and distant past can we begin to appreciate how the changing shape of time affects successive cohorts' sense of their identities.

Biblical actors, our Founding Fathers, and United States veterans faced quite dissimilar "problems" of generational succession. Nonetheless, each group represents an "actual generation," in Mannheim's sense of the term. Note that three themes recur in all three analogies. First, there is not much self-conscious uniformity of opinion *within* any age group. Genealogies in the Gospels of Matthew and Luke differ because they connect with different strands of Judaism and Hellenist culture. Intense fights over policy between Federalists and Anti-Federalists and among factions in the early American republic were waged by men with remarkably similar backgrounds, including their ages. Those who beat the draft have rarely joined in demanding assistance for their age peers whose lives were shattered in Vietnam.

Second, factors besides age and aging that affected how generations or cohorts in one case study negotiated their place in society were not usually salient in another case study. However much Adams, Jefferson, and Madison might have wished that antebellum Americans would frame their debates over slavery in terms of their own deliberations in 1776 and 1787, the rising generation chose not to follow their lead. Differences in historical memory and future expectations influenced how people interpreted Jesus' ministry. Class, race, and budgetary constraints seem more salient than age in characterizing the dilemmas of Vietnam veterans.

This suggests, third, that the developmental stakes expressed by various generations or cohorts tend to be highly negotiable. Adapting past traditions is a reasonable way to accommodate present-day circumstances and to adapt to future challenges. But history accords most groups a greater range of options for sparking conflict or fostering solidarity than they could possibly need or use. Nor is position in historical time or in the social order a good predictor of collective ideas or behavior. None of the groups studied here committed itself to a lifetime contract. Each negotiated with an eye to the past and to the future that was frequently tested by fresh issues, by new dilemmas.

I do not mean to imply that these three case studies cover all the possibilities as we contemplate the future of age relations. None of the analogies takes account of the fact that adult longevity has strikingly increased since 1940 and that age-specific norms and roles are undergoing fundamental transformations (Chudacoff, 1990; Neugarten & Neugarten, 1986; Riley & Riley, 1986). Even the VA case study is not quite on point, since the modus operandi of that institution seems to remain as it was fixed in 1945; structural lag is a serious problem (notably its presumption that the hospital can serve as the cornerstone of health care delivery for an increasingly geriatric veteran population). Hence we must guard against *the fallacy of cohort-centrism*, which Matilda White Riley defines as "erroneously assuming that members of all cohorts will age in exactly the same fashion as members of the cohort under study" (1992, p. 233). To the extent that the process of generational or cohort reconfiguration is continuous in the face of ever-shifting political agendas, then we might expect more, not fewer, unanticipated shifts in future patterns of succession.

There is, moreover, a gender bias in each of these analogies. Though some biblical scholars have suggested that Jesus' descent from David is to be traced through Mary, not Joseph, we mainly are dealing with patrilineal materials. Revolutionary women lived most of their days in a "separate sphere," divorced from the political and ideological disputes of their fathers, brothers, and husbands (Premo, 1989). The VA only belatedly is addressing the needs of women veterans (DePauw, 1985; U.S. Committee on Veterans' Affairs, 1987). Yet it seems reasonable to hypothesize that gender-specific differences will affect future patterns of generational succession (Goldscheider, 1990). Women increasingly outnumber men in the older ranks of society. The male-based case studies presented here ignore an important element that is bound to affect future generational relations. That admission, in turn, underlines a major theme in Mannheim's essay: How generational factors interact with other factors affects the transmission of values from one age group to its successors over time.

In thinking about the future of age relations, we must pay more attention to the context in which historical continuities, changes, and constraints converge. For it is these factors that will give distinctive shape to the process of succession experienced by successively longer lived cohorts. "Grasping the contingent nature of the past can break the tyranny of the present; seeing how historical actors made and remade social life, we can gain a new vision of our own present and future" (Benson, Brier, & Rosenzweig, 1986, pp. xiii-xiv). The impact of population aging on social institutions and cultural norms, no less than the dictates of the political economy on work, capital formation, rights, and resource allocation, merits careful consideration. But even analysts keen to discover cycles in history and uncover rhythms in generational patterns must leave room in their interpretations for unpredictable developments, the seemingly mundane events that transform the lives of ordinary people. Manifestations of the human capacity for tragedy, for foolishness, for dignity cannot be predicted with much certainty. However plausible it may seem to forecast an increase in age-based conflict, such a scenario is not inevitable from an historical perspective. Not even for a United States baby boom generation that has often defined itself (in spite of itself) in the (mirror) image of its elders.

Acknowledgments

I wish to thank Fred Bookstein, Victor Marshall, Lillian Troll, and Vern Bengtson for their critical reading of the first draft of this paper.

PART II

Social Contexts of the Generational Contract

The first two chapters of this volume (by Vern Bengtson and Andrew Achenbaum) sought to establish the definitional and operational boundaries for the possibility of a changing "generational contract" as societies fare in the 21st century. The three essays in Part II are equally sweeping in design. More than the two chapters that precede them, however, a revisionist tone pervades this section. The authors attempt to debunk conventional wisdom by extending the temporal and geographical parameters of the debate.

In Chapter 3, historian Maris Vinovskis takes as his starting point demographer Sam Preston's oft-cited argument that, since the 1980s if not before, children have been getting much less than older people in terms of public expenditures. To test this hypothesis historically, Vinovskis traces continuities and changes since the early years of the American republic in terms of the commitment of older voters to underwrite expenditures for public schools. Making historical comparisons is indeed a reasonable way to proceed in testing Preston's assertions. Evidence concerning whether voters have chosen between self-interest and altruism is readily available: for nearly 60 years commentators have expressed fears that rising Social Security tax rates would force policymakers to sequester educational funds. Vinovskis reports that for the most part older people have actually made schooling for the young a high priority. Although there was some softening of this position in the 1980s, he finds little actual evidence of a trade-off between supporting the old and training the young—contrary to Preston's argument. If anything, framing priorities in age-based terms obfuscates the basic issue: For the sake of its future, this country must continue to invest in *quality*, regardless of age.

Economists Richard Easterlin and Diane Macunovich and sociologist Eileen Crimmins (Chapter 4) also challenge conventional wisdom. Pundits and politicians have made much of the fact that those born after 1945—the *baby boomers* and *baby busters*—seem destined to become members of the first generation who will not attain a standard of living that will surpass that enjoyed by their parents. Population aging, it is often said, has burdened those who are currently middle-aged. To the contrary, Easterlin, Macunovich, and Crimmins report alterations in life cycle decisions since World War II that essentially have maintained the initial levels of relative economic well-being of different age groups. Despite adverse labor conditions and growing inequalities within the cohort, the material standard of living enjoyed by baby boomers has advanced at roughly the same rate as that of older adults in the working-age population. The trio thus questions the very economic premises that have made the generational equity debate so powerful.

The essay on generational relations in the People's Republic of China (Chapter 5) provides a much-needed cross-cultural perspective on age-based conflicts and negotiations in advanced industrial societies. Sociologists Judith Treas and Wei Wang take pains at the outset to suggest that there is likely to be a convergence between Eastern and Western dynamics of generational succession in years to come. The real split in China, it appears, is to be found between rural and urban settings. The challenge facing policymakers and community leaders in East Asia, conclude Treas and Wang, is to find ways to reduce the anomie that pervades intergenerational relations among urban residents.

3

An Historical Perspective on Support for Schooling by Different Age Cohorts

Maris A. Vinovskis

The strain on government resources during the 1970s and 1980s has raised concern about direct or indirect competition for assistance among subgroups of our population. In particular, there is a widespread and growing belief that the elderly have been the primary beneficiaries of government assistance at the expense of our children. Figures showing a decrease in poverty among the elderly and an increase in poverty among children frequently are cited as evidence of this trend. Critics often accuse the elderly of using their political power to maintain their relative advantages over groups such as children, who cannot personally participate in the political process (Bengtson, 1989; Marshall, Cook, & Marshall, Chapter 7 in this volume; Preston, 1984a; Torres-Gil, 1989, and Chapter 12 in this volume).

One of the largest public expenditures on children is support of education—most of it funded by state or local governments. Since much of local funding of public education depends upon passage of school millages and bond issues, voters frequently are called upon to express themselves in this area. Therefore, an analysis of support of and opposition to public-school expenditures by different age cohorts will provide an interesting and useful opportunity to examine the nature and extent, if any, of the so-called "generational" conflict.

Most of the current discussion about the conflict between different age cohorts regarding support of social services focuses almost exclusively

on the present. In addition, many studies of the age-related voting behavior of the American electorate look at only a single issue, such as
support for education or Social Security, rather than comparing several
different areas of social expenditures simultaneously. Furthermore,
some analysts look only at the factor of age without taking into consideration other possible influences that may affect an individual's views or
voting. As a result, many studies of the public conflict between different
age cohorts over social expenditures are ahistorical, narrowly defined,
or focused exclusively on the impact of age.

In order to understand the origins and development of our complex
system of organizing and financing public education, this chapter first
will examine our changing attitudes toward the responsibility of parents
and governments for the education of children in colonial and 19th-
century America. Next we will analyze changes in education in 20th-
century America, with particular attention to the growth of secondary
and higher education and to the increasing role of the state and federal
governments in financing public education. Finally, we will look specifically at the role of the elderly in supporting or opposing public education in the post-World War II era and try to ascertain, based upon an
analysis of survey data from 1988, whether or not there is a real and
serious difference between age cohorts. While some analysts believe
that there are important differences by age in regard to support for
additional educational funding, others dismiss this interpretation and
argue that few, if any, differences exist between younger and older
people on this issue—especially once we take into account the impact of
the other characteristics of the voters.

Education in Colonial and 19th-Century America

In 17th-century America, education was primarily intended to teach
individuals how to read and interpret the Bible. The responsibility for
education rested with the household rather than with schools or the
government (Axtell, 1974). The father, as the head of household, had
the primary responsibility of educating the other members of the household, although the mother often assisted him. The community inter-
vened only when the household failed to carry out its duties (Moran &
Vinovskis, 1986).

Some schools were established in early America—particularly in New
England. But most of these were grammar schools intended to educate
future clergymen, rather than elementary schools designed to teach children the basics of reading and writing (Bailyn, 1960). Nevertheless,

many parents found it easier or more convenient to send their youngest children to a private dame school or their older ones to a private elementary school for training. By the end of the 18th century, in the Northeast, private schools began to supplement or replace the educational training in the home. Local governments then often sent indigent children to these schools for their education rather than trying to place them in suitable households (Cremin, 1970).

The 19th century witnessed the rapid expansion of schooling in the North (Soltow & Stevens, 1981). Although some scholars (Bowles & Gintis, 1976) have tried to link the rise of schooling with the needs of industrial capitalism, most of the schooling occurred in New England and the Middle Atlantic states before they were heavily industrialized (Vinovskis, 1987a). Furthermore, most of the educational expansion in the antebellum period did not occur in the more economically developed Northeast, but in the Midwest, which was still heavily rural and agricultural (Fishlow, 1966).

In the early 19th century, there was not a clear and distinct separation between public and private financing of education. Local governments funded education but parents of students were often expected to contribute as well. Over time, however, private and family contributions to elementary schooling declined as public support for common schools increased (Benson & O'Halloran, 1987; Cremin, 1980). At the same time, public-school reformers like Horace Mann succeeded in eliminating any public assistance to private academies and many of these institutions were replaced by public schools (Jorgenson, 1987). As a result, by the time of the Civil War, common-school education was mainly under local control and financed almost entirely by the public.

Although school reformers tried to increase state expenditures and control of education, local resistance against any centralization was intense. Drawing upon the revolutionary ideology of the fear of any centralized power, most Americans insisted that their public common schools be financed and controlled by the voters in the small school districts in which these institutions were located (Kaestle & Vinovskis, 1980).

Since most 19th-century Americans had relatively large families and school-age children were present in most homes, opposition to local school taxes came mainly from those who felt too much was being spent on schools, from those wealthier families that still sent their children to private academies, and from those who opposed public education for religious reasons (Glenn, 1988; Kaestle, 1983; Katz, 1968; Vinovskis, 1985). There is little evidence of concern among 19th-century educational reformers that elderly voters in particular opposed higher local school taxes.

Yet there are a few tentative suggestions that older voters sometimes may have been less supportive of some of the new educational innovations, such as centralization and the establishment of public high schools, than younger voters. We do not have any definitive, direct evidence of differences in public support of schools by age. But there are several studies that provide some intriguing indirect evidence on the role of age in support of public schools in 19th-century America. An individual-level study of schooling in eight communities in Essex County, Massachusetts, in 1860 and 1880 did not find the age of the parents to be a strong predictor of their children's school attendance. Moreover, after controlling for the effects of other variables, parents ages 60 and above in 1860, but not in 1880, actually were more likely to send their children to school than the rest of the population (Kaestle & Vinovskis, 1980, pp. 87–89). A study of the Massachusetts House of Representatives in 1840 on the vote to abolish the state board of education, however, found that older legislators were considerably more likely to oppose the state board of education. Yet this probably reflects the concerns of older legislators about recent efforts to centralize control of education rather than opposition to public education in general (Kaestle & Vinovskis, 1980, pp. 222–223).

Finally, an analysis of the recorded public-meeting vote to abolish the Beverly Public High School in Massachusetts in 1860 found that those ages 60 and above were the most likely to oppose that institution. The meaning of the vote itself was very complicated because it involved the question of complying with the state law establishing high schools (the town had been sued for noncompliance) rather than just whether or not someone favored a public high school (Vinovskis, 1985, pp. 86–88). Overall, there are some hints in these fragmentary data that older voters may have been less supportive of some of the newer and more centralized aspects of public-school reform efforts, but they do not necessarily indicate opposition to public schooling in general. Moreover, when there were serious disputes over education in 19th-century America, those divisions do not seem to have been strongly age related.

One intriguing recent development in the study of aging in the past is the argument that parents invested in their children's education with the expectation that they would be repaid by those children with old-age assistance. Thus, there would have been an explicit or implicit contract between the young and their parents in 19th-century America. Unfortunately, there is little or no evidence for such an interpretation at this time. As one reads through the extensive published literature promoting schooling in 19th-century America, one is struck by the lack of references to such a contract or to the future benefits in old age for parents who educated their children. Moreover, historians have not found any evidence of such thinking in the private letters or diaries of the period. As a result, while the idea of an explicit or implicit individual contract between parents and children in regard to the children's education is appealing and seemingly plausible, so far there is little reason to believe it existed for most 19th-century Americans.

Twentieth-Century Changes in Education

In colonial and 19th-century America, most households contained at least some children under age 18 and therefore helped to foster support for schooling. The long-term decline in fertility as well as the increasing likelihood of individuals living by themselves, however, meant that fewer households in the 20th century included school-age children (Vinovskis, 1987b). In 1940 slightly less than half of the households (47.2%) included children under age 18 (Sweet & Bumpass, 1987, p. 340). By 1980 that figure had declined to 38.4% and in 1988 the number of households with their own children under age 18 had dropped to 35.1% (U.S. Bureau of Census, 1990, No. 61). In other words, today almost two thirds of households do not have any school-age children in them and therefore may be less willing to support educational expenditures for other people's children—perhaps also in part because many of those are minority children.

If the proportion of households with children has decreased in the 20th century, the amount of education each child receives has increased dramatically. Few students graduated from high school in 1900, but 38.1% of the population ages 25–29 in 1940 had completed high school; by 1988 the comparable rate was 86.1% (U.S. Bureau of Census, 1990, No. 215). Similarly, while college education in the early 20th century was limited to few individuals, by 1940 the percentage of the population ages 25–29 who had completed at least four years of college was 5.9% and in 1988 it was 22.7% (U.S. Bureau of Census, 1990, No. 215).

Along with the increase in the length of schooling, the costs of education have risen. In constant dollars (1987–1988), the total expenditure (per pupil in average daily attendance) for public elementary and secondary schools skyrocketed from $389 in 1919–1920 to $4,724 in 1988–1989 (National Center for Education Statistics, 1989, Table 145). Furthermore, the sources of that funding have changed dramatically. In 1919–1920, most of the revenue for public elementary and secondary schools came from local sources (83.2%) with only a small amount from either the state (16.5%) or the federal government (0.3%). By 1986–1987 the situation had changed considerably, with almost equal amounts coming from local governments (43.9%) and the state government (49.8%). Even federal funding of public elementary and secondary education reached 6.4% (Garms, Guthrie, & Pierce, 1978; National Center for Education Statistics, 1989, Table 138; Salmon, 1987).

If one looks at total expenditures for education (including public and private elementary, secondary, and higher education), there has been a significant increase during the past three decades—particularly in the area of higher education. As a percentage of gross national product, the cost of all educational institutions rose from 4.8% in 1959 to 5.9% in 1987, with most of that percentage increase due to the expansion of higher education. It is interesting to observe, however, that educational expenditures as a percentage of gross national product peaked in the mid-1970s and have decreased slightly since then (National Center for Education Statistics, 1989, Table 25). Moreover, educational expenditures relative to Social Security and Medicare costs have declined considerably from 1960 to 1987.

Voter Reactions to Increased Educational Spending

The funding of education, especially at the local level, is very diverse and complicated. In the mid-19th century, most of the funding for public schools came from allocations at either the township or county levels, with only a very small proportion of expenditures from state funds (Kaestle & Vinovskis, 1980). During the 1870s and 1880s, however, as part of conservative efforts to curb excessive municipal spending, most states set limits on the amount of property taxes or borrowing without a referendum by the local voters. One of the unanticipated consequences was the difficulty of raising funds for public schools and thus a growing reliance upon state sources of funding. Another consequence was the necessity of holding frequent local school tax and bond elections, which gave voters more opportunities to participate in the financial affairs of their public schools (Hamilton & Cohen, 1974).

There is considerable variation in the frequency of school referenda. According to a comprehensive survey of school referenda in the early 1970s, there were about 7,000 annual tax levies and budget elections throughout the United States, with about eight states accounting for over 5,000 of these referenda. Factors such as the size of school districts, the proportion of operating revenues based on local sources, the minimum school tax mandated by state statute, the length of time of voted levies, the possibility of school boards to call repeat elections, and the frequency of defeats (which necessitate another campaign) all affected the frequency of school-tax-levy and bond elections. In a few states less than a dozen school referenda were held each year, while at the other extreme 1,800 such elections were held in Oklahoma alone (Hamilton & Cohen, 1974).

Although public-school expenditures per pupil rose during the 1960s and early 1970s, as indicated earlier, there was growing resistance among taxpayers. One index of this discontent was the growing disapproval of school bond issues. In the early 1960s, approximately 72% of school bonds passed, but starting in 1967 that figure declined to 67% and then leveled off at approximately 50% in the 1970s. Furthermore, in constant dollars, the amount of school bonds passed dropped by about one half from the early 1960s to the late 1970s (calculated from Piele & Hall, 1973, p. 3; U.S. Bureau of the Census, 1981, No. 254). In other words, concerns about public schooling and high taxes persuaded many voters in the late 1960s and 1970s to reconsider the extent of their financial commitment to education.

As school levies and bond issues faced increasing public resistance, scholars initiated a series of studies to ascertain the characteristics of the small minority who voted in these local elections and to differentiate between those who supported and those who opposed increases in school funding. In general, these studies found that the most likely participants in these elections were more affluent, better educated, parents of school-age children, home owners, whites, and highly interested in schools. Among the voters, those who supported the bond issues were likely to be better educated and more affluent than those who did not support it, and were more likely to be parents of school-age children, African American, and highly interested in their schools and community. Conversely, those who opposed increased taxes for education were likely to be less educated, less affluent, without school-age children, white, and more alienated from the community and the schools (Hamilton & Cohen, 1974; Piele & Hall, 1973).

In regard to age, almost all of the studies found that older voters were less supportive of educational expansion than younger voters. Even after controlling for the effects of other factors, such as socioeconomic status and parenthood, most of these analyses found elderly voters less supportive of increases in educational expenditures than younger voters. A few did find, however, that the effects of age became relatively unimportant once other personal and family characteristics of the voters were controlled for (Button & Rosenbaum, 1989; Hamilton & Cohen, 1974; Piele & Hall, 1973).

We can use the Gallup/Phi Delta Kappa Polls of Public Attitudes Toward the Public Schools 1969/88 to see if there are any recent changes in public support for education. Starting in 1969, they asked: "Suppose the

Percentage Supporting Local School Tax Increase

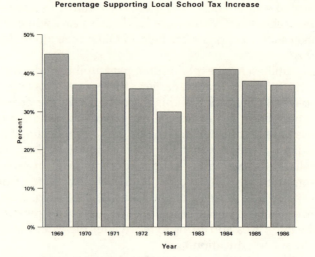

Year

Figure 1. Percentage supporting local school tax increase. *Note:* The data in
Figure 1 are from the *Gallup/Phi Delta Kappa Polls of Attitudes Toward the Public
Schools, 1969–88* by S. Elam, 1989, Bloomington, IN: Phi Delta Kappa Edu-
cational Foundation.

local public schools said they needed much more money. As you feel at
this time, would you vote to raise taxes for this purpose, or would you
vote against raising taxes for this purpose?" (Elam, 1989, p. 17)

In 1969, 45% of the public replied that they would vote for additional
school taxes, but this support declined to 37% the next year and remained at approximately that level for the next three years (see Figure
1). By 1980 support for additional school taxes dropped to 30%, but
recovered quickly in 1983 with the publicity surrounding the publication
of *A Nation at Risk* (National Commission on Excellence in Education,
1983). (The education survey was conducted two weeks after the release
of that report.) For the next three years, support for additional school
taxes remained at about the same level (Elam, 1989).

Overall, it appears that public willingness to support schooling
through additional local taxes decreased from 1969 to 1970, then briefly
stabilized before dropping to a new low in 1980, and recovered after
1983 to a level comparable to the early 1970s. Throughout most of the
1970s and 1980s, approximately 4 out of 10 Americans favored additional
local taxes to support the public schools. Those without any school
children and those with children in parochial schools generally were less
supportive of local school tax increases than those with children in the
public schools. Furthermore, for the one year (1969) for which we do

have age breakdowns, 56% of those ages 21–29, 47% of those ages 30–49, and 39% of those ages 50 and up supported additional local taxes for education.

Roughly comparable changes in support for additional educational expenditures are found in the General Social Surveys for 1973 and 1986. Those surveys inquired about the willingness of the public to support certain programs:

> We are faced with many problems in this country, none of which can be solved easily or inexpensively. I'm going to name some of the problems, and for each one I'd like you to tell me whether you think we're spending too much money on it, too little money, or about the right amount. First, space exploration . . . [education, Social Security, welfare]: are we spending too much, too little, or about the right amount on (item)? (quoted in Ponza, Duncan, Corcoran, & Groskind, 1988, p. 444)

According to a recent analysis of these data (Ponza et al., 1988), public support for increased spending on education rose from 49% in 1973 to 67% in 1986. The study also found that older age groups were consistently less likely to support increased educational expenditures than younger groups (see Figure 2). The authors, however, also point out that older respondents, along with every other age group, increased their support for educational funding from 1973 to 1986; moreover, the older age groups were also less supportive of increases in Social Security payments than other age groups. Noting that these particular questions about spending are so broad, the authors caution us against simply concluding that the elderly are acting in their own narrow self-interest in deciding upon which social programs to endorse. Unfortunately, this otherwise interesting and useful study does not attempt to examine in more detail the pattern of responses by age to these different domestic social programs.

Age Differences in Support for Increased Federal Spending for Public Schools in 1988

In order to explore the importance of age in determining support for education today, we can use the American National Election Survey for 1988, which interviewed a representative sample of 2,040 United States citizens of voting age living in the 48 coterminous states (excluding people living in Alaska or Hawaii).[1] Unlike most of the studies of school bond issues or analyses of the Gallup poll results, this survey focused

Percentage Supporting Increase in Educational Spending

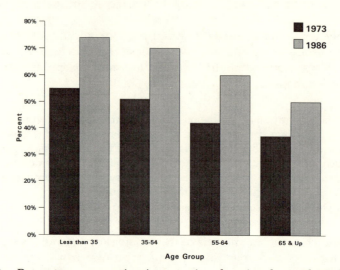

Figure 2. Percentage supporting increase in educational spending. *Note:* The data in Figure 2 are from "The Guns of Autumn? Age Differences in Support for Income Transfers to the Young and Old" by M. Ponza et al., 1988, *Public Opinion Quarterly,* 52(4), 492–512.

specifically on the role of the federal government in providing assistance to public education or to college students as well as to other programs.

The survey prefaced its questions about federal expenditures with the following statement: "If you had a say in making up the federal budget this year, for which of the following programs would you like to see spending increased and for which would you like to see spending decreased."

The interviewer then asked about a series of programs. For example, the question on public education specifically asked: "Should federal spending on public schools be increased, decreased, or kept about the same?" Comparable questions were asked about federal spending for aid to college students, for improving and protecting the environment, for assistance to the unemployed, for space and scientific research, for assistance to African Americans, for child care, for care of the elderly, for the homeless, for the war on drugs, for Social Security, for food stamps, for aid to the Contras, for Star Wars, and for fighting AIDS. Thus, altogether, questions about federal spending for 15 different activities were asked, as well as the standard inquiries about the demographic, socioeconomic, and political characteristics of these respondents.

There was considerable variation in the willingness of the public to increase federal spending on these programs. At one extreme, only a very small minority of Americans favored increased federal spending for aid to the Contras (10.9%) or for the development of the Star Wars program (15.7%). At the other extreme, most citizens favored more federal expenditures for fighting drugs (73.8%) or helping the elderly (75.2%). In terms of education, 63.9% favored additional federal spending for public schools and 44.8% supported more federal assistance for college students.

We can study the age variation in support of increased federal spending by subdividing the sample into six age groups: 18–29, 30–39, 40–49, 50–59, 60–69, and 70 and above. Coefficients of variation by age group were calculated for each of the 15 issues. For some items (such as more aid for the Contras, for the war on drugs, for help for the homeless, and for Social Security) there was relatively little variation by age. Support for additional federal spending on Star Wars had the most overall variation by age. Interestingly, approval of increased spending for public schools or for college students had the next highest amount of variation by age.

In general, individuals ages 50–59, 60–69, and 70 and above were less supportive of increased federal spending for almost all of these issues than the population as a whole. In addition, in most situations, support for increased federal aid tended to diminish for these three age groups as one moved from the youngest age group (50–59 years) to the next older group (60–69 years), and then to 70 and above. The only clear exception to this pattern was the question about the war on drugs, where those ages 50–59 and 60–69 were slightly more supportive than those in all of the other age groups.

We can also look in more detail at the age pattern of support for more federal funding of public schools by comparing it with responses to the questions about more federal funding for the elderly or for the unemployed (Figure 3). For additional federal assistance for the unemployed, there is much less overall support than for public schools, but also less variation by age. For more federal aid to the elderly, there is more overall support than for the public schools, but again less variation by age. For all three issues, but especially for more federal funding of public schools, there is a general decrease in support with age.

It is interesting to observe that support for additional federal assistance for public schools does drop rather dramatically from 77.1% among those ages 18–29 to 46.9% among those ages 70 and above. At the same time, one should note that support for additional public-school spending by those in their 50s and 60s is nearly identical, and about one half of those age 60 and above still do endorse increased federal aid for public education. Therefore, any discussions of older respondents as a homogeneous group are incorrect and misleading.

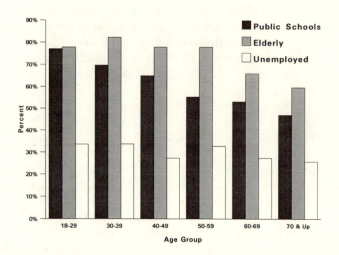

Figure 3. Percentage favoring more federal spending for public schools, elderly, and unemployed. *Note:* The data in Figure 3 are from *American National
Election Study, 1988: Pre-and Post-Election Survey,* by W. E. Miller and The
National Election Studies, 1989, Ann Arbor, MI: Inter-University Consortium for Political and Social Research.

We can take another look at the issue of age and support for increased
federal expenditures for public schools by comparing those with and
without children under 18 in their households (only for those under age
60 because very few of the older individuals had any children under 18
in their households). In each age group, those with children under 18 in
the household are more supportive of increased federal assistance for
public schools than those without. Nevertheless, even those under age
50 who do not have any children in their household are still more supportive of increased federal funding of public schools than those age 60
and above—perhaps in part because the childless individuals in the
younger cohorts still may expect to have children eventually who will
use the public schools.

One might argue, as some have, that the age differences in support
for increased funding of public education are only the result of the
impact of other factors, such as educational level or family income,
which may be highly correlated with age. Therefore, to ascertain the
relative impact of age compared to other characteristics in accounting for
differences in support of more public school funding, a multiple classification analysis (MCA) was run, with support for or opposition to in-

Table 1. Support for Increasing Federal Aid to Public Schools in 1988: Eta^2, Beta, Changes in R^2, and Adjusted R^2

Variable	Eta^2	Beta	Changes in R^2 if variable removed
Age	.0395	.1691	−.0227
Sex	.0027	.0412	−.0011
Race	.0277	.0666	−.0019
Education	.0062	.0366	+.0029
Income	.0096	.0569	−.0006
Liberal/conservative index	.0391	.1098	−.0062
Party identity	.0452	.1469	−.0122
Population of residence	.0160	.0682	−.0018
Census region	.0102	.0664	−.0027
	Adjusted R^2 = .1019		

Note: The data in Table 1 are from *American National Election Study, 1988: Pre- and Post-Election Survey,* by W. E. Miller and The National Election Studies, 1989, Ann Arbor, MI: Inter-University Consortium for Political and Social Research.

creased federal spending as the dependent variable (1 = support/0 = opposition). The nine dependent variables were age, sex, race, education, family income, liberal/conservative index, party identity, population size of the community, and the region in which the individual lived.

After controlling for the effects of the other variables, age is the best predictor of whether or not someone supports additional federal funding for public schools (Table 1). Whether one looks at the beta weights or the changes in the adjusted R^2 when this particular variable is removed from the analysis, age is the single best predictor. Moreover, the tendency of older individuals to oppose additional federal funding for public schools remains almost the same once we adjust for the impact of the other variables (Table 2).

The sex of the respondent was not an important predictor of support or opposition to increased federal spending for public schools (Table 1). Women were more likely than men to support additional funding (Table 2).

Several studies have suggested that African Americans are more apt to support increased educational expenditures than whites. This study found that African Americans and others were more supportive of federal funding for public schools than whites (Table 2), but the variable of race as a whole was only the fifth best predictor (Table 1).

It had been anticipated that education would be a strong predictor of support for increased federal school funding, but instead it was the weakest of the nine independent variables (Table 1). In addition, the pattern of support by educational level was not consistent. Those who

Table 2. Support for Increasing Federal Aid to Public Schools in 1988: Class Means, Adjusted Means, Net Deviations, and Number of Cases (0 = Do Not Increase Aid; 1 = Increase Aid)

	Class mean	Adjusted mean	Net deviation	Number of cases
Age				
18–29	78.0	75.6	+10.2	410
30–39	70.0	69.4	+4.0	466
40–49	66.0	67.1	+1.7	313
50–59	55.0	55.2	−10.2	238
60–69	55.0	57.1	−8.3	219
70 & up	51.0	53.5	−11.9	204
Sex				
Male	63.0	63.1	−2.3	795
Female	67.0	67.1	+1.7	1,055
Race				
White	62.0	64.0	−1.4	1,561
African American	84.0	72.7	+7.3	231
Other	83.0	72.6	+7.2	58
Education				
8 grades or less	55.0	61.4	−4.0	155
9–11 grades	69.0	67.3	+1.9	210
High school graduate	67.0	66.3	+0.9	665
Some college	66.0	64.4	−1.0	436
BA, no advanced degree	61.0	64.0	−1.4	275
Advanced degree	69.0	68.1	+2.7	109
Income				
0–$9,999	69.0	65.7	+0.3	301
$10,000–$19,999	68.0	68.1	+2.7	380
$20,000–$29,999	69.0	67.1	+1.7	319
$30,000–$39,999	67.0	66.0	+0.6	263
$40,000 & up	61.0	63.6	−1.8	449
Not ascertained	53.0	57.6	−7.8	138
Liberal/conservative index				
Extremely liberal	82.0	72.5	+7.1	33
Liberal	81.0	74.2	+8.8	108
Slightly liberal	78.0	72.5	+7.1	178
Moderate	69.0	67.9	+2.5	423
Slightly conservative	62.0	65.1	−0.3	298
Conservative	50.0	58.2	−7.2	260
Extremely conservative	43.0	49.6	−15.8	58
Haven't thought much of it	66.0	64.0	−1.4	492
Party identity				
Strong Democrat	77.0	74.5	+9.1	325

Table 2. (Continued)

	Class mean	Adjusted mean	Net deviation	Number of cases
Weak Democrat	74.0	71.9	+6.5	331
Independent-Democrat	74.0	68.4	+3.0	217
Independent-Independent	66.0	65.2	−0.2	196
Independent-Republican	59.0	60.4	−5.0	256
Weak Republican	57.0	58.8	−6.6	261
Strong Republican	48.0	54.8	−10.6	264
Population of residence				
0–2,499	61.0	63.4	−2.0	617
2,500–10,499	59.0	63.0	−2.4	234
10,500–50,499	64.0	63.5	−1.9	481
50,500–350,499	70.0	69.9	+4.5	311
350,500 & up	79.0	71.5	+6.1	207
Census region				
Northeast	62.0	61.2	−4.2	332
North Central	59.0	62.6	−2.8	526
South	70.0	67.7	+4.5	636
West	70.0	69.2	+6.1	356
Total	65.4			1,850

Note: The data in Table 2 are from *American National Election Study, 1988: Pre-and Post-Election Survey*, by W. E. Miller and The National Election Studies, 1989, Ann Arbor, MI: Inter-University Consortium for Political and Social Research.

had an advanced degree were the most supportive of more federal funding for education (after controlling for the effects of the other factors), but those who had at least some college education or had received their BA were less supportive than those with some high school education or those who had graduated from high school (Table 2).

Family income was not a particularly strong predictor of support for increased federal funding for public schools (Table 1). Interestingly, the most wealthy Americans were the least supportive of further federal expenditures for public schools—perhaps either because they could afford to send their own children to private schools or because they were the most likely to pay for much of the increases through additional taxes.

Whether individuals identify themselves as liberal or conservative was the third best predictor of support for or opposition to more federal dollars for public schools (Table 1). Not surprisingly, those who identified themselves as liberals were more supportive of increased federal expenditures than those who identified themselves as conservatives (Table 2).

Similarly, party identification was the second best predictor (Table 1). Democrats were more favorable to additional federal money for public schools; Republicans were more opposed to additional federal funding for public schools (Table 2).

The population size of the communities in which respondents lived was moderately important in predicting their position on additional federal expenditures for education (Table 1). Individuals in rural areas or small towns were generally less favorable to further federal financing of public schools than those who lived in the larger cities (Table 2).

Finally, the region of the country in which respondents lived had a moderate impact on support or opposition to increased federal funding for the public schools (Table 1). While those in the Northeast and the North Central states were the least likely to support additional federal funds, those in the South and West were the most likely to favor additional federal expenditures (Table 2).

Overall, the ability of these nine independent variables to predict support of federal funding of public schools was relatively modest. The adjusted R^2 for the multiple classification analysis was .1019.

Several other analyses were done to explore further the importance of age in predicting support for additional federal funding of public schools. To see if the presence or absence of children under 18 years old in the household made any difference, this variable was added in another MCA run. Presence of children under 18 in the household was the fifth best predictor among the 10 independent variables; after controlling for the other variables, 62.7% of those from households without children under 18 years old supported more federal funding, while 69.1% of those from households with children under 18 supported such additional assistance. Interestingly, the inclusion of the presence of children under 18 years old in the household did not increase the overall adjusted R^2 very much ($+.0020$), but it appears to have reduced the overall explanatory power of the age variable (beta $= .1407$) slightly so that it was now just below that of the political identity variable in importance (beta $= .1405$). After controlling for the effects of all of the other variables, including the presence or absence of children under 18 years old in the household, the gap between younger and older individuals in support for additional federal spending for public schools decreased very slightly.

One of the potential problems in the addition of the variable of the presence or absence of children under 18 years is the overlap between that variable and the age variable. Individuals who were ages 60–69 or 70 and above were very unlikely to be living in households with any children under 18 in them. To cope with this potential problem, a new variable was created to replace the two dealing with age and children in the household. The same age categories were used as before, but individuals below the age of 50 were subdivided by whether or not a child under 18 was in their household. For those 60–69, and 70 and above, no subdivision by the presence or absence of children was made.

Another MCA was run using the new age/child variable in place of the age and presence-of-child variables (the other independent variables remained the same). Compared to the previous MCA, in which the presence or absence of a child under 18 in the household had been added, there was almost no change in the adjusted R^2, but the age/child variable now was the single best predictor of support for or opposition to increased federal funding for public schools. After controlling for the effects of the other independent variables, individuals living in households with children under 18 were more likely to support additional federal funding, but the differences at the younger ages (18–29 and 30–39) were quite small.

Support for federal aid to education varies considerably by whether one is asking about assisting public schools or college students. Some Americans, drawing upon certain aspects of our historical experience, believe that parents are the ones who are responsible for paying for the higher education of their own children and therefore oppose any federal aid to college students (as differentiated from funding for public elementary or secondary schools). Whereas 65.4% of the public supports increased federal aid for public schools, only 45.3% supports increased federal assistance for college students. Again, an MCA was run with support for or opposition to increased federal spending for college students as the dependent variable (1 = support/0 = opposition) and age, sex, race, education, family income, liberal/conservative index, party identity, population size of the community, and the region in which the individual lives as the nine independent variables.

Generally, the results of this MCA were similar to those of the earlier analysis. The adjusted R^2s were almost the same and most of the independent variables were roughly similar in their relative predictive power. (Interestingly, race became a stronger predictor, since support for more federal spending for college students was particularly pronounced among African Americans.) Age, without controlling for any of the other factors, was a weaker predictor. Nevertheless, after controlling for the effects of the other variables, age continued to be the single best predictor overall in accounting for support for or opposition to increased federal spending for college students.

So far, we have found that age is the best overall predictor of support for increased federal funding either of public schools or of college students, and that the older population is much less supportive of these increases than the younger population. But what about other issues?

Does age continue to play such an important role in predicting support for increased federal funding of other domestic social programs?

Two comparable MCAs were run to determine the support for or opposition to increased federal expenditures for the elderly or for the unemployed. While in both instances older individuals were less supportive of additional federal funding than younger ones, age by itself was a less powerful predictor of support for more aid to the unemployed than of support for more assistance to the elderly. Moreover, age by itself was a weaker predictor in both of these situations than in explaining differences in support for more federal aid either for public schools or for college students. Controlling for the effects of the other variables, age continued to be the best overall predictor of more federal support for the elderly, but only the fifth best predictor of more federal money for the unemployed.

Our more detailed examination of the 1988 data on the willingness of the public to support increased federal funding for certain programs suggests that the impact of age varies from one issue to another. Usually, but not always, older age groups are less supportive of increased federal funding than younger age groups; but the age group differences vary, depending upon which issue is being considered. Particularly in the cases of increased federal aid for public education and for college students, age differences were quite strong and age was the single best predictor of support after taking into consideration the impact of the other eight independent variables in our MCAs. Therefore, while some scholars have tried to minimize the role of age in affecting support for educational expenditures, this analysis suggests that age is indeed a very important factor—even after taking into consideration the impact of the other characteristics of the respondents.

Conclusion

Americans have usually made the education of their young a high priority, but the organization and financing of schooling has changed dramatically over time. Our continually evolving mixture of parental, local, state, and federal responsibility for schooling makes the governance and delivery of educational services very complex and difficult today. Moreover, the shifting coalitions of support for educational expansion and reforms are equally diverse and defy any simplistic explanations, whether based upon social control by capitalists or the so-called conflict between "generations." At the same time, basic demographic and ideological changes in our society and economy suggest that the current concern about age cohort differences in support of education may continue and even be exacerbated in the future.

Since the mid-19th century, most Americans have accepted the notion that every child is entitled to a free public education, but there is considerable disagreement over how much education is needed, how we should pay for it, and who should control our schools. Although there are some hints that age differences may have played some role in the 19th-century decisions about schooling, they were not perceived by contemporaries to be particularly important or threatening. Nor is there any evidence in the past of an explicit or implicit contract between the young and their parents about investing in the children's education so that parents could be repaid in their old age. Today, there is growing concern and even some evidence that age may be a primary factor, among several others, in determining one's position and behavior on educational issues.

Nevertheless, given the variety of the current school systems and our complex and multiple mechanisms for financing them, there is little reason to suspect many, if any, direct and explicit trade-offs between support for education and support for programs to help the elderly. Indeed, the diverse and specialized institutions of the American political structure at all levels usually make it more difficult, if not impossible, for voters and policymakers to make such direct and explicit trade-offs between programs. Moreover, much of the future expenditures on schooling and other social programs depend on such basic changes as the rate of economic growth and our willingness to tax ourselves for further government services, rather than on taking money from one program and transferring it to another. If we are about to experience a period of relative stagnation in overall public expenditures in the near future, however, then demands for additional educational spending may clash with demands for other important societal goals such as increased welfare support, more funding for the war on drugs, and additional assistance for the elderly.

If we were relatively content with the current levels of educational spending as well as with the quality of our existing schools, then it might not be too difficult to maintain our present system. There are strong indications, however, that satisfaction with the status quo in our educational system is unlikely. Growing recognition of the importance of education for enhancing the economic productivity of our workers and of the need to maintain our international competitiveness has already led to calls for major educational reforms. As the proportion of minority students in our schools increases, many of them from economically disadvantaged households, there will be a need for additional educational expenditures. Efforts to provide equal access to quality education in local elementary and secondary public schools will necessitate increased state and federal aid to compensate for the inadequate local financial resources in many school districts today. At the same time, the growing demand for equal access for everyone to higher education may lead to efforts to increase federal aid for college students.

All of these efforts to increase public funding of education will be complicated by continued differences among us over the locus of control for schooling; over the relative role of local, state, and federal financial assistance; and over the responsibility of parents for providing for the higher education of their own children. As a result, the future battles for additional educational funding will be as complex and difficult as ever because they will be based in large part upon many different and often contradictory principles and values that are part of our historical heritage.

Given the increasingly small proportion of households with school-age children and the reluctance of some voters to provide for much more than a minimal level of education for other people's children, it is likely that the issue of equity between different age cohorts will be raised in the future. As supporters of increased school funding are frustrated by the difficult and never-ending task of convincing voters and policymakers at the local, state, and federal levels that more funds for education are needed, it is inevitable that some will raise questions about the relatively privileged status of entitlement programs such as Social Security and Medicare. As a result, there will be the temptation to reduce the complex set of factors that account for past and present educational expenditures under the rubric of a "generational" conflict—especially since we have seen that there is considerable empirical evidence that older voters are less supportive of more educational funding than younger ones.

Rather than being diverted from the real and serious problems facing education in the future by focusing mainly on age differences in voter support for educational spending, we should instead concentrate on convincing everyone of the importance of improving the education of our children in our homes and in the schools. It would also be particularly unfortunate if we confuse educational quality only with increased spending and then single out the elderly as a monolithic group opposed to educational improvements, when in fact many of them have always supported such reforms. The genius of 19th-century school reformers such as Horace Mann was that they were able to build diverse coalitions for improved schooling and to develop a broad public consensus on the value of education for everyone, and that they did not try to pit one segment of the population against another in the name of school reform. It is in this spirit that we should tackle our complex problems of providing quality education for all of our children in the future rather than looking for any simpleminded and misleading excuses for our educational difficulties and deficiencies today.

Notes

1. The data utilized in this chapter were made available by the Inter-University Consortium for Political and Social Research. The data for *American National Study, 1988: Pre- and Post-Election Survey* were originally collected by Warren E. Miller and the National Election Studies (1989). Neither the collector of the original data nor the Consortium bears any responsibility for the analyses or interpretations presented here.

4

Economic Status of the Young and Old in the Working-Age Population, 1964 and 1987

Richard A. Easterlin, Diane J. Macunovich,
and Eileen M. Crimmins

In the last two decades, as the baby boom generation has entered the labor market, wage rates and unemployment rates of younger relative to older workers have deteriorated (Berger, 1989; Lillard & Macunovich, 1989). Government transfer programs—though much less important for the working-age population than labor market conditions—also trended against the younger population, e.g., Aid to Families with Dependent Children (AFDC) has been scaled back, while the Social Security disability program has expanded.

These developments have led to a common perception that, compared with their predecessors at the same age, the economic status of the baby boom generation (their material level of living) has declined, both absolutely and relative to older generations; that their retirement prospects have correspondingly diminished; and that tensions across age groups have risen (Bengtson, 1990; Heclo, 1988; Kingson, 1988; Levy & Michel, 1991; Longman, 1985b). This paper aims to evaluate such views. It addresses the following specific questions: (1) How has the economic well-being of younger adults changed over the past 25 years, and how does this change compare with that for older adults in the working-age population? (2) What do the data imply for the economic prospects of the baby boom generation when they reach retirement? (3) What are the implications of the changes in relative economic well-being by age for past and prospective tensions between younger and older age groups?

Theoretical Considerations

It is important to distinguish economic well-being from total welfare. By economic well-being, we mean one's material level of living. One's feeling of total well-being includes, in addition, other considerations, such as the amount of leisure time one has, the extent of one's privacy or independence, the pleasure derived from work, and the number and well-being of other family members, including both one's offspring and parental and older generations. In keeping with the economic theory of welfare, we see these different dimensions of welfare, not as absolutes, but as varying in their relative importance among individuals at a point in time and for the same individual over time (Schneider & Krupp, 1965). Depending on the strength of one's relative preferences, one aspect of welfare, such as one's material living level, may be sacrificed for other aspects, such as having children. Thus the relative strength of one's different sources of well-being can be thought of as implying trade-offs; for example, in considering sharing one's home with one's parents, concerns for parental well-being are weighed against desires for privacy and independence.

To a considerable extent, the causes of one's material well-being are beyond personal control. For the individual, market wage rates are given; so too is the state of the economy and thus the strength of labor demand and job prospects generally. Similarly, the terms of government programs providing income support—poverty, retirement, unemployment, and disability programs—all are beyond personal control. But one's economic status is influenced also by a number of life cycle decisions that are within personal control. Of particular interest here are a number of demographic life cycle decisions that affect one's economic status: whether and when one forms a union and has children; whether both members of the union work, and, if so, how much; and whether one lives doubled up or in one's own household. Many of these demographic life cycle decisions are concentrated in the early adult years and thus may be especially important in affecting economic status at these ages. But there are some decisions that bear also on economic status later in life, most notably decisions regarding retirement (whether to work) and living arrangements (doubling up).

It is important to note that, while such life cycle decisions influence material living levels, they bear also on noneconomic dimensions of well-being. If to improve their economic status young people postpone family formation and continue to live in their parents' homes, then they are forgoing the benefits of having families of their own and the privacy and independence of their own households. Thus, noneconomic aspects of welfare are being traded off for material living level benefits. Conversely, a decision to retire may mean some sacrifice in material living level, but brings with it the reward of much more leisure.

At any given time, an individual has internalized a certain desired level of living, largely as a result of his or her prior economic socialization experience. If factors beyond one's control yield an income level that falls short of one's material aspirations, then, to the extent possible, life cycle decisions might be modified to raise one's actual income level to that desired. Thus noneconomic aspects of welfare may be sacrificed for economic. If, however, circumstances yield a potential income level in excess of that desired, then prospective economic gains may be forgone in favor of other sources of enjoyment—more children, more leisure, privacy, etc.

This conception, that life cycle decisions, or more generally, economic and social behavior, are importantly affected by one's available resources relative to one's target level of living, derives from relative income or relative deprivation theory (Duesenberry, 1966; Merton, 1968; Modigliani, 1961; Stouffer, Suchman, DeVinney, Star, & Williams, 1949). Currently, in studies of the older population, the effect of relative income on decisions to retire or to double up is recognized in the concept of the "replacement rate," the ratio of retirement to preretirement income (Fields & Mitchell, 1984; Munnell, 1982).

Relative income theory has a direct bearing on the view noted at the start of this paper that the baby boom generation has experienced a decline in material living levels, both absolutely and relative to older age groups. It is true that recent decades have seen a divergence in the resources available to different age groups—more favorable trends in earnings and transfer payments for the older adult population than for the younger. In the absence of altered life cycle decisions, this development would cause a divergence in material living levels between older and younger adults. However, assuming similar trends in material aspirations by age, relative income theory suggests that, at both ends of the age distribution, life cycle decisions would be altered by the differential trend in available resources. Those having difficulty in achieving their material aspirations—the younger adult population—would be more hesitant about forming unions, having children, establishing their own households, and so on (Christian, 1989; Easterlin, Macdonald, & Macunovich, 1990a; Hernandez, 1989). Those finding it easy to achieve their material aspirations—the older adult population—would retire earlier, would be more likely to live in their own rather than in another's household, and would be more willing to have their adult children live at home with them (Goldscheider & Goldscheider, 1989).

The effect of these decisions would be to increase the observed rate of advance in material living levels among the younger population relative to that of the older, thus modifying or eliminating the divergence in resource trends. A hypothesis that this paper seeks to test is that life cycle decisions at younger and older ages have substantially modified the divergence in economic well-being that would otherwise have occurred because of labor market factors and government programs beyond individual control. If this is so, then the economic prospects in retirement of the baby boom generation may be better than is commonly assumed.

In the case where resources are deficient relative to one's target level of living, not all life cycle decisions would be unambiguously positive in their effect on living levels. If increased strains within a marriage arise from the difficulty of achieving desired living levels, the result might be marital dissolution. Similarly, in a nonmarital union, the occurrence of an unplanned conception when there is already a shortfall relative to desired living levels might precipitate a crisis leading to dissolution of the union. In both cases an increased prevalence of single parents would imply worsening living levels, particularly for mothers and their children. But single parents confronted with a threat to their living levels might seek to compensate, in turn, by doubling up with their own parents or by forming an unmarried-couple union. The impact on living levels of single mothers and their children of such adjustments is often overlooked in the literature (Macunovich & Easterlin, 1990).

We are not claiming that life cycle demographic decisions depend wholly on relative income considerations; clearly any given decision is affected by a variety of considerations. Our expectation, however, is that, over time, changing relative income influences have been strong enough to affect observed patterns of economic well-being by age as hypothesized above.

Concepts and Data

Because we want the measure of economic status to take account of the life cycle decisions made to influence one's economic well-being, the economic status of an individual is defined here as the total money *income per adult equivalent* (IAE)—adjusted for price level change over time—in the household in which the individual resides. The definition of *income* is that of the Bureau of Census's Current Population Survey: pretax, posttransfer money income, including public and private pension income, public assistance, other welfare payments, and alimony and child support payments. Income in kind is excluded. To adjust for price level change over time (in earnings rates as well as income per adult equivalent), the CPI-X1 index is used (for a discussion of why this index gives a more accurate picture of the trend in living costs than the standard Consumer Price Index, see U.S. Congressional Budget Office, 1988). The definition of *household* is also the same as that of the Current Population Survey, except that, here, unmarried-couple households have been identified whenever possible, and differentiated from other types of households. Clearly the decision to form an unmarried-couple union affects one's material living level and such unions need to be taken into account in the analysis of economic well-being. Unmarried-couple households are identified according to the Bureau of Census definition: two unrelated adults 15 years of age or over of the opposite sex living together in a household in which no other adults are present.

The income measure used here is not a simple per capita measure, in which total household income is divided equally among all members, whether children or adults. Rather, it is a per-adult-equivalent measure, with IAE computed for each household by dividing the household's total money income by the number of adult equivalents in the household, derived according to Fuchs's scale (1986). This conversion to a per adult equivalent basis yields a better measure of individual differences in economic status by allowing for variations in household size and adult-child composition; in addition, it allows for economies of scale in consumption.

The economic status of an individual is assumed to correspond to the average economic status of the household in which the individual resides. This is similar to the assumption in governmental estimates of the poverty rates of persons that one is in poverty if the family of which one is a member is so classified.

The average economic status of an age group or cohort, such as those born in the baby boom, is measured as the mean value of the IAEs of all of the persons composing that age group (excluding only the very small fraction in group quarters). Although this procedure for determining the average status of an age group may seem obvious, it is not the way that inferences are commonly made about differences by age in the population. This is because age of head of household (or family) is typically used as the basis for inferring such variations. It goes almost without saying that an individual of a given age may be living in a household or family headed by a person of a much different age. As will be shown later, this difference in classification procedure can have an important effect on impressions of differences in economic status by age.

The data used here are from the March Current Population Survey tapes for 1965 and 1988. All measures are for March of the survey year, except for income, earnings, and work experience, which refer to the previous calendar year. The state of the economy gives rise to differen-

tial fluctuations in income by age, but, to judge from the average unemployment rate, the two income years considered here, 1964 and 1987,
were quite similar with regard to the state of the economy.

In the analysis below we present data mostly for 5-year age groups
from age 20 through 59, and we make inferences about changes in
economic status by comparing the economic status of a given age group
at two different points in time. The baby boom generation, typically
taken to include those born between 1946 and 1964, was 24 to 42 years
old in 1988. As an approximation to the comparative economic well-
being of the baby boomers, we compare the IAE of persons age 25–39 in
1988 with that of persons of the same age in 1965, whose birth years fall
entirely in the pre-World War II period. We also examine the living
levels of the baby boomers relative to their older contemporaries, those
age 40 and older, and compare their relative economic status with that
of their prewar predecessors.

Findings

Absolute and Relative Economic Status by Age

In this section, first we take up changes in earnings of young and old,
then changes in their average economic well-being and the way in which
changing life cycle decisions both at younger and older ages have affected the relative economic well-being of young and old. Finally, we
examine changes in the distribution of income within different age
groups.

Trends in earnings.   To measure the relative pay rates of young and
old, we use the average real earnings of full-time full-year workers.
Among males the rate of increase of real earnings between 1964 and 1987
is higher the older the age group, with only one important exception
(Table 1, column 3). The exception is the oldest age group, those 55–59
years old, and for this group the rate of increase is still second highest.
Moreover, for this group the rate of change may be biased downward by
more retirement in 1987 than in 1964 of those at the highest earnings
levels. (A downward bias may also exist for those age 20–24 because of
a growing proportion enrolled in college, but allowance for this would
be unlikely to alter the disadvantaged position of this age group.)

Among females, the trends for those in their 20s are, like those for
men, the least favorable of any age group. The rates of increase for
women in their 50s, however, are somewhat below those for women in

Table 1. Average Earnings of Full-Time Full-Year Workers by Sex and Age, 1964 and 1987 (1987 Dollars)

	Males			Females			
	(1)	*(2)*	*(3)* *(2)/(1)*	*(4)*	*(5)*	*(6)* *(4)/(5)*	*(7)* *Average (3) and (6)*
Age group	*1964*	*1987*	*(%)*	*1964*	*1987*	*(%)*	
20–24	$14,000	$15,551	111	$11,172	$13,421	120	116
25–29	19,528	23,171	119	11,984	17,657	147	133
30–34	23,286	27,414	118	11,743	19,813	169	144
35–39	24,522	31,786	130	12,064	20,358	169	150
40–44	25,593	34,640	135	12,221	20,879	171	153
45–49	25,468	35,139	138	12,076	20,406	169	154
50–54	22,701	34,492	152	11,859	19,003	160	156
55–59	21,962	31,749	145	11,860	18,469	156	150

their 30s and 40s (Table 1, column 6). If one simply averages the indexes for males and females in each age group to obtain a consensus measure of trends by age, a clear picture emerges of more favorable trends among older age groups than younger (column 7). So far as individual earnings rates are concerned, it is clear that the trend since 1964 has favored older age groups. This conforms with the findings of other researchers (Berger, 1989; Levy & Michel, 1991; Lillard & Macunovich, 1989).

Trends in average economic status. If one turns to a measure of economic welfare, do the differential trends of Table 1 translate into corresponding differentials in economic status? The answer is in the negative. Aside from those age 20–24, there is remarkable similarity among age groups in the rate of increase over time of average income per adult equivalent. In terms of material living levels, the seven 5-year age groups between ages 25 and 59 have absolute increases ranging between about 60 and 70%. Put differently, those between 25 and 39 do just about as well, on average, as those between 40 and 59 (Table 2, column 3). Even those age 20–24, with an increase of 46%, do not do so much worse. In general, the pay rate trends by age in Table 1 are not replicated in the trends of economic status in Table 2.

There is, rather, much more similarity in the growth of economic well-being, as measured by IAE. This similarity is a reflection, we believe, of the way in which changing life cycle decisions in the various age groups have affected the relative economic status of these age groups. In the preliminary analysis that follows, we look simply at the direction in which each life cycle decision tended to alter income, without attempt-

Table 2. Average IAE in Households in which Persons in Specified Age Group Are Living, 1964 and 1987 (1987 Dollars)

Age group	(1) 1964	(2) 1987	(3) (2)/(1) (%)
20–24	$ 9,288	$13,604	146
25–29	9,753	15,892	163
30–34	10,149	16,582	163
35–39	10,266	17,312	169
40–44	10,511	18,002	171
45–49	11,223	18,726	167
50–54	11,667	19,280	165
55–59	11,624	18,455	159

ing a comprehensive multivariate analysis to identify separately the quantitative importance of each decision.

Children and earners per household. As was suggested, one of the mechanisms by which economic status is affected is via decisions on childbearing—other things equal, the presence of fewer children in a household raises a household's average income. Although all age groups had fewer dependent children per household in 1988 than in 1965, the decline is typically much more pronounced for younger persons than for older (Table 3, column 3). For the baby boomers between ages 25 and 39, the reduction comes close to averaging a full child.

A second mechanism for influencing economic status is changing the proportion of adults who are working in a household —other things equal, the larger the proportion of adults working, the higher the household's average income. In households in which young adults are living, the proportion of adults in the labor force has gone up more than in those in which older persons are living (Table 3, column 6). Indeed, for the oldest age group, those 55–59, there is a very slight decline, perhaps due to an increase in early retirement.

In general then, there was a larger decrease in number of children per household between 1965 and 1988 in households in which younger adults lived than older adults and a larger increase in the proportion of adults working. In themselves, these trends would tend to raise the average economic living level of younger persons, both absolutely and relative to older persons.

Living arrangements. Shared living arrangements—doubling up or undoubling with relatives or nonrelatives—is yet another way that rel-

Table 3. Characteristics of Households in which Persons in Specified Age Group Are Living, 1965 and 1988

	Children under age 18 per household			Labor force participants per adult		
	(1)	*(2)*	*(3)*	*(4)*	*(5)*	*(6)*
Age group	*1965*	*1988*	*(2)−(1)*	*1965*	*1988*	*(5)−(4)*
20–24	1.07	0.68	−0.39	.67	.78	.11
25–29	1.76	0.94	−0.82	.65	.80	.15
30–34	2.39	1.37	−1.02	.64	.81	.17
35–39	2.36	1.52	−0.84	.70	.85	.15
40–44	1.91	1.24	−0.67	.73	.87	.14
45–49	1.23	0.72	−0.51	.71	.82	.11
50–54	0.69	0.42	−0.27	.69	.75	.06
55–59	0.39	0.22	−0.17	.65	.64	−.01

ative economic status of different age groups is influenced. Table 4 is designed to bring out the changing importance of doubling up among younger persons and its effects on their average income. In 1965, about two thirds of persons aged 20–39 were living with a partner and children in their own household, but by 1988 the percentage in this type of living arrangement had declined by 19 points (Table 4, columns 1–3).

Offsetting this decline was a big increase in those doubling up with parents or nonrelatives. The largest increase (8 percentage points) was for those living with their parents ("living in household of others and member of primary family"). In addition, there was an increase of 3 percentage points in those living with roommates ("living with nonrelative(s) in own or other's household"). There was also an increase in those living alone (5 percentage points), reflecting the rise in those never married, and an increase in those in childless unions living in their own households (2 percentage points). If one compares average income in these different living arrangements, one finds that, without exception, higher income living arrangements grew at the expense of lower (columns 4 and 5). Thus, younger persons were, on average, improving their economic status through their decisions regarding with whom they lived.

The greater doubling up with their parents by young adults means, of course, that the "nests" of older age groups were less likely to empty as much as previously, a situation probably made more acceptable to older parents by their relatively favorable earnings position. Between 1965 and 1988 the proportion of those aged 40–59 who had adult children in their own household (and had no other adults present) rose by 6 percentage points, while the proportion of those with no adults present

Table 4. Persons Aged 20–39: Percentage Distribution by Living Arrangement and Average IAE by Living Arrangement, 1965 and 1988

				IAE in specified living arrangement as percentage of IAE for those in own or partner's household	
		Percentage distribution			
	(1)	*(2)*	*(3)*	*(4)*	*(5)*
Type of living arrangement	*1965*	*1988*	*(2)−(1)*	*1965*	*1988*
Total	100	100	0	105	107
Living in own or partner's household and:[a]	(77)	(60)	(−17)	100	100
Children under 18 present	66	47	−19	95	90
No children under 18 present	11	13	2	148	145
Living alone	3	8	5	152	142
Living with nonrelative(s) in own or other's household	2	5	3	155	124
Living in household of others and:					
Member of primary family	15	23	8	110	106
Member of related or unrelated subfamily	3	3	0	69	60

Note: Detail may not add to total because of rounding. [a] Includes persons in married couples, unmarried-couple unions, and those in broken unions who are not in subfamilies or living with nonrelatives.

other than head or partner declined correspondingly (Table 5, columns 1–3). Although this shift had an adverse impact on average income of persons 40–59 (columns 4 and 5), it was mitigated by a reduced burden of elderly dependents (a 3-percentage-point decline in those "sharing with other than adult children") and an increased percentage of those living alone (3 percentage points). Thus, the change in living arrangements among younger and older adults in the working-age population tended to raise the relative economic status of the young. However, it seems likely that the quantitative effect was small.

Living arrangements of females in broken unions. The incidence of marital disruption has risen in the past 20 years, and more so among young than old (Table 6, columns 1–3). Moreover, younger women in broken unions usually have young children to support, while older women usually do not (columns 6 and 9).

In itself, the effect of marital disruption on *average* income of persons of a given age, both male and female, is negative, partly because of the loss of economies of scale, and partly because labor force participation of

Table 5. Persons Aged 40–59: Percentage Distribution by Living Arrangement and Average IAE by Living Arrangement, 1965 and 1988

	Percentage distribution			IAE in specified living arrangement as percentage of IAE for those in own or partner's household	
	(1)	(2)	(3)	(4)	(5)
Type of living arrangement	*1965*	*1988*	*(2)−(1)*	*1965*	*1988*
Total	100	100	0	101	101
Living in own or partner's household with or without children under 18 present[a] and:	(87)	(83)	(−3)	100	100
No other adults present	51	45	−6	108	111
Sharing with adult children only	23	29	6	94	92
Sharing with adult children and others	4	4	[b]	84	75
Sharing with other than adult children	9	5	−3	76	69
Living alone	6	9	3	117	123
Living with nonrelative(s) in own or other's household	1	2	[b]	115	109
Living in household of others and:					
Member of primary family	6	5	−1	88	83
Member of related or unrelated subfamily	1	1	0	93	72

Note: Detail may not add to total because of rounding. [a] Includes persons in married couples, unmarried-couple unions, and those in broken unions who are not in subfamilies or living with nonrelatives. [b] Less than 0.5.

single mothers may be less than that of those in intact unions. However, among younger women a partly compensating shift in living arrangements has occurred. Between 1965 and 1988, among females aged 20–39 who were in broken unions, the percentage in an unmarried-couple union rose by 12 percentage points (Table 7, columns 1–3). As can be seen from average income by living arrangement (columns 4 and 5), this shift has typically involved a growth in higher income living arrangements at the expense of lower.

Among females ages 40–59 who are in broken unions, the changes in living arrangements and their income effects are quite different. Although the pattern is somewhat mixed, the biggest increase (7 percentage points) is in the relatively low income group of those heading their own household (Table 8). The biggest decline (8 percentage points) is in those doubled up in the household of others, usually their adult chil-

Table 6. Percentage of Females in Specified Age Group in Broken Unions,[a] by Presence of Children Under 18 Years Old, 1965 and 1988

	All females in broken unions			Females in broken unions with no own children under 18 years present			Females in broken unions with own children under 18 years present		
	(1)	*(2)*	*(3)*	*(4)*	*(5)*	*(6)*	*(7)*	*(8)*	*(9)*
Age group	*1965*	*1988*	*(2)−(1)*	*1965*	*1988*	*(5)−(4)*	*1965*	*1988*	*(8)−(7)*
20–24	6	15	9	2	3	1	4	12	8
25–29	9	20	11	2	5	3	7	15	8
30–34	9	21	12	2	5	3	7	16	9
35–39	11	23	12	3	7	4	8	16	8
40–44	13	24	11	5	11	6	8	13	5
45–49	15	24	9	9	17	8	6	7	1
50–54	19	23	4	15	20	5	4	3	−1
55–59	23	26	3	21	24	3	2	2	0

Note: Detail may not add to total because of rounding. [a] Includes widowed and divorced females, married females with no spouse present (except those with spouse absent in armed forces), and never-married females with own children present.

dren. It seems likely that among older females in broken unions this shift reflects the more favorable trend in their relative income position. Thus, relatively favorable income trends for older females have made it more feasible for them to live on their own; conversely, relatively unfavorable trends for younger couples have made them less willing to have a divorced or widowed mother double up with them.

Trends in income distribution within age groups. Although *average* IAE has increased over the past 25 years at about the same rate for all working-age groups, there have been important differences among age groups in the trend in income inequality. Table 9 presents the most commonly used summary measure of income inequality, the Gini coefficient, for each age group in 1964 and 1987. (For a good discussion of the Gini coefficient and other inequality measures, see Osberg, 1984.) For most age groups, inequality rose between 1964 and 1987, but the increase was much greater among the younger age groups. As a result, the members of today's baby boom generation have considerably greater inequality than did those currently approaching retirement age when they were at a comparable stage of the life cycle (those aged 50–64 in 1987 would have been 23 to 37 in 1964). Thus, although average income has grown for the baby boom generation, it has grown more for the higher than lower income segments of the group.

Table 7. Females Aged 20–39 in Broken Unions: Percentage Distribution by Living Arrangement and Average IAE by Living Arrangement, 1965 and 1988

	Percentage distribution			IAE in specified living arrangement as percentage of IAE for those in own household	
	(1)	(2)	(3)	(4)	(5)
Type of living arrangement	1965	1988	(2)−(1)	1965	1988
Total, females in broken unions	100	100	0	131	144
Living in own household	60	54	−6	100	100
Living alone	9	9	0	185	277
Living in unmarried-couple union	2	14	12	a	208
Living with nonrelative(s), own or other's household	4	3	−1	227	247
Living in household of others and:					
Member of primary family	8	5	−3	218	206
Member of related or unrelated subfamily	16	15	−1	127	122

Note: Detail may not add to total because of rounding. [a] Number of cases less than 25.

Implications for Economic Status of Baby Boomers in Retirement

The preceding analysis brought out the fact that changing life cycle decisions at various ages have led to virtually the same growth in average economic status for all age groups of the working-age population. It also indicated that the absolute income level of the baby boom generation was considerably higher than that of their predecessors at the same age (see Table 2). These results imply that in retirement the living levels of the baby boomers may be considerably better, on average, than is commonly supposed. Another paper (Easterlin, Macdonald, & Macunovich, 1990b) develops this analysis in detail, but it is appropriate to note here some of the highlights.

Figure 1 presents smoothed life cycle patterns of IAE for successive 5-year birth cohorts from 1915–1919 through 1960–1964. Because we are interested in comparing preretirement income status, the profiles are terminated at ages 55–59. Due to a lack of data, only segments of the life cycle pattern for each cohort are represented. As can be seen, whenever cohort comparisons for the same age are possible (a vertical reading of the figure), those born later invariably do better than those born earlier. The figure confirms what is common knowledge, that those currently retiring, the cohorts born in the 1920s, are better off than their prede-

Table 8. Females Aged 40–59 in Broken Unions: Percentage Distribution by Living Arrangement and Average IAE by Living Arrangement, 1965 and 1988

	Percentage distribution			IAE in specified living arrangement as percentage of IAE for those in own household	
	(1)	(2)	(3)	(4)	(5)
Type of living arrangement	1965	1988	(2)−(1)	1965	1988
Total, females in broken unions	100	100	0	119	123
Living in own household	46	53	7	100	100
Living alone	32	30	−2	143	157
Living in unmarried-couple union	2	5	3	138	169
Living with nonrelative(s), own or other's household	4	3	−1	164	157
Living in household of others and:					
Member of primary family	14	6	−8	120	107
Member of related or unrelated subfamily	3	2	−1	89	94

Note: Detail may not add to total because of rounding.

Table 9. Inequality in IAE Among Persons in Specified Age Group, 1964 and 1987

	Gini coefficient		
	(1)	(2)	(3)
Age group	1964	1987	(2)−(1)
20–24	.320	.350	.030
25–29	.312	.353	.041
30–34	.337	.357	.020
35–39	.346	.368	.022
40–44	.338	.360	.022
45–49	.359	.361	.002
50–54	.369	.379	.010
55–59	.391	.388	−.003

cessors. But it also shows what is not generally recognized, that the baby boom cohorts, those of 1945–1949 through 1960–1964, are better off than their predecessors. Moreover, the improvement continues, though at a slower rate, from the leading group of baby boomers (1945–1949) to the trailing group (1960–1964).

The general pattern is that each younger cohort—including the baby boomers—starts out better off than its predecessor, and that this advan-

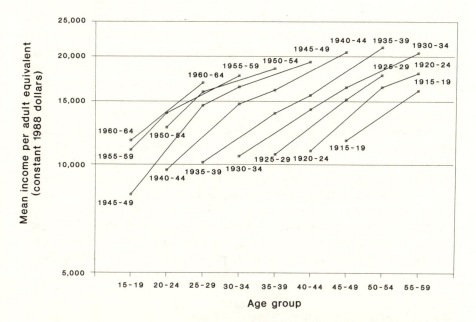

Figure 1. Mean income per adult equivalent: Smoothed profiles for 5-year co-horts 1915–1919 to 1960–1964. *Note:* From "Retirement prospects of the baby-boom generation: A different perspective," by R. A. Easterlin, C. Mac-donald, and D. J. Macunovich, 1990b, *The Gerontologist*, 30, 776–783 (up-dated to 1989). The profiles have been smoothed by omitting data for two years, 1969 and 1984, in which unemployment rates differed considerably from those for the other years.

tage is maintained throughout the life cycle. Assuming that this pattern holds in the future, the implication is that the baby boomers will approach retirement age with higher IAE than any prior cohort.

Our earlier paper also presents some evidence on the asset position of the baby boomers (Easterlin, et al., 1990b). It suggests that as the baby boomers approach retirement age, private and public pension coverage and vesting rates will be higher than for those currently approaching retirement. Home ownership rates among baby boomers are currently only slightly below their predecessors', and are likely to catch up or pass them. Financial asset holdings of baby boomers appear to be markedly higher than their predecessors. Although there is a danger that Social Security retirement income benefit rates may be reduced, coverage for women and consequently their entitlement should be considerably better. These considerations, together with the more favorable life cycle income situation, point to better economic prospects for baby boomers in retirement than is commonly assumed.

One caveat on retirement prospects of the baby boomers: While the average economic status of baby boomers in retirement is likely to be better than those currently retiring, there might be a more serious poverty problem. As has been seen, inequality among baby boomers is substantially greater than among their predecessors at a comparable stage of the life cycle. If inequality among baby boomers continues to grow over the life cycle, as it did among those currently retiring, then poverty rates may be higher among baby boomers when they retire than among those currently retiring. But because the poverty line is a given absolute amount of income, this outcome is not assured even if the baby boomers end up with greater inequality than those currently retiring. Whether poverty will be greater depends on the relative strength of the growth in average income compared with the growth in inequality. An increase in average income, holding income distribution constant, would reduce the poverty rate; an increase in inequality, holding average income constant, would raise the poverty rate. Which will predominate is uncertain.

Implications for Age Group Tensions

To understand the relevance of the present analysis to tensions among age groups, it is necessary to shift from the economic well-being of age groups to total well-being, because feelings between age groups are likely to be influenced by mutual perceptions of well-being as a whole, not just by perceptions of material welfare.

As has been seen, labor market conditions over the past 25 years would, in themselves, have widened the gap in economic well-being between young and old in the working-age population. However, life cycle decisions of the different age groups have changed in ways that essentially maintained initial levels of relative economic well-being.

If one considers the implications of this for total welfare, including noneconomic as well as economic dimensions, then it appears that to maintain their relative *economic* status, young adults increasingly sacrificed other dimensions of welfare, such as children, leisure, and the privacy and independence of their own households. Conversely, among the older working-age population, potential gains in economic status may have been forgone in order to enjoy such things as greater leisure or greater privacy and independence. Since the two groups had fairly similar trends in economic welfare, this suggests that the older age groups had a relatively greater growth in total welfare. The implication is that trends in rates of earnings (Table 1) may more accurately reflect relative total welfare by age than IAE (Table 2), because changes in the resources available to different age groups reflect the potential for welfare gains broadly conceived.

A growing gap in total welfare between younger and older adults would, in turn, lay the basis for greater feelings of inequity between age groups and a rise in tensions of the type hypothesized by Bengtson (1990). It does not follow, however, that in the future age group relations would be the same or even more tense. The key consideration in such a projection is the outlook for trends in available resources by age group. So far as labor market conditions are concerned, economic analysts foresee a reversal in recent experience (Lillard & Macunovich, 1989). As the baby *bust* cohorts born after 1964 increasingly enter the labor market, a growing shortage of younger workers will occur, reversing the previous situation of relative surplus. This should impinge favorably on the wage and unemployment rates of younger relative to older adults. If this forecast is correct, relative earnings rates among age groups will converge, and result in an amelioration of age group tensions. Thus, the postulated recent growth of age group tensions may be a transient phenomenon, linked to the movement of the baby boom cohorts through the young adult ages.

Summary

We take up in order here the three questions posed at the beginning of this paper: (1) How has the economic well-being of younger adults changed over the past 25 years, and how does this change compare with that for older adults in the working-age population? (2) What do the data imply for the economic prospects of the baby boom generation when they reach retirement? (3) What are the implications of the changes in relative economic well-being by age for tensions between younger and older age groups?

With regard to the first question, our analysis shows that despite adverse trends in labor market conditions, the baby boom generation's material level of living is substantially higher than that of its predecessors 25 years ago, and has advanced at about the same rate as that of older adults in the working-age population. The baby boomers have been able to maintain their relative economic status because life cycle decisions (on childbearing, work, and living arrangements) of younger relative to older persons have typically improved the relative economic status of the former. Comparing age groups over time, younger people have had a greater decline in children per household and a larger increase in the proportion of adults per household in the labor force. They have doubled up more with parents or roommates. And while the incidence of broken unions is greater among the young, those in broken unions have responded, in part, by greater resort to unmarried-couple unions. Thus, although labor market conditions would, in themselves, have widened the gap between young and old in material well-being, life cycle decisions have changed in ways that have come close to maintaining initial levels of relative economic well-being. Although not demonstrated here, it seems fairly clear that the quantitative impact of altered life cycle decisions has been greater for younger than for older adults.

However, the improvement in average living level of baby boomers has been accompanied by a growing inequality in the distribution of income. For the most part this increase in inequality reflected a trend in the 1980s common to most age groups, but it was most marked among younger adults.

Regarding the second question, the income trends imply that the economic prospects of the baby boomers in retirement will, on average, be considerably better than is commonly expected. Data on assets tend to buttress this conclusion. However, the recent growth in inequality among baby boomers raises the possibility that for baby boomers poverty may be a more severe problem in retirement than is true among those currently retiring. But even if inequality among baby boomers at retirement is greater than among those currently retiring, its adverse impact on the poverty rate could be reduced or even turned around by a strong upward trend in average income.

Finally, with regard to the third question, the means by which baby boomers have been able to maintain their relative economic status in the population—sacrifice of family formation, leisure, and the privacy and independence of one's own household—imply that they have forgone other dimensions of welfare in order to maintain material living levels. Conversely, among the older working-age population, potential gains in economic status exceeded their material aspirations and enabled them to enjoy greater leisure (earlier retirement) and more privacy (undoubling). In a total welfare sense, therefore, it seems likely that the older population experienced greater improvement than the younger, probably more like the trend in rates of pay than in IAE. This divergence in total welfare trends by age may have contributed to increased tension among age groups in the recent past. It is likely, however, that this is a transient phenomenon, linked to the passage through the young adult ages of the baby boom generation. As the boomers are replaced by the ensuing baby bust generation, relative trends in pay rates should reverse, and so too should trends in total welfare by age. This should contribute to a relaxation in tensions among age groups over the next couple of decades.

Acknowledgments

The authors are grateful to Donna Hokoda and Christine Macdonald for excellent assistance and to the University of Southern California for financial support. The comments of Vern Bengtson, Jack Cornman, and other conference participants were also quite helpful. The uniform file prepared by Mare and Winship (1985) was used for the 1965 Current Population Survey data reported here.

5

Of Deeds and Contracts: Filial Piety Perceived in Contemporary Shanghai

Judith Treas and Wei Wang

The implicit social contract within families has traditionally emphasized the reciprocal obligations between generations. Parents support children in return for their assistance in old age.[1] This is typically a social, not a legal, contract; individuals have always had a degree of discretion in how they fulfill their obligations. Family members work out their responsibilities in coordination with other kin and in the context of changing social, demographic, political, and economic forces. Some sections of the intergenerational contract become thoroughly institutionalized—buttressed by a supporting framework of norms, practices, and specialized organizations. As the course of least resistance, these institutionalized ways of doing things have enormous resilience, but broad-scale social change sometimes makes existing intergenerational arrangements problematic.

This paper considers late-life intergenerational relationships in the People's Republic of China. China is interesting on several counts. First, extraordinary macrosocial change has altered the context in which cohort succeeds cohort and parents cede authority to a younger generation. Second, even leaving aside strong cultural traditions, intergenerational family relations are pivotal in the material organization of Chinese society. Farm production depends on the family organization of labor. Children and old people rely on intergenerational support. The fortunes of young people rest on their parents' social, economic, and cultural capital.[2] The critical importance of intergenerational family life, coupled with remarkable macrosocial change, points to China as a crucible for the negotiation of generational relationships.

The Macrosocial Context

Extraordinary change marks the contemporary history of China. After painful years of Japanese occupation and civil war, Communist victory led to the founding of the People's Republic of China in 1949. A new government brought more wrenching social changes: Class enemies were rooted out; peasant farmers were collectivized; wave after wave of ideological campaigns espoused new values. Although famine remained a local threat, the new regime improved the lot of many people—providing, for example, schooling for children and rudimentary health care in the rural areas. Between 1966 and 1976, the Cultural Revolution shook China. Universities were closed, young people were mobilized against their elders, and city dwellers were "sent down" to labor in the countryside. Western influences were purged. By the time moderate political influences won out, families had been divided, and the life course of a generation of young people had been disrupted. Major social dislocations and government policies continue to shape the intimate family lives of the Chinese people. Since the 1970s, for example, the state's one-child policy of family planning has meant fewer grandchildren for Chinese elderly.

Because China is a poor, largely rural nation, most older people must depend on offspring for support (Jefferson & Petri, 1986). A national survey found that 67% of the rural aged report children as their major source of financial support, as compared to 22% of the urban elderly (Lin & Hong, 1989). What few public resources are available are targeted to the childless poor (Martin, 1988). Communist regimes have worked to eliminate many aspects of Confucian ideology, but filial obligation remains the cornerstone of old-age support policy. The reciprocal obligations between generations—minus some excesses of patriarchy—have been enshrined in Communist law.

The intergenerational contract has, if anything, become even more important to the well-being of the aged in recent years. The new responsibility system of economic liberalization dismantled the local welfare system that once served as a safety net for older people. With the organized cadre system of social control weakened, social pressures compelling families to support older members also declined (Sankar, 1989, p. 208). Thus, despite its importance, the intergenerational contract is under pressure. Filial responsibilities based on gender and birth order have given way to new circumstances of family life. Although eldest sons were traditionally charged with the care of aged parents, today daughters sometimes help out, especially in urban areas (Davis-Friedmann, 1983). Since the one-child policy means more couples will have no son, the 1980 Marriage Law of the People's Republic of China assigns responsibility for support of aged parents to both daughters and sons (Palmer, 1987). One study in Zhejiang finds siblings in a poorer village sharing the support of aging parents (Goldstein, Ku, & Ikels, 1990). Sometimes a husband and wife live apart in the households of different children. Sometimes older people move between their children—eating and sleeping at different households in turn.

Not all older people are dependent on children. Ironically, retired industrial workers with comfortable pensions sometimes wind up contributing to the support of grown children (Treas, 1979). These pensioners are members of an advantaged urban cohort that came of age in time to reap the fruits of socialist revolution (Davis-Friedmann, 1985). Later cohorts, including younger generations in their own families, have not been so lucky. Many young people are unemployed, because China has had trouble creating enough jobs for its growing numbers of would-be workers. Many middle-aged people had their schooling and careers cut short by the Cultural Revolution when schools were closed and students were sent to work on rural communes. Even when they find jobs in the city, contract workers do not enjoy the salaries and perquisites afforded earlier generations. Because macrosocial change has disrupted the succession of generations, generational dependencies within urban families have sometimes been reversed.

Even Chinese household structure is changing in response to demographic availability of kin, housing constraints, and other factors. Norms traditionally favor stem families, where the older person lives with a married son, his wife, and their children. Stem families continue to be the most common pattern, but older people have become more likely to live alone (or with just a spouse) and less likely to live in extended households with more than one son (Gui & Associates, 1987; Hareven, 1987; Tsui, 1989).

Changes in living arrangements may reflect changes in tastes. One poll in the city of Tianjin, for example, reported that older people desiring to live with children declined from 60% in 1983 to 50% in 1985 (Pasternak, cited in Sankar, 1989). Contemporary China, however, poses barriers to realizing housing preferences. Rural dwellers have more choice in living arrangements; they are often able to accommodate more household members by adding on to their house, or they can split households by building a new dwelling (Davis-Friedmann, 1983). In the city, however, housing choices are very constrained for older people and their families. As Sankar (1989) notes,

> because of the dependence of the elderly, especially those seventy-five and above, on their family for support and because of the severe housing shortage in most urban areas, it is difficult to clearly establish their preference for living arrangements when alternatives to their present situation are nonexistent. (p. 205)

We would not expect the normative underpinnings of the generational contract to be untouched by such dramatic changes in the needs and resources, the constraints and opportunities, of the generations. As we shall see, older people are not of one mind about the generational contract—about what older people should expect, what they should do, and what is in their best interest. Some continue to believe that the aged should count on their offspring for support, but many say older people should look to themselves and their spouses. These beliefs about intergenerational dependence have surprising implications in the lives of Shanghai elderly. Whether or not grown offspring find favor with aging parents depends on parents' beliefs about the relative merits of self-reliance and generational dependence. Whether parents regard their children as pious or respectful depends not only on the deeds of the younger generation, but also on the older generation's beliefs about the contract between generations.

Shanghai Survey Data

This paper uses two companion surveys of the aged in Shanghai. The sample surveys were conducted by Shanghai University under the direction of Yuan Jihui. Shanghai has the highest percentage of elderly (12.9% 60 and older in 1982) as well as the highest life expectancy (72.9 in 1982) in China (Gui & Associates, 1987). The city is, of course, unique even by urban Chinese standards. Because its mature industrial system has a high ratio of retirees to workers, it has many of the old-age dependency problems that other parts of China will face in a generation.

Interviews are available for 613 elderly 60 and older in urban areas of Shanghai in 1983 and 609 elderly 60 and older in surrounding rural areas in 1985. The urban data are based on multistage, cluster sampling without replacement. The rural respondents are randomly sampled from two villages in Jiadin county. The villages were selected because they had a middle level of economic development for Shanghai District.

Different sampling designs for rural and urban areas preclude pooling the samples for analysis. Separate analyses by sex are also required. Rural areas show a bias toward female respondents, perhaps because men were less likely to be at home when the interviewer called.

Depending on Children

Respondents in the Shanghai surveys were asked whether they agreed that older people should rely on themselves and their spouses, rather than depend on their children. This question, tapping beliefs about what is proper and what is in older people's best interest, is surely at the heart of the intergenerational contract. In Shanghai, older people are not of one mind about self-reliance and intergenerational dependence. In the urban areas, 79% of older men and 65% of older women endorsed self-reliance. In the rural areas, fewer respondents—47% of men and 43% of women—favored self-reliance.[3]

Unfortunately, we have no trend data to assess whether support for self-reliance is a new phenomenon. Although Shanghai is no doubt exceptional, we have no national data to gauge how exceptional. Even the wording of items may inflate estimates of the support for self-reliance since compliant respondents will prefer to agree with, rather than contradict, the statement. Despite these caveats, the evidence indicates that the intergenerational contract is open to interpretation and negotiation. Although beliefs are socially patterned with clear rural-urban differences, there is no overriding, consensual, normative mandate about what older people should do.

Together with clear rural-urban differences, the diversity of opinion suggests that the intergenerational contract is interpreted not in terms of overarching normative tradition, but rather in terms of the particular circumstances in which older men and women find themselves. Why do some older people favor intergenerational independence while others believe in intergenerational dependence? On the one hand, the aged who think old people should depend on children may be those most in need of children's support, that is, those with the *least* resources and greatest needs. On the other hand, it is possible that those who favor intergenerational dependence are those with the *most* resources since older people who are better off financially have the wherewithal to motivate their children to cater to their needs. (See Foner, Chapter 6 in this volume.)

As seen in Table 1, those who believe in depending on children are, in fact, those with the least resources and highest needs. In general, older people who are widowed or divorced are more likely to believe in depending on offspring; those who still have a spouse are more likely

Table 1. Percentage Agreeing That "Aged Should Depend on Their Children" Rather Than "Depend on Self and Spouse" by Rural-Urban Residence, Sex, and Selected Characteristics: Shanghai Residents, 60 and Older, 1983–1985

	Urban		Rural	
	Men	*Women*	*Men*	*Women*
Total	21	35	53	57
Marital status				
Married	21	25	49	48
Widowed/divorced	17	49	72	65
Age				
60–64	21	23	47	44
65–69	18	31	48	56
70–74	17	41	53	59
75–79	24	48	61	75
80+	43	71	82	68
Health				
Good	19	43	52	59
Weak or ill	23	31	54	54
Seriously ill	—	48	75	88
Education				
Illiterate	19	37	56	57
Elementary	18	43	52	46
Middle school	24	31	—	—
High school	20	8	—	—
University	29	17	—	—
Urban pension (monthly yuan)/rural income (annual yuan)				
None	60	48	38	38
1–35/≤300	8	26	62	60
36–50/301–500	22	13	33	50
51–70/501–700	18	12	17	43
71–90/701–1000	29	50	33	—
>90/>1000	19	—	—	—
Household generations				
One	18	30	37	31
Two or more	22	36	58	63

than the unmarried to endorse relying on self or spouse. (The exception is urban men, who differ little by marital status.) Advancing age is associated with the belief in relying on children. This reflects both the higher probability of being widowed and the dependency associated with disabilities, but there may also be cohort differences in beliefs within the older population. At least in rural areas, very poor health, too, is associated with skepticism about self-reliance.

In rural areas, the illiterate are more likely than those with some schooling to believe in depending on children. In urban areas, women with less schooling are also more likely than their better educated peers to believe in depending on children, but the pattern is not monotonic, and older men do not share this trend. In rural areas, low-income aged are more likely to endorse relying on children than either the relatively prosperous or the destitute. (Of course, those without any income are apt to be those who have fallen through the safety net of family supports.) For men and women in urban areas, having no pension is associated with more enthusiasm for relying on offspring.

We also hypothesize that respondents will be more likely to believe that older people should depend on children when this is consistent with their own experience. Those who live in a multigenerational household, for instance, are more likely to believe in depending on children, especially in rural areas.

In general, those older people who reject the intergenerational contract—who believe older people should rely on themselves—are those who have the least need to depend on offspring. They are younger, they have a spouse still living, and they report good health. They are better educated and, in some cases, have more money. Older people who are most likely to embrace the intergenerational contract are those who have apparently benefited from it in the past by living in multigenerational families.

Evaluating Children's Filial Behavior

There is little consensus about what older people should do. Gender, rural-urban residence, and resources color beliefs about the intergenerational contract, but the diversity of opinion points to a lack of strong cultural guidelines to direct expectations and behavior. Does this lack of consensus matter for how older people evaluate their relations with their own children?

The survey asked older people, "How do your children treat you?" In the urban area, 47% of older men and 57% of older women reported being treated with "piety" or "respect" as opposed to "so-so" or even "poorly." Among rural residents, 63% of men and 61% of women reported their children as pious or respectful. Although it is comforting that a majority of older people in Shanghai see their children in a favorable light, it is perhaps surprising that the percentages are not even higher, given the possibility of a strong social desirability bias in the question.

Why are older people more or less likely to see their children as pious or respectful? Three sets of factors seem likely influences on filial evaluations.

First, normative beliefs and expectations about the intergenerational contract must surely enter into evaluations of children's performance. In the context of some societal uncertainty about the appropriate roles of the generations, those people who embrace a generational contract emphasizing dependence may be more easily frustrated by deviations from piety. If this is the case, we would expect a belief in intergenerational dependence to be negatively associated with evaluations of children's piety. On the other hand, traditional beliefs about depending on children may be positively associated with reports of children's piety. If many people are rethinking the intergenerational contract, traditional notions about intergenerational reliance offer the only cultural framework for evaluating children's behavior. In this analysis, two indicators of intergenerational beliefs are statements regarding whether older people should depend on grown children and whether they should live with married children.

Second, what children actually do for older parents undoubtedly registers in their assessments of children's filial behavior. Children who are said to be pious are presumably those who treat their parents the best. Older people reported children's filial deeds on five behavioral items. While what children really do may not correspond perfectly to what they are said to do, these five items do provide useful behavioral measures. Indicators include (a) whether or not children talk with the aged parent; (b) whether or not children go out with the elderly, for example, for shopping or entertainment; (c) whether or not children help the aged parent with housework; (d) whether or not the children give gifts and/or especially good food; and (e) whether or not children say hello to the aged parent when they go out or come back home. Each of these variables is dichotomous except for the gift indicator, which is coded into three categories: (a) no gift or food, (b) gift or food, and (c) gift and food.

Third, the older respondent's characteristics—embodying needs and resources—will undoubtedly influence perceptions of children's filial performance. Variables include age, married status, education, income, and health. Exactly how these variables influence perceptions of children's piety is an empirical question. People with higher needs and lower resources have both more reason to be appreciative and more occasion to be disappointed with how their children treat them.

In short, beliefs about the generational contract, children's filial deeds, and personal characteristics of the aged are hypothesized to relate to older respondents' evaluations of children's piety. Logistic analysis is employed to predict the likelihood of reporting treatment by children to be pious or respectful versus "so-so" or bad. The results by sex are reported in Table 2 for urban and rural areas.

Consider men living in the urban areas of Shanghai. All things con-

Table 2. Logit Coefficients for Relationship Between Reporting Children as Pious/Respectful and Selected Variables, by Rural-Urban Residence and Sex: Shanghai Aged 60 and Older, 1983–1985

	Urban		Rural	
	Men	*Women*	*Men*	*Women*
Normative belief				
Aged should depend on children	1.196**	1.511***	.818*	.466
Aged should live with children	.128	.084	.392**	.548***
Children's performance				
Talk with aged	.474	.452	.571	1.399***
Help with housework	.645*	.666	.296	.336
Give gifts	.487*	.517*	1.208***	.826***
Greet aged	.875*	1.575***	.702	−.149
Go out with aged	.019	.339	.621	.038
Aged characteristics				
Age	.217	.210	.293	−.038
Marital status	−.218	−.299	−.519	−.464
Education	−.098	.211	−.129	−.184
Income	.022	−.288	−.037	−.207
Health	−.138	.271	1.030**	.549**
Intercept	−3.191***	−4.853***	−3.237**	−1.708

$*p<.1; **p<.05; ***p<.01$

sidered, respondents who believe older people should depend on children are more likely to perceive their own children as pious or respectful ($p<.05$). This finding is in line with the argument that adherence to a traditional intergenerational contract leads to more favorable assessments of one's children by reducing normative uncertainty about what constitutes good behavior. Beliefs about living arrangements, however, have no effect, perhaps because residential patterns in urban Shanghai are governed as much by availability of housing as by normative preferences. Three of the five indicators of children's deeds prove at least marginally significant at the .1 level. City-dwelling men whose children help with housework, give gifts, and greet them when they come and go are more likely to say their children behave in a pious or respectful manner. Characteristics like age and health apparently do not influence urban men's assessments of whether children behave in a pious and respectful way.[4]

Urban women, like urban men, are influenced by children's conduct and by their own beliefs in intergenerational dependency. They are more likely to ascribe piety if they believe in depending on children ($p<.001$). They are also significantly more likely to ascribe pious behavior to offspring if they report that their children give gifts ($p<.1$) or greet

them when they come and go ($p<.01$). Neither background characteristics nor beliefs about intergenerational living influence assessments of
children's piety.

In the rural districts, older men's beliefs in depending on children
($p<.1$) and living with them ($p<.05$) raise the likelihood that one's own
children will be seen as pious, even controlling for their actual behavior.
Men regard their children favorably when they give them gifts ($p<.001$),
but piety assessments are not affected by performance variables that
measure services and social support as opposed to material aid. Although most background characteristics fail to achieve statistical significance, reasonably good health proves to be associated with judgments
that children are pious or respectful ($p<.05$). Controlling for what children actually do, older men who have serious health problems find
more fault with their children's behavior.

Older women in rural areas of Shanghai are also influenced by their
normative beliefs about the generational contract. Those who believe
older people should live with married children are more likely to see
their children as pious or respectful ($p<.01$); the coefficient for believ-
ing in intergenerational dependence is in the same direction, but misses
statistical significance. Two indicators of children's deeds, talking together and receiving gifts, are significant ($p<.01$), raising the probability of a positive assessment of children's piety. Like older men in the
rural districts, older women view their children more favorably if they
are in reasonably good health ($p<.05$).

Insights from Rural-Urban Comparisons

Beliefs about how the intergenerational contract *should* work are associated with how personal relations with one's own children are
viewed. Even controlling for deeds—what children are said to do for
aging parents—respondents who believe older people should depend
on children see their children as treating them better.

Opinion is clearly mixed on issues of intergenerational dependence
and self-reliance. If the intergenerational contract is being rewritten in
response to new social forces, traditional beliefs in intergenerational
dependence may offer the only yardstick for gauging how well children
fulfill filial obligations. After all, if older people are less likely to live with
offspring, if aged pensioners must support grown children instead of
being supported, if daughters take on responsibilities that once be-
longed to sons, what behavior signals piety and respect?

The patterning of rural-urban piety evaluations offers some support

Table 3. Percentage Reporting Children's Performance of Various Filial Tasks, Children as Pious or Respectful, and Belief in Depending on Children by Sex and Rural/Urban Residence: Shanghai Aged 60 and Older, 1983–1985

	Urban		Rural	
	Men	*Women*	*Men*	*Women*
Performance				
Talk with aged	36	40	20	27
Help with housework	61	66	52	54
Give food and gifts	74	72	64	67
Give food or gifts	14	16	26	22
Give no food or gifts	12	13	10	11
Greet aged	80	79	41	38
Go out with aged	24	28	5	7
Pious or respectful	47	57	62	61
Depend on children	21	35	54	57

for this interpretation. Recall that the rural aged were both more likely to endorse generational dependence and more likely to report their children as pious and respectful. Rural beliefs in intergenerational dependence undoubtedly flow from the family mode of organizing agricultural production. The roots of their piety evaluations are more complex.

By all objective measures, rural dwellers are not as well treated as their urban counterparts. Table 3 shows that older people in rural areas are less likely to get help with housework. Rural dwellers are less likely to get both food and gifts rather than one or the other. On social support indicators—talking together, going out together, exchanging greetings—the rural aged are at an even greater disadvantage. Although their children do not treat them better, they are more likely to report their children to be pious or respectful than their counterparts in urban Shanghai.[5]

In farming families, piety and respect may be so rooted in the economic organization of daily life that they can be readily recognized. What city residents—with their adherence to beliefs in self-reliance—may lack is agreed-upon standards for filial conduct. Such standards enable older people to recognize piety and respect in their offspring's behavior. If this is the case, raising the filial satisfaction of older urban residents may depend less on encouraging greater consideration on the part of the younger generation and more on making the terms of the intergenerational contract clear.

In the long run, Chinese parents may come to place less value on traditional piety in their children. Over the years, for example, American parents have come to value independence and initiative in their offspring more highly than obedience (Alwin, 1988). New contracts between generations demand not merely recasting obligations, but also finding new ways of demonstrating the regard between young and old.

Notes

1.   Caldwell (1982), of course, argues that younger and older generations need not benefit equally from this exchange and that the direction in which net wealth flows may shift over time. See Bengtson, Chapter 1 in this volume, for a fuller treatment of the expectations and obligations making up the generational contract.

2.   The Communist regimes altered the parameters of intergenerational status inheritance without undermining its importance. Sins of the fathers *were* visited on the sons, and youths from "bad classes" (e.g., from families who were landlords before the revolution) have been shut out of schooling and otherwise discriminated against (Parrish & Whyte, 1978). To take another example, the Chinese until recently pursued a policy of *ding ti*, which permitted retiring industrial workers to pass on their jobs to their children (Davis-Friedmann, 1985).

3.   There is also little agreement about whether older people should live with married children or separately. Among city dwellers, a majority of older people—73% of men and 63% of women—think older people should live separately. In the surrounding rural areas of Shanghai, there is more support for intergenerational living. Only a minority of rural aged—42% of men and 32% of women—believe in living apart from married children. Recall that rural residents, who often own their own homes and can add on to their dwellings, do not face the housing shortages that constrain living arrangement preferences in the city.

4.   According to Ho (1989), Chinese fathers, as contrasted with nurturing Chinese mothers, are typically disciplinarians with respect to older children—a role that leads to less emotional closeness and sometimes even antagonism between the generations. While it is true that urban men are more critical of their children's piety than their female counterparts, no such gender differences are seen in the Shanghai countryside.

5.   There may, of course, be important rural-urban differences in the constraints on these behaviors that we are unable to measure. Going out together may depend on the availability of transportation, for example.

PART III

Age Cohorts in Conflict?

Are there "age cohorts in conflict" in the last decade of the 20th century? The title of Part III was phrased to accentuate a certain sense of irony. Questions about justice between age groups or demands for generational equity generally start from the shaky but popularly held premise that the points of divergence among specific segments of the population are well marked and that the younger, middle, and older generations are in competition for scarce resources.

The essays in this section suggest to the contrary that discord between cohorts is *not* the norm. Generational conflict is neither inevitable nor normative. Chronological age may be less salient in fueling conflicts between groups than are other cultural and structural factors (such as racism or scarcity) operating at the micro- or macrolevel.

By focusing on nonindustrial societies, anthropologist Nancy Foner (Chapter 6) is able to construct a comparative baseline useful in delineating trends in other places. She reviews much evidence of intergenerational solidarity and comity. Nonetheless, she notes that the lot of the frail elderly in nonindustrial societies is often unpleasant and difficult, far more so than our ethnocentric stereotypes of the "valued elder" would suggest. Children, impelled occasionally by the pressures of guaranteeing delayed reciprocity, certainly seem likely to help their elders, to the extent possible, even in rapidly changing "traditional" societies. Still, being sonless or being denied access to limited resources exacerbates the aged's sense of dependence. Moreover, the elders' vulnerability is sometimes mitigated by cultural values and religious beliefs, economic inducements, and negative sanctions. And even in nonindustrial societies, the state intervenes: Foner notes in passing the importance of receiving military pensions to the extended family's well-being. Death, however, often is the only source of release from elders' personal struggle with the finitude of life. And attitudes toward death in old age vary considerably.

Victor Marshall, Fay Lomax Cook, and Joanne Gard Marshall—a sociologist, policy scientist, and research librarian respectively—examine in Chapter 7 the extent to which conflicts between cohorts have been differentially reported in the North American press. In both the United States and Canada, they found more attention given to issues of youth and children than to issues of the aged. Moreover, in contrast to the greater attention paid to the reporting of "generational-equity" issues in the United States, there have been strikingly few media reports reflecting interest in this topic among Canadian reporters, academics, and commentators. The difference, the authors claim, is not due to greater age group inequities in the United States or to values differences between the two countries. Rather, greater emphasis on universality in Canada public policies, argue Marshall, Cook, and Marshall, reduces the perception that allocations there are driven by age-based mechanisms. Conversely, lobbying groups such as Americans for Generational Equity (AGE) have had a greater influence on political discourse in the United States—a trend that, we suspect, will continue into the 21st century.

There has been relatively little public debate to date over intergenerational equity in the European Community (EC). This comparative lack of discord convinces sociologist Alan Walker (Chapter 8) that the United States debate may reflect a parochial sociopolitical construct. Germany, he hypothesizes, is the most likely EC country to repeat the United States debate concerning age group inequities. Even there, a united Germany's solidaristic consensus on welfare tempers the likelihood of age-based fragmentation of the sort fomented in the pluralistic, neoliberal political culture of the United States. The family is, in Walker's view, the pivotal institution bridging the macro- and microlevels of intergenerational relations, a position similar to Bengtson's in Chapter I. The provision of care by female kin, Walker notes, is affected by state intervention. Walker's thesis thus anticipates the emphasis placed on families in Part IV of this volume. Moreover, his projections about future developments set the stage for a debate with the authors in Part V concerning how serious age cohort conflicts may become in maturing welfare states during the 21st century.

6

When the Contract Fails: Care for the Elderly in Nonindustrial Cultures

Nancy Foner

As the number and proportion of the elderly in American society continue to rise, alarms have been sounded about how they will be provided for in the future. Of special concern are the frail elderly. Suffering physical or mental losses, they can no longer fend for themselves and need special care. At the macro- or societal level, there is a growing concern as to whether—and how—the government can maintain the level of support now offered to the elderly through various entitlement programs in social security and health care. At the microlevel, there are questions about whether families will be able to care for the rapidly growing number of old people who will live, for many long years, in a disabled and weakened state.

In the face of the enormity of this apparent "aging crisis," there is a temptation to look longingly to less complex societies where, it is imagined, old age is less of a problem. In these cultures, it is often believed, the weak, sick aged are cared for willingly, faithfully, and lovingly in the bosom of their families. This nostalgia for a golden age or, as Nydegger (1983) puts it, golden isles, crystallizes our cultural concept of the good life and expresses our desires and anxieties. But the idyllic picture of the young faithfully carrying out their caretaking duties seriously distorts reality.

To be sure, the elderly in nonindustrial cultures often do receive tender and loving care. Where government does not provide social welfare benefits and where services cannot be hired, people of all ages, including the old, must rely on kin and other associates in times of need. Indeed, a number of factors act as powerful incentives motivating many young people to carry out their caretaking duties.

Yet problems arise. In fact, the lot of the frail elderly in nonindustrial cultures is sometimes extremely unpleasant and difficult. As part of a broad analysis of inequalities between old and young in nonindustrial societies, I have shown elsewhere how tensions may develop between incapacitated elders and their younger caretakers. (Even more serious conflicts arise between still active elders at the top of the age hierarchy who are powerful and privileged, and subordinate juniors; Foner, 1984a, 1985.) My concern here is different. The issue is not whether intergenerational relations are hostile or amicable. Rather, why is it that in many cultures the elderly may be neglected, mistreated, even sometimes abandoned? Why, in other words, does the informal contract or agreement between the generations—concerning the obligations young people owe the elderly—fail?

Beyond exploding simple and idyllic myths about care for the frail elderly in nonindustrial cultures, this analysis has additional implications. By pointing to factors underlying care—and neglect—in places where the old have nowhere else to turn but their kin and neighbors, it highlights, in bold relief, some of the forces involved in caregiving in our own society as we approach the next century.

The Contract Fulfilled

A look at ethnographic reports for a wide range of nonindustrial cultures shows that, in many cases, the informal contract with the elderly is, in fact, fulfilled. Children, kin, and neighbors frequently tend to the needs of the physically incapacitated aged for many years, often up until the end. This is so even in some mobile hunting-and-gathering societies, where meeting the needs of the helpless elderly could endanger the very existence of the family or band.

What causes younger people to fulfill their obligations to elderly parents? As in our own society, the answer is less often a matter of formal ethics than of emotional or practical considerations. Many children feel deep affection for aged parents and look after them with loving concern. Indeed, the senior generation often carefully nurtures good relations with their children, or grandchildren, with an eye to old-age support. Navajo grandmothers say that it is the duty of the older generation to teach their children that a "good Navajo" will care for the elderly. The grandmothers admit to having a vested interest in spoiling and coaxing grandchildren into becoming emotionally attached to them. The old women say that those who receive no aid and protection in old age ignored such precautions when younger; having made no attempt to establish warm, loving relationships with their grandchildren in the past, they are now paying the price of isolation (Shomaker, 1990, p. 28). Another related factor can come into play. By looking after their own aged parents and grandparents, younger caretakers may be consciously setting an example for their children so that they will not be abandoned in the future.

Then there is the notion of delayed reciprocity—sometimes referred to as lifetime reciprocity. Sons and daughters frequently see the care they give mothers and fathers as repayment for the gifts, provisions, and care the old people provided them in the past. In words echoed in many ethnographic reports, a man among the Gonja of West Africa said: "When you were weak [young], your mother fed you and cleaned up your messes, and your father picked you up and comforted you when you fell. When they are weak, will you not care for them?" (Goody, 1973, p. 172). From the elders' perspective, they are now rewarded for having met their earlier responsibilities. "Now you sit and eat," is how Samia elders of Kenya view the years when they can no longer work. Now sons and daughters feed them just as they fed their children when the children were too young to work (Cattell, 1990).

Broad cultural values—which young as well as old people have internalized—may also be involved. These may be moral or ethical values about the kind of care or obligations the young owe their elders. As Rosenberg (1990, p. 29) puts it for the !Kung of Botswana, entitlement to care may be "naturalized" within a culture. In other words, cultural norms are so deeply embedded that it seems "natural" that young people will care for elders, especially parents, when they become very old. By the same token, the cultural code also includes ideas about what is unacceptable behavior. Among Australian aborigines, for example, it is considered callous and reprehensible for family members to desert an ailing old person (Reid, 1985). In general, old people in nonindustrial societies often demand care as a publicly acknowledged right—and young people often feel it is the elders' due.

Whatever their origins, once cultural conceptions and attitudes about the elderly come into existence, they have a life of their own and cast a particular light over the solid features of social life. In Geertz's (1966) phrase, they are a model for, as well as a model of, action. In societies where the elderly are respected and admired—for their accumulated practical and ritual expertise, for example, their control of material resources, or their sheer age and seniority[1]—young people may believe that elders deserve to be looked after when they are weak and ill. Indeed, the physically frail (but mentally alert) may still be valued for their experience and knowledge and still control considerable economic resources. Meeting the needs of the frail old may be viewed, at least in part, as an extension of the obligations and respect young people have long owed to senior kin.[2]

When I asked a colleague who had lived for four years with the Twareg pastoralists of Niger how they treated the frail elderly, her initial response mirrored the way the Twareg themselves saw it: Old people should be served and fed. And, indeed, they were. Despite a severe 3-year drought in the 1980s and extreme scarcity of food, the physically weak elderly continued to be fed. When they were sick and dying, a daughter or granddaughter would minister to their needs. The elderly, including the extremely frail, were among the most respected individuals in the society: They had nurtured the young, were founts of wisdom about history and genealogy, and had, by this time in their lives, gained considerable status from years of giving substantial gifts of livestock to others (B. Worley, personal communication, October, 1990).

Cultural values may even dictate that the needs of frail elders come before those of the young. In a study of the Akamba of Kenya, traditional healers and health workers were asked what they would do if a dying old man over 60 and a dying 25-year-old man came for treatment but there was only enough medicine or herbs to cure one person. Many favored saving the old man, even where the young man was first in line (Kilner, 1984).

Complaints by the elderly forcefully remind young people of their duties, thereby greasing the wheels of the system of mutual responsibility and caregiving. Such complaints are a conscious or unconscious strategy to maximize support—an effort to bring about positive consequences by accentuating the negative, as when public complaints prod the young into fulfilling their duties. Despite being well looked after, !Kung elders constantly grumble and denounce others for neglecting them: "Can't you see that I am starving and dressed in rags?" is one typical comment in what Rosenberg (1990) calls !Kung complaint discourse. By negative example—often in melodramatic tales of neglect and woe—complaint rhetoric restates the social contract of caregiving obligations.

In many societies, moreover, there is an economic inducement to look after frail parents. The son or daughter who cares for the old couple receives, in exchange, special treatment in the division of property. Among the Kirghiz herders of Afghanistan, studied in the 1970s, most of the responsibility of looking after aged parents fell on the younger son (and his wife and children). That son never left the parental household, but as compensation he inherited the family herd, tent, and camping ground (Shahrani, 1981). In the past, in parts of Europe and France, the child who sat by the hearth received similar property benefits; if there were no sons, an unmarried daughter might stay and inherit the whole tenement (Goody, 1976).

If sentiments of affection and obligation or the promise of economic benefits are not enough, negative sanctions may be applied, ranging from the threat of disinheritance to community disapproval or even supernatural punishment. In small, closely knit communities, where people live together in continuing face-to-face contact, public opinion matters very much to an individual, so that collective opinion is an important spur to duty. Those who neglect obligations to the elderly may come in for severe criticism, as Reid (1985) mentions for the Yolngu of Arnheim Land, Australia. There family members are expected to mobilize to provide comfort, care, and material support for sick and feeble elders. In many African societies, the fear of the anger of deceased ancestors, who are believed to cause all manner of disasters, may also reinforce norms of respect and obligation. In Nigeria, children who fail to support their elderly parents when they are deemed able to do so earn the wrath of both their parents and the community. They risk a parental curse or perhaps a community accusation of witchcraft (Peil, Bamisaiye, & Ekpenyong, 1989).

The burden of supporting the elderly may be spread over the whole community, as in societies, like the !Kung, with a tradition of communal food sharing and food distributions. Where the sharing ethic is strong, those who are generous to the old may be honored and applauded. And finally, in societies where certain foods are taboo to younger people, the elderly are sure to be given those foods.

The Contract Fails

If a variety of factors assure that the informal contract between the generations is often fulfilled, other variables may intervene to upset the balance. Pressures of limited resources and the absence of children are perhaps most important in explaining why the frail elderly may be neglected, forsaken, even abandoned and killed. Also playing a role in poor treatment are broad cultural values and expectations. Indeed, some anthropologists have suggested that far from being a violation of the social contract, the neglect of extremely incapacitated old people is, in some societies, a fulfillment of this contract. The elderly themselves may acquiesce in—sometimes even request—death-hastening treatment.

Childlessness

The state of childlessness or sonlessness (in many societies, it is a son's duty to care for elderly parents) is a terrible misfortune in nonindustrial societies. Parenthood is a crucial aspect of adult status. Children remember and honor their parents when they die—and are expected to care for them when they are incapacitated and can no longer look after themselves. Old people without children (or sons) face the dilemma of being forced to depend upon more distant kin, with whom the bonds of affection and obligation are not so close. The aged will have provided fewer services in the past to more distant relatives than to immediate kin, and they lack the strong moral, jural, or economic authority that they could exert over children.

Admittedly, family arrangements in many societies are flexible enough so that couples unable to bear children of their own can rear youngsters who will support them in old age. Formal adoption occurs in many European and Asian societies; foster parenting, which involves no permanent change in identity, is common in Africa. In societies where daughters are supposed to leave home at marriage, couples who bear only daughters can sometimes arrange a marriage in which the daughter and her husband remain with her parents to support them later on. Yet the best of plans do not always succeed. Foster or adopted (as well as natural) children sometimes die before their parents do, or are unable to care for them for other reasons.

In nonindustrial as well as industrial societies, old men are often cared for by their wives, since men are typically older than their spouses. Where men have several mates, younger wives may still be around by the time their much older husbands need care. Even then, however, sons (or sons-in-law) may be essential for herding, farming, or hunting, so that a sonless or childless old man may find himself in difficult circumstances whether or not he has a young wife to look out for him.

Childless elderly have a peripheral identity among the Gende of Papua New Guinea; they are neglected, often suffering isolation and shame and sometimes even outright physical abuse. Without children to assist them in financing interclan exchange competitions and ceremonies and repaying bride-price loans, they are regarded as "rubbish persons" who have failed to maintain exchange relations in good order. When they become frail and ill, few feel obligated to care for them or sacrifice pigs to restore their strength. When they die, their death is unimportant and unattended (Zimmer, 1987).

To reach old age and have no adult sons is an unfortunate state in many African farming and herding societies.[3] In his classic account of the Tallensi, Fortes reported that sons—own sons or, second-best, proxy sons—were old men's chief economic asset. A son was morally bound to look after and farm for his father. "Yet how can I leave him since he is almost blind and cannot farm for himself?" asked one man who had just quarreled bitterly with his father. "Can you just abandon your father? Is it not he who begot you?" (Fortes, 1970, p. 177). Old men, no matter how incapacitated, still exercised authority over sons, who had an interest in their fathers' land. Old men without adult sons had to depend on the unreliable assistance of kin and neighbors for help on their farms, and as a result they were unlikely to have more than a "minimum of food and other necessaries." When they became too weak to farm at all, relatives ordinarily gave them shelter and food. However, although refusing gifts of food to needy kin was viewed as an offense against the ancestors, people were not bound to be overgenerous to kin who did not contribute to the common pool (Fortes, 1949, pp. 216–217).

Like sonless old men, old women without sons are also at a disadvantage in many African societies. Among the Gusii of Kenya, sonlessness is a disaster second only to barrenness; an old woman needs at least one son who will care for her and whose wives will work for her (LeVine, 1980, p. 94). A case history from another Kenyan group, the Samia, makes this painfully clear. Miriamu was a blind old woman in her late 80s. Of the four children to whom she gave birth, only two grew to maturity, but the son died in 1965. The surviving daughter was married and lived a day's journey away. By the late 1980s, Miriamu could not move about at all and lay naked in her house, save for a dirty, ragged blanket. Sometimes a co-wife or the co-wife's son, who lived nearby, sent food; other kin helped a little. Her daughter did what she could, sending a little money and visiting once or twice a year to clean the house and do a few odd jobs. Some days, according to the anthropologist, Miriamu "sits and eats," but too often she sits cold, and the food does not come (Cattell, 1990).

Even those who do have sons may be without their help. Sons may be alive and well but living far away, often working in towns. Zimmer (1987, p. 72) speaks of "de facto childlessness" among the Gende of Papua New Guinea in cases where parents were left childless when migrant children reneged on their obligations. Even if they do send gifts and financial help, migrant children are not available to attend to the daily, physical needs of aging and sick parents (although in some societies grandchildren are occasionally sent home to provide services or the elderly themselves are brought to live in town) (Peil et al., 1989).

Sons may not be around because they have quarreled with their parents. Moore (1978) tells of an old Chagga man, Siara, who was in his midseventies when she knew him. Siara had no living sons nearby to rely on in old age. His firstborn had died. His eldest living son, a Catholic priest, came home only on holidays. According to Chagga custom, the youngest son, Danieli, should have stayed at home, looking after his old parents and caring for their needs. In return, he would ultimately inherit their garden and whatever was attached to it. Relations between Siara and Danieli had long been marked by conflict, however. In the late 1950s, Danieli left the community. At the time of the study, in 1974, he lived far away and had not even been home to see his father in 14 years.

It is not that the sonless or childless are totally isolated or alone; in small communities, they usually have considerable contact with kin and neighbors, most of whom they have probably known since childhood. Among the Chagga, hardly any of the elderly were alone in their homesteads, and all lived near relatives who were obligated to care for them. However, those who lacked nearby sons had to depend on kin whose interest in them was "secondary rather than primary in the Chagga hierarchy of intensity of relationship and obligation" (Moore, 1978, p. 73). To younger people who must help support distant kin or neighbors, the obligation tends to be seen as a particularly heavy burden, especially if they must also support their own parents as well. The childless or sonless old must often beg for help from people who resent giving, and in some societies such old people are ridiculed, neglected, or even accused of witchcraft. There are some indications that they also run a risk of being abandoned or killed. Zimmer (1987) describes two older Gende men, without wives or children, who depended on their brothers' reluctant help and contributed little to communal festivities. According to villagers, men such as these, in precontact days, before whites imposed their law, would have been thrown from a cliff into the river when they were no longer able to fend for themselves.

Resources

Even the frail elderly who have children can end up neglected, mistreated, and sometimes abandoned and killed. Why some societies make more elaborate provisions for the care of the elderly than others—and why some provide only the bare minimal necessities—is unclear. What we do know is that old people's control of valuable resources (people, property, and knowledge) as well as their drain on the group's resources play a role.

In societies where old people control property, they can use these rights to compel others to support them or provide them with goods and services (Amoss and Harrell, 1981). The extent of old people's political influence or family authority can affect the degree of support they get and the grace with which it is provided. Take the case of the Hopi, as described in the 1930s. As long as aged men controlled property rights, held special ceremonial offices, or were powerful medicine men, they were respected. But "the feebler and more useless they become, the more relatives grab what they have, neglect them, and sometimes harshly scold them, even permitting children to play rude jokes on them." Sons might refuse to support their fathers, telling them, "You had your day, you are going to die pretty soon." Aged Hopi were heard to remark, "We always looked forward to old age, but see how we suffer" (Simmons, 1945, pp. 59, 234). It should be noted, too, that personal qualities can affect a person's fortunes in old age. The basic needs of irascible and querulous elders may be met, but they are less likely than the good-tempered to attract the spontaneous concern and goodwill of younger relatives (e.g., Reid, 1985; Simic, 1978).

Resources affect neglect in another way. There is the problem of limited resources, for basic food and survival, in the community or family—and the drain the incapacitated elderly place on these resources. This is what is sometimes referred to as the cost/contribution balance between what the aged contribute to the resources of the group, on the one hand, and the cost they exact, on the other (Amoss & Harrell, 1981, p. 6). No longer essential workers, or contributors to subsistence, the frail elderly may sap limited resources and be regarded as a burden by the young. This is especially so in societies where subsistence is precarious and/or where there is frequent mobility. In this regard, old women sometimes fare better than old men. Old men who lose physical vigor can no longer do strenuous male productive work such as hunting or farming. Frail old women, however, can still perform useful women's work, performing light domestic chores.[4]

Even with the best intentions, younger people cannot always give elderly parents the kind of attention they expect. They are often too busy with productive or other tasks. And environmental factors beyond anyone's control, such as drought or low food reserves, often require decisions that result in difficulties for the elderly. A poor harvest among the Gwembe Tonga in Zambia, for example, meant that many households simply did not have enough food. To reduce the number of bellies dependent on household granaries, the very old were sometimes sent to live with relatives in distant, more prosperous regions (Colson & Scudder, 1981, p. 128).

In allocating limited resources, young adults may be torn between obligations to parents and to their own children. As land has become scarcer and consumer needs have escalated, the problem has become more serious, leaving the young with less to spare for the old at a time when the elderly are making increased cash demands. "It is a difficult job to look after them," one Kikuyu man from Kenya said of his aged parents. "They are often as unreasonable as children. They forget what it is like to have nine children and little land" (Cox & Mberia, 1977). A study of urban Nigerian workers found them to be torn between the duty to send food and money to their parents, on the one hand, and the expectation to maintain a life style commensurate with their occupational status, on the other. The result was that many did a little of each: often skimping on support for parents and feeling, at the same time, that they had compromised their own quality of life (Togonu-Bicker-steth, 1989).

The problems posed by limited resources and old people's dependence are sometimes resolved in an extreme way: killing, abandoning, or exposure of the elderly—what anthropologists call gerontocide. Cross-cultural studies show that such treatment is more common than we might suppose. Maxwell and Silverman found evidence of gerontocide in a little over 20% of 95 societies in a worldwide sample (Silverman, 1987). Glascock uncovered abandonment of the elderly in 9 of the 41 nonindustrial societies in his sample—and reports of killing old people in 14 of these societies (Glascock, 1990).

Both studies found that gerontocide tends to occur in societies that can be characterized as technologically simple—hunting and gathering, pastoral, and shifting horticultural, as opposed to those with intensive agriculture. "The need for the social group to move frequently," Glascock writes, "poses a threat to the elderly as does the inability of most of these societies to store sufficient food to allow all members to survive severe food shortages" (1990, p. 56). A decline in health and strength results in old people becoming a burden on other members of the social group.

Details concerning the killing of the elderly are largely lacking in ethnographic material so that we do not know how the elderly themselves viewed their fate. My own guess is that they sometimes had mixed, perhaps angry, feelings about being killed or left to die, but they felt unable to resist pressures to acquiesce in the decision. What evidence is available, however, shows that far from invariably fighting against such treatment, old people in many societies accepted their fate, or at least did not actively resist it. Indeed, part of the informal contract between old and young in a number of societies is a tacit understanding, accepted by the elderly as well as the younger generation, that when the old become a drain on the community's resources it is time to go. This is much like Durkheim's (1951) description of altruistic suicide, where people have an obligation or duty to the social group to kill themselves. Gerontocide, according to the evidence, is usually a family affair. Typically, children and the elderly individual jointly decide that the time is right to die. Where killing is involved, commonly the son carries out the act (Glascock, 1990).

In some places, anthropologists have found, the disabled elderly were abandoned upon their request. Among the Mardudjara hunters and gatherers of Australia, the incompetent old were fed and spared the difficulties of moving too often, but when frequent travel became unavoidable, some of the elderly asked to be left behind to perish (Tonkinson, 1978). In the past, among the Eskimos of northern Canada, the old person usually initiated the abandonment process. During a storm or when the family was busily occupied, the aged parent would quietly slip off into the tundra to die from exhaustion and exposure (Guemple, 1977).

In some societies, being buried alive was considered an honorable way to die. In earlier times in Samoa, an old and ailing chief was able to orchestrate his own funeral. He told his children and friends to get ready to bury him, thus ending his life amid the acclaim of his family and community in an elaborate mortuary ceremony. In much the same way, extremely frail elders among the Yakut of Siberia would, in ancient times, beg their relatives to bury them. Before being led into the wood and thrust into their graves, they were honored at a three-day feast (Simmons, 1945, pp. 236–237). Such dignified ceremonial deaths, Myerhoff suggests—where the dying person is the "hero, the death not an intrusion but a fulfillment of his life" (1978, p. 229)—are far preferable to the isolation and loneliness of dying that most Americans experience in modern hospitals and nursing homes.

Sometimes, younger people help the death process along when the elderly are in pain and discomfort. In this sense, death hastening can offer an escape from intense suffering (Logue, 1990). A Hopi man told of the time when his uncle—a man who had been frail and sick for several years—was finally dying ("his breath is about the length of my finger and he is getting cold"). After the dying man's face was covered with a blanket, the nephew propped him against the wall "so that the breath will escape quickly . . . he is too old and weak to feel any pain; and it is better for him to be on his way" (Simmons, 1945, p. 234).

Cultural attitudes toward death may soften the blow or make the aged indifferent to dying. In the past, elderly Eskimos in northern Canada were willing to be abandoned when they became weak or ill because they did not believe they would really die. They were convinced that their "name substance"—"the essential ingredient of a human being which includes the personality, special skills, and basic character"—would live on, and would enter the body of a newborn child (Guemple, 1983).

Cultural Beliefs

The Eskimo case makes clear that, critical as social and economic factors are in explaining neglect and mistreatment, cultural beliefs may also be involved.

In an intriguing analysis of aging on the Polynesian island of Niue, Barker (1990) argues that religious beliefs concerning death and the ancestors help explain why the disabled elderly were treated so poorly. Despite free and easily available medical services, caretakers did not bother to ask for medical help for physically ill elders. The demented and incontinent were left unattended and received minimal care. Little effort was made to bathe them, clean their homes, or provide them with material comforts. Old people who were bent over or who walked oddly were figures of fun. When blind or unstable elders hurt themselves, they were ridiculed and teased.

Such mistreatment Barker admits is, in part, a response to the economic burden the frail elderly place on the able-bodied. On Niue, with its fragile ecosystem, there is not much surplus available for nonproducers, and periodic droughts bring food scarcities. Yet younger handicapped people—also an economic burden—are not subject to neglect or special ridicule. The disabled elderly are singled out for neglect, Barker argues, because of Niuean cultural conceptions of death, the life cycle, and spirits of the dead. Old people who no longer look or behave like competent adults are believed to be dangerous and threatening. Courted by spirits of the dead, they are in transition—the nearly dead—inhabiting a twilight world of not-quite-human-but-not-quite-ancestor. By abandoning the nearly dead or limiting contact to the point of neglect, younger adults prevent being contaminated by ghostly influences from beyond, and distance themselves from powerful and potentially dangerous transformations.

Social Changes

Like our own society, nonindustrial societies are not static. The social patterns anthropologists observe at one point in time are not fixed or permanent and can undergo significant change. Brought up to expect that care will be forthcoming, the elderly may find that, when frailty sets in, changes have undermined or reduced the strength of social arrangements, cultural values, and resources that, in the past, guaranteed care.

A reduction in old people's control over productive resources, for example, may affect the willingness of the young to look after them—and the kind of care that is provided. With growing consumer needs and scarcer land in many societies, young people, as I already noted, may have less to spare for elderly parents. And new ideas, values, and conceptions may give legitimacy to young people's neglect—as well as reduce the effectiveness of mystical sanctions at old people's command.

Also crucial is that increased migration to new cities and towns removes many potential caretakers from the scene. Children are less likely to be around to provide care, leaving the elderly in difficult straits when they become frail and ill. The case of the Gende of Papua New Guinea is pertinent here. Since they were first contacted in 1932, there has been a steady increase in migration away from the area, with many moving to work in town or on plantations. Indeed, in the 1980s, about one quarter of the population—two thirds of whom were men and women between the ages of 18 and 45—were absent. The consequences for the elderly have been devastating. With more and more daughters living at a distance and sons away in town, Zimmer (1987) writes, the daily needs of aging and sick parents are likely to go unattended.

Conclusion: Looking Ahead

This bleak scenario is not inevitable. Social changes do not always leave the frail elderly in the lurch, a point that must be emphasized. Too often anthropological writings on aging and change assume that the position of the old will invariably deteriorate as their societies become more economically developed and integrated into the "modern" world. I have argued elsewhere that such predictions must be challenged: The worsening of old people's position is only one possible outcome (Foner, 1984a, 1984b). This is true for the frail as well as for the hardy elderly.

There is no better proof than the very fact that most ethnographic reports describing young people meeting their caretaking obligations— and having a strong sense of filial duty—are based on data collected in societies that have already experienced extensive contact with Western industrial powers, some based on very recent research. Thus, drawing on fieldwork conducted among the Samia of Kenya throughout the 1980s, Cattell (1990) concludes that despite the stresses from labor migration, geographic separations, poverty, and other factors associated with modernization, families still struggle to meet their obligations to the senior generation. Children remain the prime source of old-age security, allowing many elders who can no longer work to achieve the cultural ideal of sitting by the fire and having food brought to them. Indeed, throughout less developed parts of the world, the absence of old-age pensions for most of the rural population—a situation that, given the high costs, is unlikely to change for a long time—means that children continue to be the main support of the frail old.

There are some cases where change has actually led to improvements for the disabled old, as in a number of cultures where pensions have been introduced or where the elderly attract much-needed overseas remittances. Before old-age pensions were introduced among the Western Apache, the very old were poor and economically dependent on the young. When Goodwin lived among them in the 1930s, however, old people who received monthly army pensions were often the wealthiest members of their families, and younger relatives came to them for money. The very frail old usually received better care. Younger people had an interest in keeping old relatives alive: When they died, the pensions ceased (Goodwin, 1942, p. 517).

When we turn to our own society, it is difficult to foretell exactly how changes in the next decades will affect care for the frail elderly. What is clear, as Bengtson notes in Chapter 1 in this volume, is that dire predictions about the abandonment of elderly family members are unfounded. As in the nonindustrial world, children here are likely to continue to feel strong obligations to look after and help their elderly parents.

True, there are marked differences from nonindustrial cultures. The advent of Social Security and other government programs has reduced pressure on children to support their parents financially. Unlike nonindustrial cultures, where the elderly have long been used to, indeed have demanded, material and other help from their children, there is, as Clark (1973) puts it, a strong cultural imperative for most elderly Americans to be self-sufficient and economically independent. Old people in American society are generally reluctant to live with their children or even to ask them for financial help (see Keith, Fry, & Ikels, 1990). Moreover, a wide array of nonfamilial long-term care arrangements, including large numbers of nursing homes, are available. Nonetheless, children in American society will doubtless still play an important role in caregiving—ranging from providing actual day-to-day care to regularly visiting nursing homes and managing paid home-care arrangements long-distance.

Many of the same forces that motivate children in nonindustrial societies to look after their parents operate and are likely to continue to operate here: emotional bonds between children and parents; cultural norms of filial obligation and duty; and younger people's sense that they owe parents care in repayment for help and assistance parents provided them over the years (see Rossi & Rossi, 1990; and Rossi, Chapter 10 in this volume). Indeed, increased longevity may well strengthen emotional ties between the generations as parents and children have more years of shared lives (Bengtson, Chapter 1 in this volume). Occasionally, the lure of inheritance is a factor underlying care for frail parents. And the opinion of others may play a role. This includes their own children, for whom adult caregivers may be consciously or unconsciously providing a model to guarantee their own care in the future.

If looking at nonindustrial societies points to factors motivating care, it can also reveal some of the reasons why the elderly can be neglected when they most need help and attention. The lack of children who are alive and available is, as we saw, crucial. In our own society, spouses are the first line of defense for the elderly in times of need, children are the second (Bould, Sanborn, & Reif, 1989). The childless run a much greater risk of institutionalization; about 40% of nursing home residents have no living children, compared to less than 20% in the community (U.S. Senate Special Committee on Aging, 1987–88). As we look to the future, the proportion of the elderly with no living children is expected to increase as the low-fertility baby boomers become old. In fact, voluntary childlessness—unheard of in nonindustrial cultures—is on the rise here (Bengtson, Chapter 1 in this volume). Also, with increasing rates of female labor force participation, adult daughters are apt to be less available to their aged parents. Add to this the complications from increased geographic mobility as well as divorce (on the ramifications of divorce for future cohorts of American elderly see Riley & Riley, Chapter 9 in this volume). Moreover, the aging of the population means that chronically ill parents, themselves extremely old, will be more likely to have children who are already retired and who are limited in their ability to provide help due to their own low income or health problems.

The pressure of resources is also an issue. As in nonindustrial cultures, children here are often torn between the demands and needs of their parents, on the one hand, and those of their spouses and children, on the other. This may be especially difficult in times of economic downturns, when financial resources are scarce. How these resources are allocated will vary from case to case, but the sick elderly are likely to suffer when there is not enough to go around or to pay for the kind of care they require. As more and more middle-aged women are forced to juggle care for a disabled parent with responsibilities to dependent children as well as a job, they may simply be unable to provide the kind of attention and assistance that the parent needs or wants.

It is at the societal, rather than family, level that the question of resources has received the most attention in this country. The frail elderly, many claim, are already monopolizing too much of the nation's resources at the expense of the young—and this will get much worse in the future as costs mount for the rising numbers of elderly.[5] Callahan (1987) puts it bluntly when he says that the full provision of health care, by government funds or institutions, for the ever-growing number of elderly—who are being kept alive for an ever-longer period of time— promises to be insupportable. His controversial solution is to call for a revamping of our obligations to the elderly and our cultural conception of a "natural life span." He proposes rationing health care by age: de-

nying life-extending health care to those who have completed this natural life span, somewhere in their late 70s or early 80s.

This, ironically, brings us back to nonindustrial societies. In the wake
of the miracles of modern medicine, which is able to keep large numbers
of people alive in grossly incapacitated states, and the problem of scarce
government resources, many Americans may well look at practices in
nonindustrial cultures with a different eye. Once popularly condemned
as savage and barbaric, ceremonial killings and the abandonment of the
severely ill aged in these societies may, at the other extreme, come to be
glorified as enlightened acts of kindness.

As modern-day anthropologists remind us, the way we interpret different cultures reflects our own concerns, ideas, and predilections. This
is true of scholarship as well as popular thought. The very emphasis in
this chapter on analyzing failures in the caregiving contract in nonindustrial societies is a response to dilemmas facing the frail elderly in this
country. Yet, this analytical process is a dialectical one, as the discussion
has also suggested. Much as our views of different cultures are shaped
by our own concerns, these views can, at the same time, allow us to
reflect back on our customs, values, and attitudes in a slightly different
way. Indeed, a cross-cultural perspective can provide a different angle
or lens for, and perhaps bring into sharper focus, problems and processes concerning caregiving and relations between the generations that
are of such critical importance in our own society.

Notes

1.   Because they have lived a long time, the elderly in preliterate societies
are (as long as they are mentally alert) regarded as possessors of knowledge,
wisdom, and experience. It is they who know about the past and how things
should be done—and they are valued for their expertise and advice. Growing
old also usually brings with it certain ritual powers and knowledge. And with
aging comes the opportunity to establish durable relations with kin, descendants, social debtors, and allies—and sometimes control over material resources
as well. In many nonindustrial societies, age and seniority are, in themselves,
bases for deference—juniors may have to greet or speak to elders in a respectful
manner or allot them the best or largest portion of food at public ceremonies (see
Foner, 1984a).

2.   Providing the senior generation with material support and help, moreover, is nothing new. In nonindustrial societies, the dramatic role reversals of
later life observed in our own society occur less often. Because services cannot
be hired and government does not provide social welfare benefits, people must
rely on kin and other associates not just in their later years but throughout their

lives in times of danger, emergency, and disaster. In these societies, children are a major human resource, and they usually contribute to their parents' material support, in good and bad times, for much of their lives. This is unlike the situation in middle-class America, where material exchanges between parents and children typically involve parents as the main givers, with a startling shift occurring in late old age if aged parents must turn to adult children for support.

3. In practice, much of the son's obligation of providing day-to-day care usually falls on his wife (or wives) and children.

4. In societies where men have many wives, however, they may have a definite edge in that when they reach an advanced age they often have at least one wife to bring them food and look after them (see, for example, Cattell, 1990, on the Samia of Kenya, and Reid, 1985, on Australian aborigines).

5. For an alternative conceptualization of this issue as it relates to pensions, see Walker (1990a, and Chapter 8 in this volume). Walker argues that an economic and demographic imperative has been manufactured to facilitate restructuring the welfare state.

7

Conflict over Intergenerational Equity: Rhetoric and Reality in a Comparative Context

Victor W. Marshall, Fay Lomax Cook, and
Joanne Gard Marshall

In the mid-1980s the issue of intergenerational equity arose on the agenda of policymakers and scholars in the United States but not in Canada. We describe the emergence of the issue in the United States, document the differential importance of the issue in the two countries, and seek an explanation for the difference.

The Issue of Intergenerational Equity

The intergenerational-equity issue refers to the concept that different generations should be treated in similar ways and should have similar opportunities. It arose as an issue when claims were made that government policies treat the young and old very differently and thus cause them to have different and unequal opportunities. The issue is more specific than general concerns about the economic costs of an aging population (e.g., Walker, 1990a), and refers to one of several forms of "generational conflict" based on other generational-cohort-based interests (Tindale & Marshall, 1980). It also differs from conflict between familial generations (Bengtson, Cutler, Mangen, & Marshall, 1985; Bengtson, Marti, & Roberts, 1991). Its specific feature is that it links the economic costs of the aged to those of the young, with the argument that the young are being deprived of opportunities for well-being because of excessive allocation of resources to the old.

Our analysis shows that, in 1984 in the United States, two events occurred quite independently of each other, causing ripple effects that catapulted the issue of intergenerational equity to visibility in both the policy community and the academic community. In the policy community, Senator Dave Durenberger (R-MN) founded Americans for Generational Equity (AGE). In the academic community, Professor Samuel Preston's Presidential Address to the Population Association of America was entitled "Children and the Elderly: Divergent Paths for America's Dependents." The address was later reprinted in the journal *Demography* (1984a) and published in revised form in *Scientific American* (1984b). The role that Preston's address played in relation to the development of the intergenerational issue will be discussed in a later section.

According to its founder Senator Durenberger, AGE's goal is "to promote the concept of generational equity among America's political, intellectual, and financial leaders" (quoted in Quadagno, 1989, p. 360). Senator Durenberger's management intern, Paul Hewitt, became president and executive director of AGE. AGE's research director, Phillip Longman, had written in a 1982 article that the old are "taking America to the cleaners" because "the old have come to insist that the young not only hold them harmless for their past profligacy, but sacrifice their own prosperity to pay for it" (p. 24).

Within three years, AGE's initial budget of $88,000 had quadrupled in size due to funding from 85 organizations and businesses, which included banks, insurance companies, defense contractors, and health care corporations (Quadagno, 1989). According to its 1990 annual report, AGE attempts to call "into question the prudence, sustainability, and fairness to future generations of federal old age benefit programs" (Americans for Generational Equity, 1990, p. 2). Nothing akin to the development of AGE occurred in Canada.

Relative Importance of the Intergenerational-Equity Issue in the Two Countries

The importance of an issue may be addressed at four levels, of which we consider three in some detail in this paper. The three that we address are: (1) attention to the issue as gauged by reports in public media; (2) academic discourse, which is reflected in published scholarly papers and books; and (3) political and government policy attention. The fourth level, considered briefly here but more extensively in a separate paper (Cook, Marshall, Marshall, & Kaufman, 1991), is the level of public opinion, which may be gauged through survey data. It is reasonable to assume that public opinion is shaped by media attention and that media attention and academic discourse influence one another.

Studying Media Attention

For pragmatic reasons we examined the print media, because they can readily be accessed through on-line computer searching techniques. Several databases provide access to the contents of newspapers and popular magazines in the United States, Canada, or both. For Canada, we selected the CANADIAN BUSINESS AND CURRENT AFFAIRS (CBCA) database, an index of 10 newspapers including *The Globe & Mail* (which purports to be Canada's national newspaper) and *The Toronto Star* (Canada's largest circulation newspaper). Over 500 magazines are also indexed in CBCA.

For the United States, we selected NEWSPAPER ABSTRACTS and COURIER PLUS, which together index about 25 national and regional newspapers (including *The New York Times*) and over 300 magazines and periodicals. An additional database, MAGAZINE INDEX, provided access to 435 North American popular magazines and selected major scholarly journals, most of which are United States publications, but at least 11 of which are Canadian. The time periods covered by the databases vary, but together the databases provide a reasonably comprehensive view of media coverage since 1980.

We searched for any articles that dealt with the social relationship between the young and the old. Key words vary by database. *Young* is often captured by the words *children* and *youth; old* is also often captured by the words *aged, senior, older people,* and *aging.* We also searched for specific phrases such as *generation gap, (inter)generational conflict,* and the obvious *(inter)generational equity.* (Details of the search strategy are available from the authors upon request.)

Findings From the Analysis of Media

The four databases searched contained approximately 7.3 million records of newspaper or magazine articles. Of these, the number of records referring to the old totaled 15,615 (0.2%) and the number referring to the young totaled 77,465 (1.1%). When these two concepts were combined to retrieve only articles in which the old and young were discussed together in the same article, 356 articles were found. Of these 356, just 30 (8.4%) dealt with intergenerational equity or conflict. The number of articles addressing children and youth is far greater than those dealing with the elderly in both Canada and the United States.

Table 1. Media and Academic Attention to the Issue of Intergenerational Equity in Canada and the United States (Number of Articles) by Year[a]

	Media attention[b]		Academic attention[c]	
	Canada	United States	Canada	United States
1990	0	6	0	1
1989	0	4	0	20
1988	0	13	1	17
1987	0	4	0	13
1986	0	2	0	9
1985	0	0	0	9
1984	0	1	0	7
1983	0	0	1	3
1982	0	0	0	0
1981	0	0	0	2
1980	0	0	0	1
Total	0	30	2	82

[a] All searches were performed on the Dialog on-line information retrieval service in January 1991. For details of database scope and coverage, consult the *Dialog Database Catalog.*
[b] Database sources for media attention: For Canada, CBCA and *Magazine Index.* For the United States, *Magazine Index, Newspaper Abstracts,* and *Courier Plus.*
[c] Database source for academic attention: AgeLine, excluding articles considered to be about family intergenerational conflict or appearing in popular, as opposed to academic, sources.

The CBCA search did not retrieve a single Canadian citation dealing with generational equity or conflict, although 15 citations were found that discussed the young and the old together. The percentage of articles that addressed equity or conflict issues, in relation to all of the articles in the respective databases dealing with the old and young together, was just 4.8% for *Magazine Index,* 20.6% for *Newspaper Abstracts,* and 7.1% for *Courier Plus.* The total number of articles on the specific issues of intergenerational equity or conflict is therefore very small in relation to the larger content of the databases, even when the comparison is restricted to the number of articles addressing both the young and the old.

Table 1 shows the distribution of the retrievals coded as dealing with generational equity or conflict, by year and by origin of the article (i.e., whether it appeared in a United States or Canadian publication). For Canada, we do not find a single article in the media on intergenerational equity or conflict for the period from 1980 to 1990. Instead, the articles on young and old have to do with cooperation and positive communication patterns. They have titles such as "Young and Young at Heart Give Education a New Twist: Children, Seniors, Learning from Each Other," and "Age Barriers Knocked Down as Youngsters Mix with Elderly."

For the United States, on the other hand, 30 articles appeared in the media during that time segment. The number increased from 1 in 1984 to 13 in 1988, and then decreased again after 1988. Although not large in number, the articles were dramatic in content and a number carried a clear theme of intergenerational conflict. For example, a *Washington Post* story entitled "Older Voters Drive Budget" (1990) reported that the budget package for 1991 could widen the gap in federal spending on old and young Americans, especially poor children. *The Atlanta Constitution* carried a story entitled "United States Coddles Elderly But Ignores Plight of Children" (1990). The title of an opinion piece in the *San Francisco Chronicle* was even more dramatic: "America Is at War with Its Children" (1989).

But not all of the articles with the more general theme of intergenerational equity in the United States pointed to conflict. Many described positive, reciprocal relationships between the old and the young in which members of the two age groups provided support and assistance to each other. Still others were neutral in that they saw both the old and the young as deserving recipients of support by the state. Some articles attempted to dissipate tension and reconcile differences. For example, a *New York Times* commentary titled "The Old and Young Aren't Foes" (Hutton, 1987) argued that it is futile to scrap programs for the elderly in order to help the young; and a syndicated column by Ellen Goodman (1988) was entitled "Time to Call in Bridge Builders for the Warring Generations."

In summary, the lack of any discussion in the Canadian media of intergenerational equity or conflict is notable. At the same time, the relatively small number of articles in the United States databases suggests that the issue may not be of as great concern to the wider public as those close to the issue have come to assume. Nevertheless, the 30 articles that did refer to the relationship between the generations have on the whole been dramatic in their portrayal of conflict within the context of equity issues. We now turn to the question of academic attention to the intergenerational-equity issue.

Academic Attention in the United States and Canada

Our approach to gauging academic attention to the issue of intergenerational equity relied not only on database searching but also on our own knowledge as academics immersed in age-related studies. An initial overview search of 17 social science databases indicated that Age-Line had the greatest number of citations containing the phrase *(inter)generational conflict* or *(inter)generational equity* ($n = 153$).

Intergenerational conflict, defined as "stresses and disagreements between generations in the family and in society," was introduced as an indexing term in the AgeLine thesaurus in 1980. A computer search using this indexing term yielded 95 citations. A second search using the thesaurus term *intergenerational transfers* yielded an additional 39 unique citations. A final search using the broader strategy, in which the word *intergenerational* appears with *conflict* or *equity* anywhere in the subject fields of the record, yielded another 39 citations not found under the indexing term.

The results of these three searches were reviewed, and citations dealing with the family (as opposed to the social aspects of intergenerational conflict) and any popular or nonacademic publications were eliminated. This left 82 citations covering the period 1980 through 1990, with a peak of 20 in 1989 (see Table 1). Over the same period, only 2 articles dealing with intergenerational conflict or equity in Canada were found. Note that this searching strategy retrieved articles in a category of generational conflict that includes, but goes beyond, the intergenerational-equity issue. This is so because not all discussions of conflict are framed in terms of resource allocation, pitting the young against the old. The 2 Canadian citations, for example, dealt with conflict but not with equity.

Neugarten (1973), one of the first academics to raise the possibility of conflict between the generations, did not frame the issue as one in which the young would be deprived because of inappropriately generous provisions for the old. Demographer Samuel Preston brought this formulation to prominence, and to a wide audience of academic readers. Preston never mentioned the term *intergenerational equity* in his Presidential Address before the Population Association of America, or in the two printed versions of his talk (1984a, 1984b); yet his theme was clearly intergenerational equity.

Preston amassed data on changes in three domains—well-being, the family, and politics. He made a strong case that conditions have deteriorated for children and improved dramatically for the elderly and that "in the public sphere at least, gains for one group come partly at the expense of another" (Preston, 1984a, p. 450). He argued that "the transfers from the working-age population to the elderly are also transfers away from children . . . and let's also recognize that the sums involved are huge" (pp. 451–452).

Many scholarly presidential addresses are delivered, published, and then forgotten; but Preston's work struck a chord among academics in at least three areas—poverty, child welfare, and gerontology—and among a number of foundations and agencies with these specializations. Between 1985 and 1990, our analyses of the *Social Science Citation Index* show that Preston's articles in *Demography* and *Scientific American* were cited by academics 122 times (the former 75 times and the latter 47 times). This amount of attention is high in scholarly terms. Only 3% of scientific papers are cited more than 24 times, and only 1% are cited 50 or more times (Garfield, 1985).

Preston's argument piqued the interest of scholars. In August 1985, the National Academy of Sciences brought together about 20 social scientists for a workshop in Massachusetts (Palmer, Smeeding, & Torrey, 1988). Over the next two years, the Alfred P. Sloan Foundation, the Ford Foundation, and the John D. and Catherine T. MacArthur Foundation funded two more workshops held in the United States and a conference held in Luxemburg.

The Luxemburg conference led to a volume in which the data bear out Preston's conclusion that the economic experiences of the elderly and children in the United States have diverged widely over the past 20 years. However, the scholars who wrote the summary chapter were quick to say that "it is not at all clear that children's doing worse has enabled the elderly to do better; our poverty rates for the elderly remain on the high side among industrial nations" (Gould & Palmer, 1988, p. 422). The authors criticize the intergenerational-equity framework as encouraging "us-versus-them" thinking; yet, they also say that "the policy-making process will be fraught with much more intergenerational tension than was true in the past" (p. 422).

In Canada, the issue of possible or actual conflict between the generations—i.e., between age groups—was raised by the first author in academic forums (Marshall, 1979, 1980, 1981; Tindale & Marshall, 1980). In 1981, Marshall specifically suggested that the high dependency of the aged on the state might lead to increased age identification among the old, while the growth in the size of this dependent population "has the potential to make it a target for the resentment of younger groups who are 'paying the bills'" (Marshall, 1981, p. 94). However, this analysis stressed, first, that the social construction of aging by elites had a dampening effect on generational consciousness among the aged (by promoting an individualistic ideology of a leisure-oriented "good old age"); and second, that the major source of conflict was interjurisdictional squabbles over age-targeted resource allocation (a point discussed below).

It cannot be said that the broad issue of generational conflict, or its more narrow formulation as intergenerational equity, received much attention in Canadian academic circles over the past decade. A review of *Canadian Journal on Aging*, Canada's leading gerontology journal, and of two major policy journals, *Canadian Public Policy* and *Policy Options*, shows not a single reference to generational-equity issues or to a generational-equity debate over the past several years. These journals carry articles about the financial costs of an aging population, but not in intergenerational-equity terms (e.g., Seward [1986] and McDaniel [1987] whose articles are not included in Table 1).

Policy reports are not easy to track, but we found three areas in which the language of intergenerational equity was used. The Economic Council of Canada 1989 annual report, entitled *Legacies*, expressed concerns that younger generations may be saddled with a large national debt burden and a devalued natural environment. The report, however, does not consider, let alone advocate, reallocation of resources from the old to the young.

The second area is a string of federal government documents dealing with pension reform. The final report of a major interdepartmental task force on the Canadian retirement income system (Task Force on Retirement Income Policy, 1979) used the term *intergenerational equity*, but with an intent quite opposite of that which characterizes the debate in the United States. The Canada Pension Plan (CPP) (and Quebec Pension Plan, QPP) had just been approved and was being phased in, providing a benefit to future generations that was not available to people currently old. Thus, the task force opined,

> given the way in which the C/QPP were phased in—there is a presumption that the future elderly will be relatively better off than are today's elderly. This is the position adopted by this report and obviously argues strongly for improving the financial position of those who are now elderly in order to maintain equity between generations. (1979, p. 145)

A 1982 Canadian government report aimed at a wider public audience, *Better Pensions for Canadians* (Government of Canada, 1982), repeated this same concern in a brief, two-page section, "Intergenerational Equity." This report recognized that "today's generation should not place an undue burden on future generations through the pension arrangements it establishes"; but it also argued that "the current generation should treat the elderly today at least as well as it expects to be treated by future generations." A year later, the *Report of the Parliamentary Task Force on Pension Reform* (House of Commons, 1983) devoted three paragraphs to the issue. None of these reports suggested that anything more than prudent fiscal planning was called for; and none of them pitted the old against the young in any conflictual context.

The third area in which we found one mention of intergenerational equity is discussed in a later section.

The virtual lack of academic discussion in Canada of intergenerational conflict, let alone equity, parallels our finding that little attention is given to the issue in Canadian media. The number of scholarly articles on intergenerational conflict in the United States is very small in relation to the larger content of the databases. Still, we do find the emergence of the issue within the United States social science community in the early 1980s, in parallel with coverage of the issue in the American media.

The Extent of Political Attention in the United States and Canada

To gauge political attention to intergenerational equity in the United States, we looked at activity within the United States Congress. We used the *Congressional Record Index* (index to all addresses and discussions on the floor of Congress) and the *Congressional Information Service Index* (index to congressional hearings and committee reports). Looking under *generational equity* and *intergenerational equity* in these indexes, we found not a single entry. We found no references to *generations* in the *Congressional Record Index* but four references to *Generations United* in the *Congressional Information Service Index*. (Generations United aims to promote greater consciousness about the ways generations are linked and to foster the development of social programs that integrate the concerns of young and old.)

In 1986, the Select Committee on Aging in the House of Representatives held a hearing entitled "Investing in America's Families: The Common Bond of Generations." In his opening statement Congressman Edward R. Roybal, chairman of the Select Committee on Aging, made specific reference to intergenerational equity:

> [T]he purpose of today's hearing is to highlight the emotional and financial interdependence of families across generations and their common stake in programs for both young and old. It is also to take a critical look at what some see as an emerging conflict between old and young due to financial pressures on families.

We found no recorded follow-up to the hearing in the form of reports, future hearings, or legislation. The terms of the debate, however, may have shifted as a result. According to Nancy Smith, a staff member for the House Select Committee on Aging, "the term *intergenerational* is now in the vernacular." Smith said after the hearing:

> The view was that we need to be talking about taking care of all the generations. . . . Right now, our strategy is to look for ways to benefit all the age groups. For example, we are supporting a National Health Program similar to Canada's where there would be health care for all ages. (personal communication, February 18, 1987)

We were not able to conduct an analysis for Canada comparable to that using the *Congressional Record Index*, because of the nature of indexing of *Hansard*, the official record of the Canadian Parliament. We therefore interviewed two highly placed policy advisors in the Department of National Health and Welfare and in the Office of the Minister of State for

Seniors (the cabinet minister with responsibility for the aged). Neither had any knowledge that intergenerational-equity issues had been discussed in the House of Commons or in the Senate. They indicated an awareness of the intergenerational-equity debate at the senior bureaucratic level of the federal government, perhaps reflecting the government reports discussed earlier in this chapter. One noted that she occasionally hears "seniors have more than their share," but that so far "no one has rocked the boat" by introducing the issue into Canadian policy discourse.

The second advisor suggested that federal policy initiatives for income security are turning toward children and youth because poverty among the aged has been reduced (see below). Recent policy changes have dealt with redistribution within the aged category, taxing back pension benefits from the elderly above a given level of income (the "pension clawback") but increasing the level of support for the means-tested Guaranteed Income Supplement; while recent or planned changes within the children and youth category are intended to redistribute income within that category.

In summary, we have shown that the intergenerational-equity debate in public media and scholarly publications has become much more important in the United States than in Canada. In addition, we have shown that while governmental and public policy initiatives in Canada have not been influenced by the intergenerational-equity issue, this issue has been on the policy agenda in the United States, albeit to a limited extent. We now turn to the explanation of these differences.

Explaining the Differences

Why has the intergenerational-equity issue emerged in the United States but not in Canada, a country that shares many of the same social issues with the United States and many of the same social conditions? (Canada has a similar proportion of elderly adults and a similar large budgetary deficit.)

We examine four possible explanations for the differences in importance of the intergenerational-equity issue, when comparing Canada and the United States. The first is that the issue is more important in the United States because of a greater inequity among age groups. The second possibility is that basic value differences between the two countries account for different approaches to support for the old and for the young. We will demonstrate that there is little support for either of these explanations.

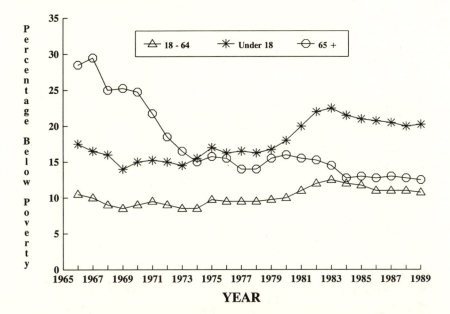

Figure 1. Percentage of persons below the poverty line in the U.S. by age group, 1966–1989. *Note:* From *Money Income and Poverty Status in the United States: 1989*, Current Population Reports, Series P-60, Number 168, Table 19 (p. 59) and Table 20 (p. 59), by U.S. Bureau of the Census, 1990a, Washington, DC: U.S. Government Printing Office.

The third possibility is that differences between the two countries in mechanisms of resource allocation affect the degree to which resource allocation is viewed in age-based terms. The fourth possibility is that differences in the nature of the political process between the two countries account for the lower level of intergenerational-equity debate in Canada. The third and fourth possibilities, we shall argue, do affect the extent to which intergenerational equity is on the public agenda.

Do Objective Differences in Poverty Account for the National Differences in Importance of the Issue?

In the United States, part of the intergenerational-equity argument is that while the aged were once a high-poverty group, their poverty has fallen due to lavish resource allocation from the public purse, while, simultaneously, the rate of poverty among children has increased. Figure 1 shows the percentage of persons below the poverty line in the United States, by age group, over the period 1966–1989.

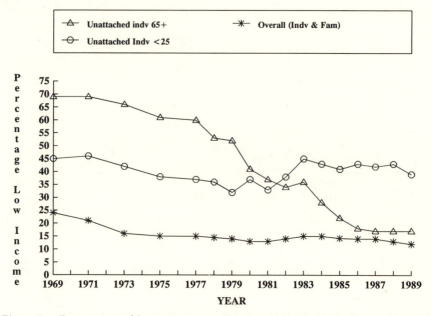

Figure 2. Percentage of low-income unattached individuals in Canada by age group, 1969–1989. *Note:* From *Income Distribution by Size in Canada,* Catalogue 13-207, by Statistics Canada, 1989, Ottawa: Ministry of Supply and Services Canada.

The most striking feature of the rates over this period is the crossover caused by slight increases in poverty among those aged 18 and younger, along with dramatic falls in poverty among those 65 and older. The picture is so dramatic that we can ignore otherwise important issues such as the definition of poverty. Such a crossover effect might well be expected to contribute to the perception of intergenerational inequity in the United States. We now ask if there is a similar pattern in Canada. The data are presented in Figures 2 and 3.

The available Canadian data distinguish persons living in families from those living as unattached individuals, and the upper boundary of the younger age category is 25 rather than 18 as in the United States figure. The definitions of poverty are also not the same in the two countries. Nonetheless, while the crossover appeared a few years later in Canada, the similarity to the United States pattern is remarkably similar. In this respect at least, the objective basis that has led some United States lobbyists and scholars to argue that there is inequitable resource allocation across the generations is also present for Canada. We therefore conclude, as a matter of logic of inference, that similarity in

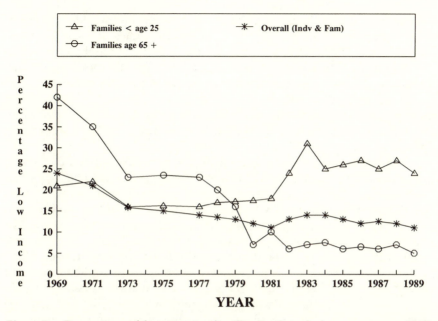

Figure 3. Percentage of low-income families in Canada by age group, 1969–1989. *Note:* From *Income Distribution by Size in Canada,* Catalogue 13-207, by Statistics Canada, 1989, Ottawa: Ministry of Supply and Services Canada.

objective conditions cannot account for differences in the importance of this policy issue.

Is Canada a "Kinder, Gentler Society" Than the United States?

Only brief mention will be made here of a second possible explanation for the differences between the two countries in the level of rhetoric on intergenerational equity. (We explore this possibility in greater detail in Cook et al., 1991.) Could it be that Canadians hold values of beneficence toward the aged (Dowd, 1984) that override concerns about unequal allocation of societal resources to the old and the young?

A review of public opinion data in Canada and the United States, presented elsewhere (Cook et al., 1991) found that, while comparison is difficult to make due to differences in question wording, the elderly have a special place in the hearts of both Canadians and Americans. Public opinion about support for the elderly is strikingly similar in the two countries.

The debate about any potential distinctiveness in societal values be-

tween Canada and the United States, and about the possible sources of
these values, has constituted one of the major topics of Canadian sociology (Brym, 1989). The principal theorist fueling the debate has been
the American sociologist Seymour Martin Lipset. His thesis posits historically conditioned value differences between Canada and the United
States, set more than 100 years ago through a series of historical events
having much to do with the revolutionary aspects of American society,
as contrasted with a more conservative, continuing British influence on
Canada.

In the domain of values pertinent to the generational-equity debate,
Lipset sees Canada as midway between the United States and European
countries in regard to individualism versus collectivism, citing data on
percentage of wealth in government hands and extent of government
ownership of industry. Cross-national public opinion polls, several of
which are reviewed by Lipset, support the notion that Americans are
more individualist, Canadians more collectivity oriented (Lipset, 1990,
p. 142). Behavioral data, however, are conflicting as indicators on the
individualism-collectivity dimension. The Canadian federal government, which is Conservative, has through a number of policies and
programs increased the emphasis on individualism and on economic
competitiveness. However, its popularity in the polls is currently very
low. In 1990, Canada's largest province, Ontario, swept a democratic
socialist government, the New Democrats, into power, replacing the
Liberals, who had replaced the Conservatives just half a decade earlier;
and in 1991 the New Democratic Party was returned to power in two
other provincial governments, British Columbia and Saskatchewan.

Strong reservations may be expressed concerning Lipset's selectivity,
and overinterpretation, of data (Brym, 1989, pp. 29–30). In particular, he
ignores tremendous regional variability in both countries (e.g., Matthews, 1983).

Few Canadian social scientists endorse Lipset's characterization of
Canadian-American value differences. Available data, including the
public opinion data specifically dealing with attitudes toward the aged,
suggest more parallels than differences. Differences in values across the
regions of Canada are great, as is the case in the United States as well.
There are not two uniform value communities to compare. Moreover, it
is unlikely that the values climate in the United States could have
changed so dramatically over the past 10 years as to provide an explanation for the emergence, only within that time period, of the intergenerational-equity issue. Similarity cannot explain difference.

Brym, who has recently reviewed the debate over the Lipset thesis
(1989, p. 62) suggests that the British tradition, cut off by revolution for
Americans, has indeed influenced Canada. However, he sees the British

influence as much stronger on institutional structures and political institutions than on values.

Do Resource Allocation Mechanisms Account for
Differences in the Importance of the Issue?

In Canada, universal programs play a much larger role in resource allocation than in the United States. Two major universal programs are age specific: Old Age Security (OAS) and Family Allowances. A third, Medicare, covers citizens of all ages (for more detailed treatment, see Banting, 1987; Fedyk, 1990; Marmor, Mashaw, & Harvey, 1990; McGilly, 1990).

Old Age Security. Whereas in the United States Social Security and Supplemental Security Income (SSI) are the sole public plans providing income in the retirement years, the Canadian public system has three major components (some provinces add a fourth). The CPP and the QPP are contributory pension plans to which all workers and their employers contribute. Like the United States Social Security program, benefits depend on an individual's retirement history and earning levels. The CPP/QPP, however, provides (as of 1982) only 9.4% of retirement income (Messinger & Powell, 1987, p. 572). The most important source, accounting for about one third of retirement income in Canada (Messinger & Powell, 1987, p. 572), is the universal OAS program. This program provides a standard pension to all citizens and landed immigrants aged 65 and older. The third component, income-tested programs, principally the Guaranteed Income Supplement, brings low-income pensioners up closer to the poverty line. About half of old-age pensioners receive full or partial supplements. Together, these programs represent an allocation of about 4% of GNP to the elderly (Messinger & Powell, 1987, p. 576).

The CPP is similar to the Social Security system of the United States in that neither is a true insurance system. Quadagno (1989, p. 357) has noted that in the United States the public image of Social Security was manipulated during the early 1980s so that, rather than being seen as a solution to a social problem, by providing support to victims of an economy that failed the poor, it came to be seen as the problem, as a contributory cause of the failings of the United States economy. Canadian formulation of the problem of CPP funding was not put in such terms.

As Gifford (1990, p. 245) has noted, the OAS is not as visible to the taxpayer as is the United States Social Security tax. Gifford maintains that this allows the Canadian benefit to be viewed as a "handout" rather than as a result of earlier taxation of the older person. Perhaps the relative lack of visibility of the benefit is the more important feature in explaining Canadian indifference toward intergenerational-equity issues.

The Family Allowance Program. The Family Allowance Program provides a benefit to parents on behalf of each child below the age of 18. This is a universal, age-specific program that, Neysmith (1987b) suggests, reflects a sense of age-specific need. The program is small by comparison to federal government benefits directed toward the elderly, and it has by no means avoided the emergence of a serious problem of child poverty in Canada.

Child poverty has become an important policy issue in Canada, as it has in the United States. Some academics have noted the disparity between support for children and support for the elderly (Eichler, 1983), but this disparity has not been a matter for active scholarly comment, nor has it found its way into the media. The National Advisory Council on Aging (NACA), which is government appointed but highly independent, in a recent position paper pointed out:

> Today, older people are not the poorest segment of Canada's population. Single-parent families with children and young adults currently experience higher rates of poverty. . . . If Canada continues to sustain its income security programs through taxes, the tax burden needed to support retired baby boomers may become onerous. (1989, pp. 6–7)

This passage appears in a section called "Intergenerational Equity," the last of the policy references we have discovered in Canada that explicitly refer to intergenerational equity (the others were discussed in an earlier section). It may be noteworthy that practically the only policy voice to raise the question of generational equity was a major advocacy body for seniors.

As the federal policy advisor mentioned earlier put it, efforts to ameliorate child poverty are being framed as within-age-group reallocations rather than between-age-group reallocations. Meanwhile, despite the small level of benefits to children (and their young-adult parents), the sense that the aged are not the only group to receive across-the-board benefits may act to reduce the sense of intergenerational inequity.

Medicare. Surely a major reason that intergenerational-equity issues are less visible in Canada than in the United States is that Medicare is not, in Canada, an age-specific program. In the United States, rising health care costs for the aged are a major cause of policy concern, and

Medicare and Medicaid policies provide age-group-based benefits. In Canada, Medicare provides benefits to every citizen regardless of age. It is estimated that about one third of all public health care expenditure is directed to the elderly population, and that this amounts to about 2% of GNP (Messinger & Powell, 1987, p. 575).

The Canadian Medicare system is a fully universal program which has consistently enjoyed overwhelming popular support, with some polls registering support by 95% of the population (Lipset, 1990, p. 138). In addition to public support, in recent years support from the three major political parties in Canada has been overwhelming. Recent legislation to preserve the universality of Medicare in Canada received all-party support.

Health care costs have risen in Canada at a rate higher than population growth, but the increases have not been so great as in the United States. This is attributed to the greater controls over the allocation of societal resources that are possible when allocation is controlled by the (largely provincial) governments rather than through an open market (Marmor et al., 1990). Provincial medical associations annually negotiate fee schedules with the provincial governments, and this procedure has had an impact of some restraint on medical fees. In addition, hospitals are placed on global budgets received from the provincial ministries of health, an approach allowing more effective planning for fiscal responsibility (including avoidance of duplication of services and expensive equipment, accountability for lengths of stay, and the allocation of authorized beds).

Claims are made, in the political process and in the media, that recent and projected increases in health care costs in Canada constitute a "crisis" for governments; and frequently the cause of increased costs is held to be the aging of the population. This inaccurate attribution persists in spite of a growing consensus among academics that population aging has not, in fact, led to great increases and will not do so, and that any increases will be slower than the general expansion in the economy (Auer, 1987; Denton, Li, & Spencer, 1987; Evans, 1985; Messinger & Powell, 1987). While rising health care costs are largely attributed by Canadian academics, and by both federal and provincial bureaucrats, to inadequate controls on physician and hospital spending (the latter seen as highly controlled by physicians), these costs do provide a focal point for media attention to the aging of the population. Newspaper accounts, and even some government reports, do couple policy discussions of increased health care costs to population aging.

It is one thing, however, to "blame the aged," and another to pit the aged against the young. While Canadians have frequently fallen into the trap of blaming the aged, or population aging, for rising health care costs (McDaniel, 1987), this problem is not linked to deprivation of the young. Rather, it is viewed in a more general context of perceived fiscal mismanagement by government. It may also be the case that the overall level of discontent with health care costs is smaller in Canada than in the United States, especially among academics and policymakers, who are likely to know that, as a percentage of Gross National Product (GNP), Canadians spend about 20% less per capita than Americans do for health care; yet they enjoy slightly lower morbidity and mortality rates and smaller social class inequities in health care delivery (Marmor et al., 1990; Vayda & Deber, 1984).

Objective (or should we say "projective") demographic or economic conditions do not lead inevitably to political or policy developments. We suggest that the resource allocation mechanisms in Canada, with their greater emphasis on universality, and with a balancing of benefits to the young as well as to the old, have been partially responsible for the lower level of rhetoric about intergenerational equity in Canada than in the United States.

Does the Different Nature of the Political Process Account for Differences in the Importance of the Issue?

There are important differences in political structure and process between Canada and the United States. For a start, Canada has three viable, national political parties with discernible (though small) differences in political ideology. Parties meet in caucuses and the British principle of loyalty to the party is operative (Brym, 1989, p. 61). A result is a weaker emphasis on lobbying, as it is more difficult for a lobbyist to make a difference by lobbying an individual member of Parliament than might be the case, for example, by lobbying an American congressman.

An obvious factor in developing the intergenerational-equity issue in the United States, but not in Canada, has been the presence of AGE, and its activities as a lobby group. AGE is, essentially, a lobby group. The major vehicles for AGE's message have included conferences (14 between 1986 and 1989); books, articles, and opinion pieces in newspapers; and speeches and comments in the United States Congress by such AGE leaders as Durenberger (R-MN) in the Senate and Penny (R-MN), Chandler (R-WA), Porter (R-IL), Richardson (D-NM), and Saxton (R-NJ) in the House. These five representatives are listed in AGE's 1990 annual report as constituting the Board of Congressional Advisors.

A factor affecting AGE's lobbying impact must surely be the energy and publishing prowess of its former executive director, Phillip Longman. Our search strategies uncovered seven articles and one book written by Longman over the period 1985–1989 (Longman, 1985a, 1985b, 1986, 1987a, 1987b, 1988, 1989a; see also 1989b). These include five popular articles in magazines such as *New Republic, Futurist,* and *Atlantic Monthly.* Two works appeared in academic sources. His works have been cited, according to our searches, 42 times. Thirty-seven citations appeared in material that we classify as academic, while only 5 appeared in popular sources. Thus, while publishing mainly in popular sources, Longman is being cited, and presumably discussed, mainly in academic sources. He has been more successful in agenda setting in academia than in the wider milieu.

What has been the impact of AGE within the policy community? The AGE annual report for 1990 credits the AGE argument with moving Congress to adopt a financing mechanism for the Catastrophic Care Act under which the cost of the new benefits would be borne totally by persons eligible for Medicare; the more affluent retirees would, in effect, subsidize poor retirees without depending on younger workers for tax contributions. As ranking minority member of the Health Subcommittee of the Senate Finance Committee, Durenberger played an important role in the passage of this legislation.

As the financing of the Catastrophic Care Insurance came to be understood by senior citizens' organizations, elderly people protested the large tax that some of them would have to pay. Under pressure from senior citizens and some of their organizations, Congress repealed the legislation in late 1989. Quadagno (1989) argues that over the long term the more important effect of AGE than this one piece of legislation "may be its influence in reshaping the parameters of the debate so that all future policy choices will have to take generational equity into account" (p. 364).

Major analysts of senior or gray power observe that it is much less developed in Canada than in the United States. Pratt, who has studied both United States and Canadian seniors' movements, notes that Canadian seniors' groups have less influence than their American counterparts, and "are not enfolded into Canada's process of elite accommodations" (1987, p. 73). Neysmith (1987a, p. 107) suggests that Canadian seniors may seek power and influence through organizations that are not specifically age based. We suggest that high levels of satisfaction by seniors with economic and service conditions may have diffused the potential bases for political organization.

Since issue articulation is enhanced by conflict and its resulting debate, the relative lack of a "senior power" movement in Canada may be one factor in the lower level of discussion of intergenerational equity. Gifford, who has provided the most thorough documentation of senior power in Canada, says that "although seniors have clear common interests, the movement is not yet at the stage of Canada-wide united action among its organizations, except in a crisis" (1990, p. 248).

Another reason for the difference in focus on intergenerational equity may be the preoccupation in Canada with the federal-provincial division of powers and the even more complicated division of economic responsibility. Foot (1984) estimates that, with current programs, it costs 2.5 times as much to support an older Canadian than a young one, but he notes that in Canada support of the young has been primarily a private-sector responsibility while that of the old has been primarily a public-sector responsibility. He cites a study by McDonald, which estimates that 43% of age-specific program costs are borne by the federal government, 47% by the provincial governments, and 10% by municipal governments. However, 58% of expenditures for the young were by provincial governments, while 72% of those for the old were by the federal government. Most age-specific provincial expenditures are oriented to those of working age, while most municipal expenditures are oriented to the young. With the aging of the baby boom, the federal government will see a significant rise in expenditures, while municipal governments benefit.

In short, population aging is thought by Canadian academics to be manageable within economic growth projections, but to require resource allocation among governmental sectors. They recognize that posing the question as one of purely public-sector expenditures miscasts it; rather, the issue is the capacity of the nation as a whole, the public and private sectors, to produce the wealth necessary to provide a decent quality of life for all citizens. The pressures of population aging are likely to be seen in political conflict between the different levels of government. The issue is not young versus old, but federal versus provincial versus municipal political jurisdictions.

Conclusion

On-line databases such as those used in this study have obvious limitations. They do not include all relevant sources, and indexing techniques are sometimes inconsistent and imperfect in their design and use. Nevertheless, on-line database content represents a large body of knowledge and public opinion, the examination of which has assisted us in interpreting the issue of intergenerational equity.

Intergenerational equity emerged as an issue in the United States in 1984 with the founding of AGE and the publication of Preston's Presidential Address to the Population Association of America. Intergenerational equity seems never to have emerged as a significant issue in Canada. We found virtually no record in Canada of attention in the media, in academic publications, or in policymaking communities. In the United States, on the other hand, the issue received attention in all of these arenas.

The issue concerns relative provision of economic resources to the aged and the young. We showed that the two countries are strikingly similar in changes over time in the age patterns of poverty. While many Canadians would attribute the differences in importance of the intergenerational-equity issue to the moral superiority of Canadians as a people, we have been unable to find support for significant value differences between the two countries. We therefore conclude that differences in the emergence of the intergenerational-equity issue cannot be attributed to differences in poverty levels of young and old, or to differences in societal values.

The greater use, in Canada, of universal programs that provide the greatest portion of income security in later life, and almost all medical care at all ages, may deflect attention away from age-based concerns. The fact that OAS in Canada is independent of labor force participation gives it a different tone compared to the United States Social Security program, even though it is an age-based program and the United States program is not solely an age-related program. The Canadian program of family allowances provides a compensating, universal resource allocation to children (and their young parents), and perhaps this lessens any sense of intergenerational inequity.

The Canadian political structure, and related processes, are different from those in the United States, and these too may have had an impact in lessening the amount of political discourse about inequities in resource allocation. Interest group lobbying, other than that done more directly by corporate capital, is less a fact of the Canadian political process than it is in the United States.

We have suggested that objective conditions and societal values cannot in themselves explain the differential importance of the intergenerational-equity issue in the two countries. The specific resource allocation mechanisms appear to be important, and several aspects of the political structure and process, which vary between Canada and the United States, probably play a more important part in explaining differences. These have been our major findings.

A subsidiary theme of our analysis calls for reflection. We have suggested that the greater receptivity to interest group politics in the United States has contributed to the success of AGE in getting intergenerational equity onto the policy table. Our data also suggest the remarkable extent to which this very small organization has contributed to the emergence of a high-profile issue. But beyond these observations, we have shown the complicity of the academic community in building up the issue. The energy behind the intergenerational-equity debate has come in large measure from the academic community, and the issue has been fueled as much by those who are opposed to the arguments of AGE as by those who support them. This has been an instance in which academics have helped to influence policy directions. Has this influence been benign?

Acknowledgments

The authors wish to thank Joanne Daciuk and Richard Settersten, for research assistance in Toronto and Evanston, respectively. We are indebted to Michael Wolfson, of Statistics Canada, who called our attention to the discussion of intergenerational equity in the set of retirement policy papers we have discussed.

8

Intergenerational Relations and Welfare Restructuring: The Social Construction of an Intergenerational Problem

Alan Walker

The social "intergenerational" contract lies at the heart of the welfare state. There is universal agreement that the unique late-20th-century phenomenon of population aging has raised questions about the main element of this contract: public pension provision. However, the precise nature and outcome of the challenge facing the social contract is subject to a wide variety of interpretations, ranging from those who argue, apocalyptically, that the demise of the welfare state is nigh (Thomson, 1989), to those who regard the notion of "intergenerational equity" as, at best, based on the shakiest of empirical and theoretical grounds and, at worst, representative of a dangerous diversion of policymakers' and the public's attention from the major sources of inequality and dependent economic and social status (Achenbaum, 1989a; Quadagno, 1989; Walker, 1990a).

It seems that the "intergenerational-equity gap" between these social scientists is a large one. What is certain is that the social contract is currently the subject of "renegotiation" and modification in the majority of Western societies, though the extent of the changes introduced or planned differs substantially among countries, even within the European Community (EC) (Walker, 1990b).

Throughout much of the literature on what is now widely accepted as the "new problem of generations" there is a relatively uncritical acceptance of both the conflict hypothesis and the link between demographics and policy change in the realm of welfare. The main purpose of this chapter is to question the motivation behind the revisions to the public-pensions contract. It is suggested that, at least as far as the EC is concerned, these changes have little or nothing to do with intergenerational conflict. This leads on to a contrast between the public debate concerning intergenerational equity in the United States and in EC countries, where it has hardly surfaced.

It is argued that the concern of policymakers is primarily with the perceived burden of pensions on public expenditure rather than with any manifest concern about distributional justice between age cohorts.[1] Thus, for largely ideological reasons, an economic-demographic imperative has been manufactured in some countries, with the aid of international economic agencies, to facilitate the restructuring of their welfare states. Rather than being "rooted in life-course processes" (Bengtson, Marti, & Roberts, 1991, p. 25) the intergenerational-equity debate should be regarded as a sociopolitical construct.

Seen in this light it is not surprising that, during the 1980s, the United States led the way in discussions of intergenerational equity. Concerns such as these sit more comfortably within the context of an individualistic welfare tradition and pluralistic political system, particularly one under leadership that is neoliberal (neoconservative in United States parlance), than they do within the more solidaristic or collectivist welfare traditions and corporatist political systems of Northern Europe. Britain in the 1980s represented a peculiar hybrid case—a traditional solidaristic welfare state under neoliberal management—and, therefore, welfare restructuring took an extreme form, the aim being to make the British welfare state more like the "market-oriented states" of Australia, Canada, and the United States (Therborn & Roebroek, 1986; Walker, 1990c).

The second part of this chapter focuses on the microsociological dimension of generational relations, though the main intention is to emphasize the interconnection between the life worlds of families and the macrosocial structure. Bengtson et al. (1991) correctly direct us to the dual macro- and microaspects of the intergenerational-equity debate; however, along with questioning their conclusion about the source of this debate, it is necessary to express a few cautious words concerning the importance they and others place on the norm of reciprocity in intergenerational relationships (see Riley and Riley, Chapter 9 in this volume).

Here recent research in Britain is used to demonstrate that, while affect and reciprocity are critical determinants of the *quality* of intergenerational relations within the family, the *provision* of care by female kin cannot be explained without reference to macrostructural determinants. In other words, interpersonal caring relationships within the family are as much an arena for state intervention as are financial transfers between age cohorts, though, of course, the forms these interventions take are very different. The "natural" reciprocity and altruism of female kin have figured centrally, as a social construction, both in the history of the welfare state and in recent attempts to restructure it and to enlarge the role of the informal sector in caring for older people (Land & Rose, 1985; Walker, 1987).

This chapter addresses the four questions raised by Bengtson at the conference that initiated this volume. First, the contract between generations is analyzed in terms of socially constructed roles, relationships, dependencies, and obligations at both micro- and macrolevels. Second, it is argued that the level and direction of change is primarily, though by no means exclusively, a function of social and economic policies. Third, although the informal contract between kin concerning the care of older people is distinguished from the formal social policy contract between generations orchestrated by the state, the role of the state in reproducing the contract between kin is the focus of attention in the second half of this chapter in order to demonstrate the interaction between the state and the life world of its citizens. Specifically, it is important to emphasize that contracts between kin are not negotiated in a political, economic, and ideological vacuum. Finally it is argued that whether or not both forms of intergenerational contract are repudiated is largely a matter of social and economic policy.

Before embarking on these analyses it is important (far more important than social scientific self-interest) to endorse the case for more research: We know too little about the relationships between age cohorts and generations at this unique historical juncture. The agenda for continued research on age cohorts and generational relations, set out by Bengtson and his colleagues (Bengtson et al., 1991), is a good starting point. But those of us engaged in this endeavor must beware of not only "cohort-centrism" (Riley, in press) but also cohort-determinism, in which it is assumed that members of the *same* age cohort experience age in exactly the same way. Our common interest in age group stratification should not blind us to variations within cohorts. This caution derives from the emergent political economy of aging (Dannefer, 1988; Estes, Swan, & Gerard, 1982; Guillemard, 1980; Myles, 1984; Phillipson, 1982; Walker, 1981).

This political-economy perspective arose in part as a critique of the analytical limitations of age stratification theory. Notwithstanding the major intellectual contribution made by age stratification theory, its excessively narrow concentration on chronological age and birth year diverts attention both from individual responses to the aging process and from differences within age cohorts deriving from macrostructural factors such as class, gender, and race. Thus in focusing on the importance of relations between generations, we must not fall into the "cohort trap" by assuming either that relations between members of successive birth cohorts are characteristic of all such intergenerational relations involving those cohorts or that membership in a particular cohort is necessarily more influential than other factors in determining the nature of these relations.

The Social Contract, the Welfare State, and Demographic Change

Most welfare states originated in pension provision for older people, and today, in all Organization for Economic and Cooperation and Development (OECD) countries, older people are the main beneficiaries of social expenditure. In fact, in European welfare states, the social contract is primarily a public-pensions contract between age cohorts. (In the United States the absence of a national health insurance or care program ensures that the cost of health care provision to older people remains central to the debate about the social contract.) Thus, for the purposes of this chapter, the "social contract" is interpreted as being a social policy contract based on intergenerational transfers of resources through the mediums of taxation and social expenditure. In other words, the social contract is only one, reified form of contract between generations. Moreover, as explained in more detail later in this chapter, social norms concerning the role of the family in the care of older relatives as well as in the care of children are reinforced by state policy, and have the effect of supporting the individual-level contract between generations, while at the same time limiting the scope of the macrosocial policy contract.

Although public transfers are only one of the four "pillars" (or "legs of a stool"—see Torres-Gil, Chapter 12 in this volume) on which retirement income is founded (Reday-Mulvey, 1990) they are the largest pillar in the majority of OECD countries. The proportion of the gross income of retired households deriving from social security (insurance and social assistance) ranges from over 80% in Sweden and Germany to around 50% in Canada and the United States (OECD, 1988a, p. 55). Of course, the social contract on which these transfers are based is not like any normal contract, in that it is imposed by the state on those in employment rather than being freely negotiated and is heavily sanctioned by the work ethic, or what should more correctly be called the paid-employment ethic. (Thus there is not a direct exchange between the cohorts involved; the relationship between them is mediated by the state.) The essence of the contract was clearly expressed by one of the main architects of the postwar welfare state, William Beveridge: "Social security must be achieved by cooperation between the State and the individual. The State should offer security in return for service and contribution" (1942, p. 6).

When the first pension schemes were introduced in the late 19th century, they benefited only those who had the good fortune to survive beyond average life expectancy. The 20th century has seen not only growth in the numbers of older people in the population of Western societies but also a rising proportion of those eligible for pensions as able to collect them and then subsequently able to go on doing so for longer periods (though there remain significant differences in mortality rates between social classes). In other words, the issue of equity between age cohorts is "new" simply because more age-balanced population structures have emerged only very recently in Western societies. Age cohort conflicts are certainly not new in historical terms (as discussed below).

Population aging has been greeted with pessimism and alarm in some quarters and has prompted action among a broad range of Western countries to modify their public pension schemes and, thereby, the social contract on which these schemes are based. Examples of the more pessimistic responses to the socioeconomic implications of societal aging include that of the OECD:

> Under existing regulations the evolution of public pension schemes is likely to put a heavy and increasing burden on the working population in coming decades. Such a financial strain may put inter-generational solidarity—a concept on which all public retirement provisions are based—at risk. (1988a, p. 102)

The following is typical of the more apocalyptic version of this theme:

> If no action is taken to deal with the incipient crisis of population aging, then it seems certain that western societies will experience major social and economic dislocation, and they may experience this relatively soon. (Johnson, Conrad, & Thomson, 1989, p. 13)

In the light of such dire predictions (see also Thomson, Chapter 11 in this volume) the actions taken so far by Western nations, with one or two notable exceptions, look remarkably modest. For example, several EC countries, including Denmark and Germany, have raised their retirement ages or are in the process of doing so. Others, such as France and Italy, are contemplating such a change. Action has been taken or is planned in France and Spain to make the qualification conditions for pensions more stringent; some other countries, including Belgium and the Netherlands, have restricted the level of pensions available (Walker, 1990b). This very brief review of recent policy changes demonstrates that just as there are "multiple paths to higher pension spending" (Pampel, Williamson, & Stryker, 1990, p. 547), the reverse is also true.

As Bengtson points out (Chapter 1 in this volume) the consequences of the current generational watershed may be either increased conflict between age cohorts or increased solidarity. The main argument of this chapter is that whether the 21st century holds the prospect of conflict or consensus is primarily a matter of social and economic policy rather than of any properties inherent in age cohorts themselves. The precise outcome depends on the interaction of macro- and microlevel factors. Certainly, as Bengtson argues, age group conflicts have the potential for greater visibility in the decades to come, but the key question is: Will the societal context within which these cohorts experience aging be conducive to conflict or solidarity?

The New Social Contract and Welfare State Restructuring

Despite encouragement from international economic agencies such as the International Monetary Fund (IMF) and OECD, and from high-profile political rhetoric in some countries (especially the United States) concerning intergenerational equity, the extent of the modifications to the social contract are relatively minor in the majority of Western countries. So far at least, the new social contract between age cohorts is not very different from the old one. There are exceptions though and it is when we distinguish those countries that have led the field in revising the social contract, sometimes in combination with intergenerational-equity rhetoric, that the connection between the new contract and welfare state restructuring can be demonstrated. Stripped of all its euphemisms, the newly emerging contract between age cohorts in some Western countries consists of cuts in social security for both current and future pensioners.

It was not mere coincidence that the countries that moved furthest and fastest in the 1980s to alter the terms of the social contract were those under neoliberal economic management—be it Reaganomics in the United States, Thatcherism in Britain, or Rogernomics in New Zealand. To a student of social policy the market-oriented welfare states, such as Australia, Canada, and the United States, are less interesting in their responses to population aging than those of the collectivist welfare states of Northern Europe. Among the latter, Britain stands out as an extreme case. Although the British welfare state (along with those of France, Germany, and Italy) has been accurately described as one of "socioeconomic mediocrity" in terms of its commitment to the core welfare aims of social security and full employment (Therborn & Roebroek, 1986), over the postwar period the state has played a leading role in both the financing and delivery of welfare benefits and services, as it has in other Northern European countries.

The sharp contrast between the United States and Northern European welfare states can be gauged not only by well-known differences in institutions and in levels of expenditure of the public and private sectors but also by differences in public attitudes to welfare. For example, while Americans and Britons have similar attitudes toward certain aspects of government, such as police power, parental rights, and free speech, when it comes to the role of the state in welfare Britons are on average twice as likely as Americans to favor state intervention and to endorse redistribution (Davis, 1986).

It is within this solidaristic context that the Thatcher government, first elected in 1979, set about the restructuring of the British welfare state. Because older people are the main beneficiaries of the largest item of social spending—social security—they quickly became one of the main targets. In 1980 the government changed the method of calculating annual increases in flat-rate national insurance pension from an earnings-linked to a prices-linked system. In 1988 social assistance payments to older people were reduced and, most importantly, the State Earnings-Related Pension Scheme (SERPS), which was due to reach full maturity in 1998, was severely curtailed. At the same time a bribe ("incentive" in official parlance) of 2% of earnings, together with a national insurance contribution rebate of 5.8%, is being paid to employees who contract out of SERPS and into a personal (private) pension scheme (Walker, 1991a).

These changes, coupled with a lower growth in the retired population than in most other European countries, have restricted the growth in the projected share of pension expenditure in national income over the next 50 years to the second lowest in the OECD: from 7.7% in 1984 to 7.6% in 2010 and 11.2% in 2040. Equivalent statistics for the United States are 8.1, 8.5, and 14.6%; and for Germany 13.7, 19.7, and 31.1% (OECD, 1988a, p. 35).

The restructuring of pension provision in Britain cannot be attributed to the need to curb the generosity of payments to pensioners. In comparison with other EC and OECD countries, British pensioners fare poorly. For example, public-pension replacement rates (pensions as a proportion of earnings in the year before retirement for workers with average wages in manufacturing) for a single person, in 1980, varied from 69% in Italy, 49% in Germany, and 44% in the United States, to 31% in Britain. Only the rates in Denmark and Ireland were lower than Britain's (OECD, 1988a, p. 50). Among EC countries, in 1985, the British state pension came second to last in terms of its purchasing power (Walker, 1990b). It is not surprising, therefore, that poverty remains a major characteristic of old age in Britain, with just over one half of older people living in or on the margins of poverty (as defined by social assistance levels).

Nor can the restructuring of pensions in Britain be attributed to any overt concern about justice between age cohorts. The issue of intergenerational equity did surface in the mid-1980s but only very briefly and in far less sensational terms than in the United States. When the government reviewed the social security system in 1985, as a prelude to the major restructuring carried through in 1988, it legitimated its proposals for cutting SERPS with reference to the age cohort contract:

> Our belief in One Nation means recognizing our responsibilities to all the generations represented within it. . . . It would be an abdication of responsibility to hand down obligations to our children which we believe they cannot fulfil. (Department of Health and Social Services, DHSS, 1985a, p. 18)

There were further fleeting appearances of intergenerational-equity rhetoric but it has not achieved the same high profile as it did in the United States. It is not unreasonable to expect neoliberal-inspired governments to be rather wary of any concept that invokes the principle of equity. But, in addition, there is no empirical evidence in Britain of any net transfer of state spending from younger to older people. There is no basis for the contention, dramatically expressed by Thomson (1989, p. 36; and Chapter 11 in this volume) that the "welfare generation" has "captured" the welfare state and steered it from being a youth-oriented state to one directed toward older people. The British welfare state has been neutral, distributionally speaking, between children and older people over the last two decades (Johnson & Falkingham, 1988). Any changes in the age cohort distribution of welfare state spending are a reflection of underlying movements in demographic structure rather than the result of a takeover by "greedy elders."

As far as future social expenditure is concerned, a similar picture emerges in all OECD countries. Taking the period 1980–2040, there is no country in which the growth of social expenditure is projected to exceed the rise in the population aged 65 and over (OECD, 1988b, p. 36). For instance, in the United States total social expenditure is projected to rise in real terms by 65% compared with an increase in the older population of 138%. In Germany total spending is set to fall by 3%, yet the population aged 65 and over will rise by 31%.

Thus, despite the numerous deficiencies in projections, such as these, of the impact of demographic factors on the welfare state—especially the assumptions of constant participation and productivity rates (Binney & Estes, 1988; Walker, 1990a)—projections do not indicate expenditure growth that is out of line with demographic change. In some cases, notably Australia, Canada, Japan, and the United States, projected social spending lags considerably behind growth in the older population. This is not surprising since, in retrospect, conscious policy decisions concerning eligibility for and levels of benefits were the major contributors to the increasing share of gross domestic product (GDP) taken by pensions in the period 1960–1985 in all OECD countries; the demographic factor played a relatively minor role (Myles, 1983; Walker, 1990a).

Social Construction of an Economic-Demographic Imperative

So why did the British government impose a new social contract on older people—much diluted from the perspective of current and future pensioners—when there was no public pressure to do so and when, moreover, it was advised to delay doing so by official agencies, the private-pension industry, and the OECD? The answer is in two parts: The first part explains the prevalence of pessimistic attitudes toward population aging among a wide cross section of Western societies and the concomitant growth of ageism. The second part indicates why some governments have gone much further than others in restructuring welfare in response to demographic change.

In the first place there is the long-standing economic pessimism concerning public expenditure on the welfare state. This is a phenomenon common to all Western societies, to a greater or lesser extent, and for the reasons already outlined it has come to be directed more and more at older people as the numbers of them receiving pensions have increased. This seemingly innate pessimism derives from the "public-burden" model of welfare, which lies at the heart of neoclassical economic assumptions concerning the respective economic contributions of the public and private sectors, and derives particularly from the contention that the public sector is an unproductive burden on the private sector. The concept of old age stemming from such theories is one of homogeneity, economic dependence, and unproductiveness. Thus older people are marginalized economically in the same way that women not in paid employment are, even though both may be performing vital roles in the informal economy. The "first-pillar" pensions older people receive from the state are regarded economically as a burden, as are the pensioners receiving them, whereas "second-pillar" private pensions are not, even though the latter may be heavily subsidized by the state.

The public-burden conception of old age in orthodox economics is attributable, in part, to the subordination of social policy to economic policy, and to the preeminence accorded to the latter in the political sphere. Another contributory factor has been individualistic functional theories, such as some variants of the life cycle approach, whereby economic ability and status are related to specific stages of the life cycle (Clark & Spengler, 1980, p. 67). It is from this simplistic theory that the demographic imperative originates. Unfortunately the theory has not been amenable to empirical evidence, at least in its unsophisticated form. Most importantly it overlooks the socially constructed relationship between the life cycle and the labor market and the flexible way in which the definition of productive capacity alters in response to changes in labor supply, and particularly to changes in the supply of younger workers (Graebner, 1980; Phillipson, 1982).

Second, in some countries ideological change has seriously undermined even the limited "handmaiden" role assigned to the welfare state by Keynesian economics. Neomonetarism (with its built-in opposition to public expenditure on welfare and its supply-side view of the costs of employers' social security contributions) is more important, in countries such as Australia, Canada, Britain, and New Zealand, than demography in explaining present policies aimed at installing a new social contract. The rate of GDP growth per annum in Britain required to finance projected increases in social expenditure due to demographic factors is only 0.16%; in the United States it is 0.84%. Even in Canada, which has one of the highest projected social expenditure growths among OECD countries, the average annual GDP growth rate required to maintain a constant social expenditure share in the face of demographic change over the next 50 years is only 1.05% (OECD, 1988b, p. 39).

Thus, rather than the main pressure deriving from demographic change, it is ideological shifts, particularly in economic orthodoxy, that have altered assumptions about the role of the state with regard to welfare and that have encouraged some countries to take what looks like, at best, premature action on the social contract. Britain provides a clear example of this triumph of ideology over demography in the restructuring of its pension provision to reduce the role of public pensions and to increase that of publicly subsidized private pensions (for a fuller account see Walker, 1990a).

The conjunction of these two factors in several Western countries during the last decade suggests that concern about population aging has been artificially amplified as an economic-demographic imperative intended primarily to legitimate policies aimed at restructuring the welfare state. The dual social functions performed by this amplification process are, on the one hand, to encourage gratitude and political acquiescence on the part of older people and, on the other, to prompt younger adults to provide for their old age in the private market. In addition, the process diverts attention from the real *ideological* imperative behind policy. Although the British government did dabble briefly with intergenerational-equity rhetoric, it was also explicit about the main reason for its restructuring of pension provision in the 1980s:

> The purpose of these proposals is to achieve a steady transition from the present dependence on state provision to a position in which we as individuals are contributing directly to our own additional pensions and in which we can exercise greater choice in the sort of pension provision we make. (DHSS, 1985b, p. 6)

In other words, the main driving force behind the manufacture of a new pensions contract in Britain was the Thatcher government's ideological distaste for public welfare. The converse German case, outlined below, also emphasizes the central place of political ideology in shaping the new contract between age cohorts.

Why was the Thatcher government able, with impunity, to carry out a succession of changes to the British pension system throughout the 1980s, whereas in the United States, in contrast, the Reagan administration was faced with stiff opposition? The explanation requires a detailed analysis of the politics of aging in Britain (Walker, 1991a). Briefly, the ideological determination of the Thatcher government and the social division of pension recipients into different consumption classes, based mainly on previous employment status and income level, have militated against the development of a unified age interest lobby. Thus, under the single-tier public-pension system that prevailed in Britain for most of the postwar period, the interests of working-class and middle-class pensioners were quite different. The maturation of SERPS would have incorporated the middle class into state pensions, but the Thatcher government, having limited the basic pension, severely curtailed the scope of SERPS as well. The British public-pension system was thus both vulnerable to cuts by a determined government and less likely than that of the United States to be defended by a powerful pensioners' movement.

This ideological and political context is sometimes missing from accounts of macrosocial relations between age cohorts and from accounts of policy responses to demographic change, yet it is essential if we are to understand the similarities and differences between societies in their responses to demographic change as well as in their governments' adoption of specific policies, whether in the orthodox economic mold of Western capitalism or in the more extreme neoliberal variant. Furthermore, policies intended to create a new pensions contract must be analyzed as one element of the much broader endeavor on the part of some governments to restructure their welfare provision; otherwise they may be wrongly interpreted as simply ageist attacks on the welfare of older people. Although the public-burden thesis and intergenerational-equity rhetoric may encourage age-discriminatory attitudes, the impact of current welfare state restructuring on older people is mainly attributable to the fact that they are unfortunate enough to be the main clients of the social security system. Ageist attitudes, however, may be used to legitimate particular outcomes of welfare restructuring.

Intergenerational Equity

Some form of welfare state restructuring has taken place in most Western societies but, of course, it has been pursued with greatest vigor in those countries under neoliberal-inspired economic management. The mobilization of free-market ideas and policies in Australia, Britain, Canada, New Zealand, and the United States during the 1980s produced the main representatives of the genre but many other countries have followed, more selectively, in their wake. The United States is conspicuous because it alone combined neoliberal economic management with a widespread debate about intergenerational equity.

Why the United States should be the only major Western nation so far to have spawned a high-profile political lobby group on intergenerational equity is a fascinating question; but the answer is likely to reveal more about the political economy of the United States than about relations between American age cohorts. Research by Pampel and his colleagues (1990) suggests that pluralistic political systems are more amenable to the influence of age structure in determining the level of pension spending than are corporatist systems. Therefore we might expect the United States political system, in conjunction with its individualistic welfare tradition, to provide a more conducive setting for an intergenerational-equity debate than the solidaristic and corporatist approaches characteristic of Northern Europe. This conclusion is supported by Marshall, Cook, and Marshall (Chapter 7 in this volume), who contrast the emergence of an outspoken lobby on intergenerational equity in the United States with the virtual silence on this issue in Canada. In addition to differences in the political systems of the two countries, they point to the greater use in Canada of universal welfare programs, especially health care, and also to the complicity of the academic community in the United States.

Leaving aside the hybrid case of Britain, of all the nations in the European collectivist welfare mold the one that might be regarded as the most likely to repeat the United States experience is Germany. It has had the lowest fertility rate among OECD countries since the early 1970s and has the highest projected dependency ratio. Germany spends one of the highest proportions of GDP on pensions in the OECD and is one of the countries with the highest proportion of older people in its population. In addition it has a relatively low labor force participation rate. Despite these obvious pressures there has been no intergenerational-equity debate to speak of and certainly nothing to compare with that in the United States (Hinrichs, in press). The main explanatory factors appear to be the solidaristic consensus on the current German welfare system and the absence of an electoral system that would enable a radical neoliberal government to achieve power.

The concept of intergenerational equity has been subjected to sustained criticism (Achenbaum, 1989a; Minkler, 1986; Quadagno, 1989; Walker, 1990a) and pronounced unsuitable as a basis either for conceptualizing the relationship between age cohorts or for policy development. Moreover in the United States, where it has achieved widest currency, it has signally failed in its main aim to undermine public support for Social Security (Cook, 1990; Quadagno, 1989, p. 371). This attempt, spearheaded by Americans for Generational Equity (AGE) in the United States, to establish an overtly conflictual relationship between younger and older people, and the rather halfhearted stab at doing something similar in Britain, may be regarded as reflections of the same combination of factors that created the much more influential economic-demographic imperative.

Thus it is not concern about justice between age cohorts that motivates intergenerational-equity protagonists but the fiscal implications of aging: the so-called "burden" of economic dependency in the form of pension costs and the "burden" of physical dependency in the form of health and social care costs. In short, population aging is regarded as a threat to capital accumulation. As AGE president James Jones himself has made clear, it is stagnated production and low investment in the United States that are the main causes of his group's gloomy prognoses for American society (1988a, p. 7).

Such concerns are not new, nor is the tendency in times of recession to regard older people as a burden. In Britain there is evidence from the 16th century that when village communities were faced with economic hardship older people were sometimes marginalized and their financial relief portrayed as a "burden on the community" (Thomas, 1976, p. 239). The social construction of age cohort conflicts predates AGE by at least 400 years and is not a phenomenon associated uniquely with late-20th-century population aging. Thirty-five years ago the United Nations (1956) expressed concern about the "psychological effects" on those in employment of the increase in pension contributions necessary in an aging society. Of course, it is precisely these considerations that lay behind the main tool of demographers and economists in this field—the deeply flawed dependency ratio; the scientific, governmental, and popular construction of older people as a burden on middle-age cohorts is perpetuated by its use (see Rossi, Chapter 10 in this volume).

The intergenerational-equity thesis derives from the predominantly economic concerns of the public-burden model of welfare. It is merely a politically expedient use of demographic change to conceal, on the one hand, the falling welfare surplus and, on the other, welfare restructuring. Additional support for this conclusion comes from the lacuna of policies accompanying intergenerational-equity rhetoric, policies that would improve the material position of the younger age groups that are said to be the target of the campaign (Quadagno, 1989). Policies aimed at redistributing resources according to goals such as social justice or interclass equity are simply not on the agenda of those countries in the process of restructuring their welfare states. Thus older people are being caricatured as "greedy elders" and used, to some extent, as scapegoats for both economic failure and ideological opposition to social policies that would meet the needs of older and younger people alike (Binstock, 1983).

Intergenerational Relations and the Provision of Care

Having analyzed the motivations behind the development of a new social contract between age cohorts, attention shifts now to the second dimension of generational relations: relationships between kin. The center of focus here is the caring relationship within the family. However, although these two dimensions of generational relations have been delineated, one of the primary functions of this paper is to argue against their common separation in the literature. While there are distinct macro- and microsocial features of generational relations, one effect of this dichotomous scientific construction of the social world is to underplay the degree of interaction between them. As with the newly emerging pensions contract in Western societies, the role of ideology is central to the social reproduction of the caring relationship. In this sphere, though, the state has been much more cautious about overt intervention in what is portrayed as an essentially private domain.

The lack of macrolevel policies that successfully share care between the family and the state, therefore, reflects the state's objective to minimize its financial commitment in the field of social care and to sustain the primacy of the family. The continued absence of such policies means that unnecessary strains are placed on the caring relationships between kin as they respond to the fundamental changes in intergenerational patterns and responsibilities being brought about by sociodemographic change.

Reciprocity and Affect in Generational Relations

It is widely accepted in the field of social gerontology that the provision and receipt of care within families is governed by a balance of affect and reciprocity. For instance, Bengtson et al. (1991), drawing on the work of Gouldner (1960), argue that "[t]he implied contract of generations calls for the parents to invest a major portion of their resources throughout their adult years in the rearing of children; in old age, the caregiving is expected to be reversed" (p. 25). In a similar vein, Johnson et al. assert that the social contract is analogous to the "implicit contract that exists within families" (1989, p. 6).

In contrast I want to suggest that, as far as the family is concerned, the implied individual-level contract may be a contributory factor in determining the provision of practical care or tending but it is not a *necessary* condition. However, it is featured significantly in the ideological construction of the caring relationship. The main source of these contentions is some recent research in Sheffield, Britain, surveying a stratified random sample of just over 300 people aged 75 and over with their principal carer not sharing the same household (Qureshi & Walker, 1989; Walker, 1991b). The family was, predictably, the main source of care and daughters were the relatives most likely to be providing it. Data from the surveys were used to investigate the importance of affect and reciprocity in determining the supply of care within the family. Neither affect nor reciprocity was found to be a *necessary* condition for the provision of practical help.

A simple decision model was created reflecting a traditional Western normative preference structure: Female relatives would be preferred to male ones, relatives to nonrelatives, and so on. In making "decisions" about who provides care, family members very largely behaved as if the hierarchical principles in the model operated in practice, though the principles might have been overruled by situational factors such as the health of prospective carers. Qualitative data indicated, first, that individual family members actually believed they had followed the principles implicit in the decision model and, second, that the model reflected their beliefs about what was right.

In most cases, of course, normative values and feelings of affect and reciprocity are mutually reinforcing. However, some insight into the power of these normative obligations—and into the fact that they are constructed *externally* to the caring relationship itself and to the life course processes that preceded it—can be gained by looking at the position of those who provided care despite highly antagonistic individual-level feelings. There were one in six adult children in the carers study who considered that their relationship with their parent had always been one-sided and who felt no obligation based on intergenerational reciprocity. The motivations of this minority of children who did not think that they owed any debt to their parents, yet still provided the necessary care, are illustrated in this quotation:

> I couldn't stand him but yet I knew it was my duty and no matter what it cost me I would have done that for my own conscience . . . and because of what people say, "Well he's got a daughter and she doesn't do anything for him." . . . I've seen all these articles in the Star [local newspaper]. I've seen all these pictures of old people and it's been said "Got a son who didn't do anything for them," but nothing is said about what the son or daughter had to put up with to cause them to turn that way. (Qureshi & Walker, 1989, p. 140)

It must be stressed that this sort of comment came from a minority of caring children whose relationship with a parent or parents had been poor over a long period, often as a result of violence and abuse (including sexual abuse) in childhood. In most cases the nature of the caring relationship rests on a delicate balance among reciprocity, affection, and duty (Marshall, Rosenthal, & Daciuk, 1987), though in this research few children specifically mentioned love as a reason for helping and were much more likely to refer to duty or obligation.

While the quality of the caring relationship may depend on individual-level factors such as intergenerational reciprocity, its existence owes more to normative constructions. In the first place, choices about who should care for older people are based on rules that derive from stereotyped beliefs about the reciprocal "debts" owed by children to their parents and from expectations about appropriate gender roles. Second, even though in most instances where care is given it is clear that people do feel a personalized sense of obligation toward their parents for past help, it is equally clear from the Sheffield research that a significant minority do not share these feelings, yet still feel compelled to help by pressures external to the particular relationship.

Indeed in some instances it was evident that intergenerational relationships between family members could be far more difficult and emotionally damaging than other relationships. In these cases the implied intergenerational contract was null and void as far as the carers were concerned because their parent(s) had never opened such a contract in the first place. Thus in some instances care was being provided to older people by female kin in the absence of familial contractual obligations deriving from any felt need for reciprocity, or from affection. Furthermore, in some cases care was given despite strong personal antipathy on the part of the carer for the person she was caring for.

The State and Intergenerational Care

Consideration of precisely how these powerful normative obligations are reproduced requires the focus of attention to be shifted from this brief discussion of microsocial relations back to the macrosocial ones. The state occupies a central role in the social construction of the traditional intergenerational caring relationship and, therefore, in the maintenance of the dominant role of the family, and female kin in particular, in caring for older people. There is not space here to dwell on the impact of the gender division of labor in care (see Finch & Groves, 1983; Lewis & Meredith, 1988; Qureshi & Walker, 1989); our primary concern is with how the division of labor and intergenerational obligations are reproduced socially.

How does the state influence, directly or indirectly, the provision of care by families? First, a variety of direct methods exist, ranging from outright coercion (for example, legislation in Canada and Israel that echoes the 19th-century English Poor Law obligations placed on adult children to support their parents) to the provision of incentives (such as tax allowances or additional benefits for those caring for dependents). Second, the state can influence family help, less directly, by the way it organizes and provides services to individuals in need and by the assumptions it makes about the nature and availability of such assistance in rationing care. Third, the state's general economic and social policies set the framework of material and social conditions within which individual families find themselves.

Broad welfare policy may thus help to increase or reduce strains in and around the caring relationship by, for example, the levels of the social security and social services provision it sets. Thus the state may have a direct influence on the quality of intergenerational relations within the family by the sorts of welfare policies it adopts. However, in industrial societies, it is the operation of covert forms of power, particularly at an ideological level, that gives the state its primary influence over the life world.

In the care of older people outright coercion has rarely proved successful. The idea that the state could compel families to offer love and gratitude to their older parents was given little credence even by the administrators of the English Poor Law. For example, they commented regretfully on the fact that even the most obvious needs of older people failed to call forth sufficient informal support, despite coercive measures (Checkland & Checkland, 1974). Indeed, if informal care is unwillingly given it loses its special qualities—particularly the intrinsic benefits such as emotional warmth, affection, and interest—and can no longer be claimed as a superior form of care. In fact in this situation it can become rapidly destructive of relationships, inducing resentment and guilt in both giver and receiver.

So, in Western societies the state is very reluctant to intervene directly in the caring relationship; indeed a norm of nonintervention may be said to operate. This norm is underpinned by fears that if state help is too easy to obtain it would undermine intergenerational obligations and that this would have serious fiscal implications. This assumption concerning the impact of state provision is well documented in Europe from late Victorian times (Anderson, 1977; Booth, 1984; Wall, 1990) and it appears to be as deeply embedded culturally, if not more so, in the United States (Kreps, 1977). It must be emphasized, however, that the persistence of this norm owes nothing to empirical evidence, both historical and contemporary, which has repeatedly led to the opposite conclusion: State support can enhance the quality of intergenerational relations (Anderson, 1977; Levin, Sinclair, & Gorbach, 1986; Wall, 1990). For example, Wall (1990, p. 4) points out that in the late 19th and early 20th centuries older people were frequently welcomed into the households of their children because of the Poor Law relief, and later because of the pensions that they brought with them.

A closely related argument is that state welfare provision has resulted in the breakup of the family because there are said to be fewer joint households than in past times. But the simplistic assumption of a linear progression, from preindustrial times when older people lived with their children to modern times when they live on their own, has been disproved by historical research (Laslett, 1965; Wall, 1984). (In a similar vein, Foner, Chapter 6 in this volume, explodes the simplistic myths about care for frail older people in contemporary nonindustrial cultures.)

Along with worries concerning the possible abrogation of intergenerational caring responsibilities, the reluctance of the state to intervene in the family to provide help and support probably owes something to the fact that the state is a patriarchal state, in that it is dominated both by men and by the ideology of patriarchy (Barrett, 1980). This means that the state has a direct interest in supporting traditional, that is, gendered, patterns of caring (see Rossi, Chapter 10 in this volume).

Despite the weight of contrary evidence, social security and health and social care programs are built on the principle of nonintervention or, at best, minimum intervention. This is not to suggest that there is no state intervention in the care of older people. Of course, there is an infrastructure of social service provision even in residual welfare states. But such intervention is of a minimum, last-resort kind. For example, social services are usually organized on a casualty basis: The provision of home care follows a crisis in the informal caring relationship rather than being allocated at an earlier stage to support this relationship; access to public residential or nursing home care follows hospitalization or carer breakdown.

In operating on the principle of nonintervention, the state is attempting to perpetuate the myth that the family is a private domain. This emphasizes the fact that it is not via direct intervention in the family that the state maintains the primacy of intergenerational obligations, which brings me back to the role of ideology.

In practice the state in all Western societies intervenes actively in the family but it does so mainly in the form of ideology rather than in material ways (Donzelot, 1979; Moroney, 1976). In particular the state supports the reproduction of the gender division of domestic labor and intergenerational obligations with regard to care and legitimates these as "normal" or "natural," while at the same time it promotes the myth of the private world of the family. For example, in rationing home care in Britain it is common for the proximity of a daughter to be used as a criterion.

The norm of nonintervention in some aspects of the life world reinforces itself in limiting demands for social services and in ensuring that the family (and women in particular) perform the two sets of functions essential for social reproduction. On the one hand there is daily reproduction, including the care of sick and elderly family members and, on the other, the intergenerational transmission of values and obligations. In this way the boundaries to the roles of the family and of the state are socially constructed, for the most part, not in statute but through the reproduction of "normal" patterns and duties of family life.

At the center of this process of reproduction is the hegemony of what has been called the ideology of familism (Barrett & McIntosh, 1982; Dalley, 1988). This is the ideological construction of the individualistic, privatized, Western family form—with its characteristic gender division of labor and normative belief system concerning intergenerational responsibilities for care within both the family of procreation and the family of orientation. This ideology, and particularly its prescriptive norms concerning intergenerational obligations with regard to care, is internalized by family members, as we have seen, and even when there is no individual-level contract they still act according to a general sense of duty. Nonconformity to the hegemony of familism is regarded as deviant by other family members and by society (Dalley, 1988, p. 21).

Within this ideology of familism the family is portrayed as a haven from the outside world. Women are located centrally as the providers of nurture and care. They are regarded as natural carers and their intergenerational altruism is also seen as natural. They conform, in this portrayal, to the selflessness and altruism epitomized by the Victorian ideal of women. But, as the research outlined above demonstrates, female kin are under enormous normative pressures to provide care, and therefore their actions should more correctly be regarded as what Land and Rose (1985) call "compulsory altruism."

Familism and Welfare Restructuring

It is widely accepted that key aspects of modern welfare states were founded, to a considerable extent, on the unpaid domestic labor of women (and on their low-paid employment within welfare institutions). Social policies in the realms of social security, health, and social care have reflected and reinforced the ideology of familism, for example, by assuming that the family is necessarily the right location for the care of older people and that, within it, female kin are the most appropriate carers.

As policies to restructure the welfare state have developed over the last decade or so, the social construction of the natural role of the family in caring for older people and (within the family) the implied contract between the generations have figured prominently. This is particularly the case in those countries under the influence of neoliberal ideas, in which the traditional family has a central role. For example, Friedman and Friedman argue, in the face of the evidence, that in the past:

> Children helped their parents out of love and duty. They now contribute to the support of someone else's parents out of compulsion and fear. The earlier transfers strengthened the bonds of the family; the compulsory transfers weaken them. (1980, p. 135)

Or as Mrs. Thatcher (1981) put it when she was the prime minister of Britain:

[I]t all really starts in the family, because not only is the family the most important means through which we show our care for others. It's the place where each generation learns its responsibilities towards the rest of society. . . . I think the statutory services can only play their part success-fully if we don't expect them to do for us things that we could be doing for ourselves.

Under the direct or indirect influence of beliefs such as this, the ideology of familism has been employed by policymakers to resist increases in public expenditure on the health and social services as a result of the rise in the so-called burden of dependency. Thus policies such as "community care" have been presented as preferable alternatives to institutional care but for largely economic reasons, with insufficient resources devoted to them to ensure that a superior quality of care is provided (Walker, 1987). The family is expected to play an even greater part in caring for older people even though the research evidence shows that there is little spare capacity (Qureshi & Walker, 1989).

Just as welfare state restructuring has been part of the driving force behind the imposition of a new pensions contract between the generations, so the old "implied" contract within the family is being rein-forced. But, as Bengtson and his colleagues point out, demographic trends have produced "dramatic changes in intergenerational patterns" within families (Bengtson et al., 1991, p. 3). For example, family members are spending longer periods than previously occupying intergenerational family roles. This means that, for women in particular, both the *duration* and the *intensity* of their caring activities will increase, as demographic change is coupled with limitations in spending on support services. The implications of these two sets of antagonistic developments for relations between the generations and also within generations—especially between male and female domestic partners—are likely to be momentous.

Summary and Conclusion

The starting point of this chapter was the social contract between age cohorts that lies at the heart of the welfare state. There is widespread agreement that it is in a state of flux but much less consensus about the causes and implications of this change. The chapter has attempted to intrude, from a European perspective, on a rather introspective United States debate about intergenerational relations. Two distinct forms of intergenerational contract have been identified: the social policy contract in the form of public pensions and other measures, and the informal contract between kin.

The first aim has been to question the assumption that changes in the social contract are simply the product of demographic change and thereby to shed light on the causes of the "new" problem of generations. Two main factors were highlighted. On the one hand, there is the public-burden conception of welfare, implicit within neoclassical economic assumptions concerning productivity in the public and private sectors. The implied construction of old age is one of homogeneity, economic dependence, and unproductiveness. It is not surprising therefore that population aging is perceived as a problem in societies in which such economic orthodoxy holds sway. On the other hand, ideological change in some countries has brought hard, or harder, times for the welfare state, which have led to changes in the social policy contract well in advance of any serious funding problems. Thus older people have the misfortune to be the main recipients of state welfare at a time when it is being restructured.

The second aim has been to counteract the tendency in the age cohort literature to dichotomize the social world into macro- and microspheres and to regard the microlevel contract between generations as being constructed purely within the family. This position underplays the degree of interaction between the two spheres and, in particular, overlooks the crucial role of ideology in reproducing intergenerational dependencies, relationships, and obligations. For this reason attention was focused on the processes whereby intergenerational relationships within the family, concerning the care of older people, are reproduced.

Data from some recent field research in Britain were used to show that the caring relationship is constructed, in part at least, outside particular individual-level relations and reciprocities. In other words the microlevel contract is not simply a contract "of" generations but also "for" generations in that it is partly manufactured externally to the life world: The altruism of female kin is to some extent "compulsory altruism."

At the center of the reproduction of intergenerational obligations within families is the hegemony of the ideology of familism—the individualistic, privatized, Western family form with a gendered division of labor and normative belief system concerning intergenerational responsibilities. Thus, even when there is no material basis for reciprocity, some family members act according to a general sense of duty. The state occupies a pivotal role in the legitimation of this traditional division of labor in care, as being "normal" or "natural," through the policy of nonintervention (or reluctant intervention) in family care and by the ways it structures its interventions. At an ideological level the state is active in promoting familism.

The two main themes of the chapter are united, finally, by highlighting the prominent place given to intergenerational reciprocities within the family by policies aimed at restructuring welfare. Not only has the ideology of familism been used to resist increases in social spending, but it is also being exploited currently by some governments to justify reductions in spending on health and social services. Thus welfare state restructuring is on a collision course with the dramatic changes underway in intergenerational patterns within families. The outcome is primarily a matter of the interaction between social and economic policy and the generations concerned, rather than something that can be determined by age cohorts themselves.

In conclusion, all Western countries are either contemplating modifications to the public-pensions contract between age cohorts, or modifications are in the process of being implemented. The main motivation is the wider goal of welfare restructuring, which is, in part, a response to the perceived public-expenditure "burdens" associated with population aging. To some extent official concern about population trends is being artificially amplified as an economic-demographic imperative to legitimate restructuring. The pace of change in the introduction of a new pensions contract differs significantly among countries, depending on the ideology currently holding sway. Britain, under neoliberal-inspired policies, has already radically altered its social contract, whereas in Germany the perpetuation of a solidaristic consensus on the welfare state has meant that, so far, the reforms are more modest and the timetable more relaxed.

Intergenerational-equity rhetoric concerning "greedy elders" has proved to be something of a red herring in this process of change. It has been confined very largely to the United States, with the vast majority of European countries and even the United States' close neighbor Canada remaining immune. Moreover, despite dire predictions (some of which are repeated in this volume—see Chapter 11 by Thomson) and ample rhetoric (particularly in the United States) there is no actual evidence of overt age cohort conflicts. However, the process of welfare state restructuring may itself create the conditions for *both* intergenerational and age cohort conflicts. The modification of the social contract underway in Western society consists of important institutional reforms in the fields of pensions and social care, reforms that could have far-reaching effects on future age cohort relations.

For example, in Britain the recent emphasis on individual responsibility and the switch from public to personal pensions will encourage future cohorts to think—selfishly—more in terms of their own life cycle, rather than solidaristically (cf. Bengtson et al., 1991, p. 20). This may in turn weaken social integration between age cohorts. Similarly, the attempts to increase the role of the family in the care of older people will result in more pressures falling on female kin. This has the potential to create new conflicts between carers and older relatives and within the carer's own nuclear family.

So, rather than there being just a new problem *of* generations deriving from something inherent in the nature of current demographic trends, there is also the prospect of a new problem *for* generations being manufactured by economic and social policies aimed at restructuring the welfare state.

Research Questions

The research agenda arising from this analysis is inevitably comparative in nature. It is particularly important to develop comparative analyses between different welfare state forms such as those of North America and Northern Europe. There are four main priorities for such research:

1.   Information on reciprocities, exchanges, and obligations between generations, in different societies as well as cultures, and how these interact with social and economic policies. The main aim here would be to explore the extent of intercohort solidarity.

2.   Data on the distribution of public and private resources between age cohorts in different countries.

3.   Comparisons of the changes under way in welfare states and their impact on intergenerational relations. This could be coupled with the collection of examples of policy initiatives that enhance intergenerational solidarity.

4.   The politics of aging in different societies, designed to shed light on the differences in political responses to population aging, particularly between the United States and EC countries.

Acknowledgments

I am very grateful to participants in the "Generations" Conference at the University of Southern California for the stimulating discussion that followed the presentation of the draft of this chapter, and to Andy Achenbaum, Vern Bengtson, Jack Cornman, and Jill Quadagno for their detailed written comments, which proved to be extremely helpful in revising the draft for publication. Vern Bengtson deserves particular credit too for the intellectual stimulation provided by his various background papers. Of course, none of the conference participants, bar this one, can be held responsible for what appears in this chapter.

Notes

1.   The term *age cohort* refers to people born at roughly the same point in chronological time; an *age group* consists of people who fall within a certain age range; and the term *generation* denotes the single step in descent within family groups (Bengtson, Cutler, Mangen, & Marshall, 1985; Daniels, 1988). *Intergenerational equity* has been most widely used in the literature in the macrosocial sense to apply to distributional justice between age cohorts.

PART IV

Family Issues Across Generations

The two chapters in Part IV take off from Alan Walker's theme that families are used by social policymakers to restructure state welfare programs. Sociologists Jack and Matilda White Riley (Chapter 9) discuss the "latent matrix" of kin connections in an aging society. Unlike either simple or complex forms of kin networks, the power balance has changed among longer lived individuals. Nowadays, parents and offspring live long enough to become equals. Both can find potential linkages in flexible, complex safety nets that are not constrained by age. Sharply distinguishing between *familial* generational networks and *age-specific* cohort lines, the Rileys claim that this latent matrix of kin connectedness, an ideal type of social relations, can accommodate the increasingly diverse family structures and arrangements triggered by divorce, cohabitation, substitute kin, as well as traditional family forms. This feature, they speculate, might moderate the spectra of tensions and strains across generational lines.

More than any other contributor, sociologist Alice Rossi (Chapter 10) reminds us that gender is a significant axis in generational relations both within and outside kinship networks. Noting the powerful, perduring influence of sexual physiology, Rossi emphasizes that certain sociostructural and relational patterns—such as women's "physiological edge" in interactions with their children—persist over time. Emotions, she notes, are as critical as are rational calculations in determining behavior, especially between generations and age groups. Women early in life develop considerable affiliative and relational capabilities that grow as women mature, and as their family members age. Yet for all of her emphasis on continuities in gender dynamics, Rossi reminds us of the significant compositional changes that have occurred in conjunction with an increasingly aging society: the triads formed by three-generational bonds have become, as she suggests, the bulwark of social stability.

9

Connections: Kin and Cohort

Matilda White Riley and John W. Riley, Jr.

In this chapter we discuss the reciprocal influences of social change and kin connections, with the succession of birth cohorts as the dynamic link between the two.

Our theme is that a new type of kinship structure is emerging, which we call a *latent matrix* of kin connections (M. Riley, 1983, revisited). In postulating such a transition, we make four points along the way. First, numerous social and cultural changes—especially cohort increases in longevity—are yielding a large and complex network of kin relationships. Second, these many relationships are flexible. "Family contracts" (Burgess, 1948), and who the contracting partners may be, are increasingly matters of choice rather than obligation. A plethora of options is potentially at hand. Third, these relationships are not constrained by age or generation; people of any age, within or across generations, may opt to support, love, or confide in one another. Fourth, many of these kinship bonds remain latent until called upon. They form a safety net of significant connections to choose from in case of need. If a close relative is not available, a substitute often stands ready in the wings.

This latent matrix is not yet (if it will ever be) a reality; it is, rather, an "ideal type" or model to be analyzed and discussed. Our discussion is in three sections. In the first section we contrast the latent matrix with two other ideal types of kinship structures that reflect social changes, past and potential future. In the second section we ask how the analytical framework from the sociology of age can help in understanding how these structural changes come about, and with what implications. Here our emphasis is on the *successive cohorts* of people, each born at a particular period of history, who are continually moving through the kinship network over their long lives, bringing to it their special historical experiences, creating and recreating the variety of connections with kin, and foreshadowing the possible future. In the third section we consider several contemporary patterns of kin relations from the perspective of cohorts that will be old in the next century. Will these patterns begin to approximate our postulated matrix of latent relationships that provide wider and more flexible options? And if so, we ask in a final note, how will this matrix affect the "generational contract" to which this volume is addressed?

Changing Kin Connections

To examine past and future changes in kin connections, and their relation to broad social and cultural trends, we use three ideal types of kinship structures.[1] These are schematized roughly in Figure 1. The *simple* type consists of the nuclear family and (sometimes) a surviving older generation, with the members held together by economic as well as by social-emotional bonds. In the *expanded* type, the kin network has become larger and more complex, and the economic bonds have been somewhat loosened through supports from the state and other extrafamilial institutions. In our *latent matrix*, the extrafamilial supports remain; the kinship structure has become far more complex; and a wide array of relationships, no longer constrained by age or generation, are matters of choice rather than obligation.

These ideal types are, in Max Weber's (1920/1952) sense, artificially simplistic; they may never exist in reality, but are an idealized selection from it. Yet (keeping in mind the truism that history is by no means unidirectional) we think here of key elements of each type as either reflective of the reality of the past or prophetic of real directions for the future.

The nature of such key elements has been suggested in three papers, presented at a recent meeting of the Social Science History Association, which point to some of the ways in which the past is useful for understanding the present and the possible future (Brandes, 1989; Hareven & Adams, 1989; Riley, 1989).

Simple Forms

The first paper, by Stanley Brandes, on kinship and care for the aged in traditional rural Spain and Portugal, illustrates the nature of *intergen-*

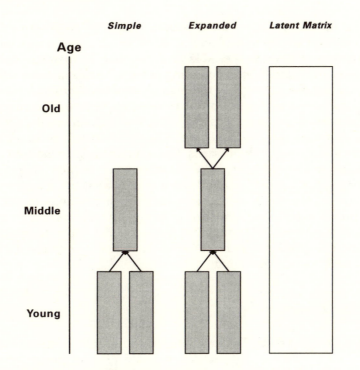

Figure 1. "Ideal types" of kinship structures.

erational contracts. It shows how, prior to World War II, care of the aged was intertwined with the transmission of property. The early pattern exemplifies a clear-cut simple structure of independent households— that of the parents and that of each adult offspring. Brandes describes the elaborate procedures operating to maintain this independence: ro- tating visits from offspring (with their families); elderly widowers mak- ing monthly visitations to each of the offspring; and selection of a single heir—even "adopting" an heir from outside the family—to preserve the family house and land until the death of the parents. Ideally, these relationships involved the exchange of property and other material re- wards for companionship and care in old age. In actuality, they all too often resulted in abuses of power by the older generation, or despair (even suicide) among elderly widowers consigned to the monthly rounds of staying with their offspring.

Later in the century, however, this early, property-based, relatively simple connection between two generations of adults broke down. With industrialization and enlarged economic opportunities, the traditional power relationship between generations was, as Brandes puts it, "turned upside down." Young people emigrated to cities or foreign countries; and old people often had to entice care and companionship from the young through special kindnesses, sharing their social security payments, or, increasingly, accepting old-age homes as the solution.

This is just one example of the many varied configurations of simple kin networks common in historical analyses of preindustrial Europe and colonial America (see e.g., Laslett, 1965), and throughout the anthropological literature (see Nancy Foner, Chapter 6 in this volume). In the extreme instance of Irish peasants, the son remained unmarried—often to age 30 or 40—until the father died and bequeathed him the farm (Arensberg & Kimball, 1940/1961). It was only after the dramatic rise in longevity[2]—coincident with the related transformations in the economy, public health, and standard of living, and the rise of the nation-state—that substantial numbers of kin networks expanded to include additional generations, and to become more deeply immersed in other institutions outside the family.

Shift Toward Expanded Forms

The second paper, by Tamara Hareven and Kathleen Adams (1989; cf. Hareven, 1982), which again focuses on aid to older people, indicates how the expanded family structure began to replace the simple type. By examining cohorts born at different times and experiencing different historical eras, these researchers tie changes in the lives of people and their families directly to history and to social change—the approach from the sociology of age that we describe later in this chapter.

Two cohorts of the adult offspring of immigrants to a New Hampshire mill town are examined: an earlier cohort (born 1910–1919), who came of age during the Great Depression; and a more recent cohort (born 1924–1929), who came of age during World War II. Members of these two cohorts, who had been subjected to these differing early-life experiences, related in very different ways to their older parents. Those in the earlier cohort, toughened by the depression, were primarily concerned with keeping the entire family afloat economically: They pooled resources, doubled up on housing, and kept their aging parents (and other needy relatives) "in the family"—an implicit contract. They held to the traditional ideologies of relying on kin rather than public agencies.

By contrast, members of the more recent cohort were no longer bound to the older generation by any contract, implicit or explicit, since they could take advantage of the economic recovery brought about by World War II. Instead, they devoted themselves to improving their own and their children's lives, and were readier to accept government help or nursing homes for their parents. They were more geographically distant from the older generation, more likely to live separately, and thus drew firmer boundaries between younger and older generations. As the authors put it, however, even this more recent cohort was "transitional" between a milieu of a deep involvement in generational assistance, and the individualistic values and life-styles characterizing the post-World War II era.

Many other researchers (e.g., Bengtson, 1990; Furstenberg, 1990) have elaborated other aspects of the shift from simple to expanded types of kinship structures, as members of successive cohorts have not only responded to recent social and cultural changes but also, most importantly, have survived to increasingly older ages. With the pronounced rise in longevity, the number of generations surviving jointly has increased to four or even five; and, despite the century-long decline in the number of children born in each family, more of the members of each generation live to be old. Increasing numbers of a child's four grandparents are alive at one time. Peter Uhlenberg (1980, p. 318) has shown that, whereas back in 1900 more than half of middle-aged couples had no living elderly parents, today half have two or more parents still alive.

Moreover, just as the generations in a family have increased in number and complexity, linkages among family members have been prolonged. Thus parents and their offspring now survive jointly for so many years that a mother and her daughter are only briefly in the traditional relationship of parent and little child; during the several remaining decades of their lives they have become status equals. Today (though families remain the major caregivers) public funds and private pensions eliminate much of the intergenerational economic dependency—save for the care needed at the extremes of the age spectrum for very little children and those of the very old who are disabled.

Matrix of Latent Relationships

This transition from a simple to an expanded kinship structure can lead eventually to the latent-matrix model we are postulating in this chapter, as it was discussed by Matilda Riley, in the third paper at the Social Science and History Association Conference (1989; cf. 1983). This emergent type, which has even greater complexity than the expanded structure, is described as a latent web of continually shifting linkages that provide the potential for activating and intensifying close kin relationships.

Many elements of such a matrix are already in evidence. As schematized in Figure 1, this new type has lost the clarity of well-defined family structures. It has lost the sharp boundaries set by generation or age or geographical proximity. Indeed, the emerging boundaries of the kin network may be more closely influenced by gender, or even by race and ethnicity, than by age or generation. Instead, the boundaries of the kin network have been widened to encompass many diverse relationships, including several degrees of stepkin and in-laws, single-parent families, adopted and other "relatives" chosen from outside the family, and many others (discussed below). As recently reported by the U.S. Bureau of the Census (1989), the "traditional" nuclear family of a couple with children under 18 has declined from 40% of United States households in the 1970s, to 31% in the 1980s, and to 26% in 1990. At the same time, with rising rates of divorce and remarriage, many a child now has two sets of parents, and even four sets of grandparents. And, looking toward the future, this latent matrix can contain still unimagined relational structures, as even now it is possible for an offspring to have biological linkages to *two* mothers: one who donates the egg and a second who bears the child!

A unique feature distinguishes these many relationships: They are latent. Most of them remain dormant unless called upon as needs arise, over the life course, for instrumental or emotional support, companionship, affection, or intimacy. Friendship between adults and their parents is not obligatory, but must be earned. Even parenthood, as James Sweet and Larry Bumpass (1987, p. 396) point out, has been transformed from an ascribed role for women to a matter of choice. If there was once a family contract, there are now many flexible options.

How closely does this third ideal type approximate the emerging realities of contemporary or potential future family life? To examine this question requires analysis of how it comes about that kinship structures and relationships change as societal conditions change, and how successive cohorts operate as carriers of such changes.

Cohorts and Kinship

For a few clues to this global process, we turn to the sociology of age (cf. Riley, Foner, & Waring, 1988; Riley, Johnson, & Foner, 1972). Figure 2 schematizes our by now familiar *age stratification paradigm* (Riley, Johnson, & Foner, 1972), designed as an analytical tool for formulating pertinent questions and seeking answers through appropriate research. Here we shall emphasize its heuristic value for understanding the shifting ideal types of kinship structures, and the successive cohorts of individuals who, throughout their long lives, both influence and are in-

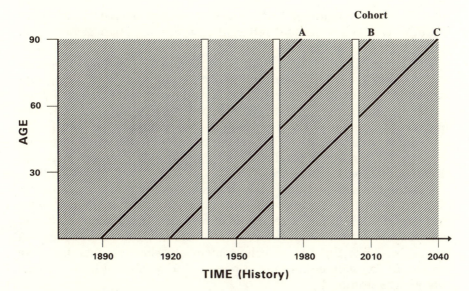

Figure 2. Cohorts in an age stratification system. *Note:* From "Sociology of Age" by M. W. Riley, A. Foner, and J. Waring, pp. 243–290 in *Handbook of Sociology*, edited by N. Smelser, 1988, Newbury Park, CA: Sage.

fluenced by these structures. In the diagram, the vertical lines refer to structures of people and roles, and the crisscrossing diagonal lines to cohorts.

Cohorts in an Age Stratification System

As a reminder, the diagram is a social space bounded on the vertical axis by years of age, and on the horizontal axis by dates that indicate the course of social and cultural change—past and future. Within this space, although the diagonals and the verticals look static, they are dynamic: Both the cohorts of people and the kinship structures are continually changing across time.

The successive cohorts consist of people, who were born in particular time periods,[3] and who are aging. In a single cohort (e.g., Cohort A), as people age they move along the diagonal—across time and upward through the social structure. That is, they move through successive roles: in family life, through school grades and work careers, through retirement, and ultimately to death. In the meantime, they change biologically, psychologically, and socially; and they develop patterns of attitudes and behaviors that reflect the particular period of history in which their lives are embedded.

The entire space is filled with such diagonals—because people in many successive cohorts are continually starting their lives, aging, dying, and replacing each other. Cohort A (and two others) are highlighted in the diagram simply to indicate how particular cohorts can be identified for any given analysis. (For example, two siblings in the same family who differ widely in age would belong to different cohorts; hence their lives would run along parallel diagonals, but would reflect markedly different historical experiences.)

It is the full series of diagonals that calls attention to the central sociological principle: Because different cohorts are born at different dates and live through different segments of historical time, *people in different cohorts age in different ways.* (To avoid confusion, we do not use the term *age cohort*, since the age of cohort members changes over their life course. In any moment of time, a person is a member of both a cohort and an age stratum.)

At any given time, these cohorts fit together in social *structures*, such as a particular ideal type of kinship. Thus the vertical lines in the diagram point to the people and the associated roles that comprise these structures. This means that a single vertical line (as in 1980) is a cross-sectional slice through many cohorts, whose members differ in age, though they coexist and may interact with one another. Of course, structures are not fixed: Over time, as society moves through historical events and changes, this vertical line moves across the space from one period to the next. Over time, the age-related structures of roles and norms are subjected to social and cultural changes. Over time also, the people in particular age strata are no longer the same people; inevitably, they have been replaced by younger entrants from more recent cohorts with more recent historical experience.[4]

Although the full meaning of this paradigm is not discussed here, certain implications of cohort succession for kinship structures and changes are readily apparent.

Cohorts and Structures

One can imagine superimposing on a vertical line in Figure 2 any one of the ideal types of kinship structures from Figure 1. Thus, for a given analysis, many of the elements of the expanded type might correspond to contemporary modal structures (as in the vertical around 1970), the latent matrix to a year in the next century, and the simple structure to some date in the early 1900s. Each structure can then be seen as a cross section of people from all the coexisting cohorts who, at differing stages of their lives, confront the particular social and cultural conditions of that period in history.

Within particular families. The configuration of cohort memberships has important implications for relational bonds within families. For example, consider the contrast between two nuclear families. In one family (suggestive of the expanded type), both parents belong to the same earlier cohort, and the closely spaced children all belong to another more recent cohort. In this family, belonging to the same cohort is one of the major factors producing solidarity, reflecting communalities of historical experience or of cohort size, and the shared meanings, attitudes, and characteristics dramatized in Karl Mannheim's (1928/1952) seminal work. Thus in this family there may be close ties between the parents, and another set of close ties among the children. Yet the pronounced division in cohort membership between parents and children may lead to tension or conflict. By contrast, in another family (as in the latent matrix) the parents differ widely in age, and hence reflect the experiences of very different cohorts; and the children, too, may belong to widely differing cohorts. Here, there is no cohort base for solidarity; but there is also no cohort base for cleavage. Indeed, such *cohort heterogeneity* might even serve to modulate potential strains and tensions. Current tendencies toward this form of heterogeneity are reinforced by additions to families of numerous stepkin, in-laws, and adopted relatives, thus seeming to presage the breakdown of generational and age barriers as postulated in the latent-matrix model.

These contrasting paradigmatic families are useful not only in considering how cohorts impinge on kin structures: they also have significant *terminological* implications. In the first family, cohorts and generations are closely linked. In the second, however, cohorts clearly do not coincide with generations (an empirical situation noted by Duncan, 1966). This contrast underscores the confusion resulting from use of the term *generation* to mean *cohort*. As Gunhild Hagestad (1982) puts it, "People do not file into generations by cohort." We avoid this confusion by using *cohort* to mean persons born at the same time, retaining the full connotations of Mannheim's early conceptualization (cf. Marshall, 1984), but reserving the term *generation* for its kinship meaning (see also Kertzer, 1983; Ryder, 1968). (This is not to preclude appropriate use of Mannheim's term *generation* to mean *cohort*, as in wide popular usage. The need is simply to make clear which definition is meant in particular contexts.)

Intersections with other structures.   Just as kinship relations are affected by cohort configurations within a family, they are also influenced by other social structures with which they intersect in the larger society. These structures too have been changing, and the multiple roles performed by persons in successive cohorts have influenced their kinship roles. The "welfare state" has taken over much of the fiscal support for little children and for the elderly poor (as discussed by Jill Quadagno at the conference and by authors of several chapters in this volume). Thus in the United States there has been a shift in emphasis from generation-based contracts to age-based contracts (e.g., Social Security and Medicare), often reducing the role of recent cohorts of kin to mediators between older people (or children) and federal, state, or local bureaucracies.

The intersection between kinship and *work* has also had profound implications for the family, as both husbands and wives in oncoming cohorts engage simultaneously in the lockstep path of education, work, and retirement (Riley & Riley, 1991). Kin structures also intersect with many forms of *institutional care*. In an earlier era, when most people died young, orphan asylums served as surrogate parents; and in medieval Europe, the Catholic church served not only as school but also as home and hospital. Today, there are childcare centers, nursing homes, life care communities, and hospices (J. Riley, 1992)—all of which share responsibilities and opportunities with recent cohorts of family members.

Ironically, many of these intersecting structures are stratified by generation or age. Seemingly, then, if the family itself is tending toward flexible structures of the latent-matrix type, it intersects with other more rigid structures that were originally suitable for the expanded type. The larger society, as we note elsewhere (cf. Riley, 1988), is marked by *structural lag*.

Cohorts and Change

Cohort influences extend, of course, beyond the boundaries of kin structures at a given time, to link secular changes in the society to alterations in the modal arrangements of these structures. If kinship structures can be understood as composed of members with differing cohort experiences, in complementary fashion these successive cohorts can be seen to transform old structures as they move through them. Thus, for example, the two cohorts studied by Hareven and Adams (1989), which respectively experienced the hardships of depression and the opportunities of prosperity, contributed to the shift away from the traditional norm of filial obligation to support elderly parents (as discussed above).

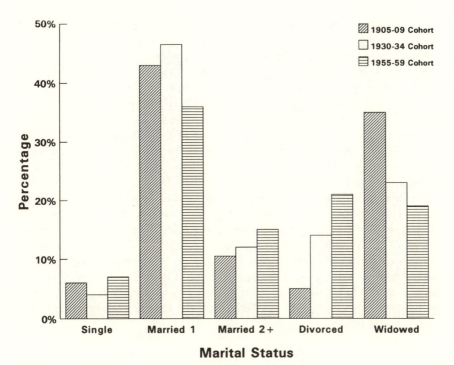

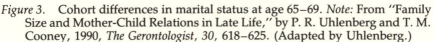

Figure 3. Cohort differences in marital status at age 65–69. *Note:* From "Family Size and Mother-Child Relations in Late Life," by P. R. Uhlenberg and T. M. Cooney, 1990, *The Gerontologist, 30,* 618–625. (Adapted by Uhlenberg.)

In another example, Uhlenberg has demonstrated how the life course patterns of three successive cohorts of white women, as they reach age 65–69, are marked by the societal changes over the past century in divorce and also in marriage and in mortality (Uhlenberg, Cooney, & Boyd, 1990). In Figure 3, although the majority in all three cohorts are married, the relative importance of widowhood and divorce in disrupting marriage has been reversed. In the earliest cohort (born 1905–1909 and reaching old age by the 1970s before the major societal upsurge in divorce), the widowed greatly outnumber the divorced. By contrast, in the most recent cohort (born 1955–1959 and reaching later life after 2020), divorcees are projected to outnumber widows.

Uhlenberg and his associates go on to consider the implications of these cohort differences for changes in kinship structures (just as we can imagine redrawing their chart to fit three appropriate diagonals in Figure 2). For example, they find that, in cohorts of people who are old today, the divorced as compared with the widowed have fewer assets and lower socioeconomic status, and are more likely to be dependent on living with others (1990, p. S10). Also widely described in the literature are the contemporary consequences of divorce for the offspring and for intergenerational relationships generally (cf. Furstenberg, 1990) as, for example, the bonds between father and son tend to be especially weakened by divorce (cf. Uhlenberg, 1990; and see discussion below).

In addition, the analysis in Figure 3 goes beyond those cohorts who form the kinship structures of today to forecast the marital status of people in the cohort born in 1955–1959 when they grow old in the next century. This illustrates one further use of the age stratification paradigm: Analysis of successive cohorts can improve forecasts, because many facts are already in hand about the earlier lives of all cohort members alive today, who will be the older people of the future.[5] Cohort comparisons are only one of many means of interpreting past changes and informing estimates of future potentials. But the notion of cohort succession alerts us to the continual influx into society of people who can be newly socialized to confront the structures and formulate the norms of the future.

Signs of the Latent Matrix

In this last section, we look toward the future, asking whether certain relational patterns current among cohorts today may portend shifts toward the latent matrix of kin relationships. We examine four such patterns: divorce, cohabitation, substitute kin, and persistent traditional ties. Running through all these patterns we find key elements of the latent matrix: complexity of structure, prolongation of relationships (though often dormant), and the replacement of ascribed obligations with flexibility of choice.

Divorce

It is clear that the long-term rise in rates of divorce[6] and remarriage is leaving in its wake many weakened, even hostile, kinship ties; but it is also leaving a proliferation of new bonds. A recent textbook on the United States family (Skolnick & Skolnick, 1989) includes the following example:

When Ellen and David are 15 and 17, their family looks like this: They have two biological parents, two stepparents, three stepsisters, a half-brother and a half-sister. Their extended family has expanded as well. They have two sets of step-grandparents, two sets of biological grandparents, and a large network of aunts, uncles, and cousins. (p. 364, reprinted from Ahrons & Rodgers, 1987)

However much this example may caricature the modal complexity (which extends beyond the nomenclature available in the English language), it illustrates the expansion of the latent matrix of relationships that provide options for activation.

Although some implications of these relational patterns are positive, many are negative. Various measures to reduce the difficulties of divorce for children and their mothers (we might call these measures "subcontracts") have not met their original promise; such measures include child support and alimony, joint custody arrangements, and no-fault divorce (Furstenberg, 1990). When couples in the middle generation are divorced, the relationship between paternal grandparents and grandchildren often becomes weaker, although relationships on the maternal side become deeper and stronger (Bengtson & Robertson, 1985, p. 98). According to some estimates, 3 to 4 million American grandmothers and great-grandmothers have primary responsibility for their grandchildren.

Focusing on the implications of divorce for older people, Frances Goldscheider (1990) points to the special risks to cohorts of people (especially males) who will become old in the 21st century. Unlike the older people of today, they will have participated fully in the gender and kinship revolutions of the last third of the 20th century. Predictably, they will have less advantaged kin connections, as their lives are increasingly linked to key family changes—in divorce, in female labor force participation, in remarriage, and in the nature of intergenerational relationships.

Increasingly too, as women are finding new independence through participation in the labor force, it will be the older men of the future who are at risk. Those divorced men who are old today, as compared with women, are already disadvantaged: Only half of the men have weekly contact with adult children, and very few mention adult children as a source of support (Cooney & Uhlenberg, 1990). The interactions between children and the recent cohorts of divorced fathers who will reach old age in the future are even more disturbing: While these offspring are still young, levels of contact are already low, possibly portending still more weakened and confused ties when they grow old.

Nevertheless, however weak or dormant the connections resulting from divorce, the connections are numerous and they persist. This fact is illuminated by the contrast between contemporary dissolution of marriage through divorce and the earlier dissolution of marriage through death of one spouse (often the continually pregnant wife). Historically, as in the early German records reported by Arthur Imhof (1986), successive remarriages by widowers resulted in numerous stepmothers but rare stepfathers, with young stepmothers sometimes confronting children from their husbands' previous marriages who were older than themselves! Although such anomalies are not unusual today, both partners to the original marriage now typically survive to contribute to the bilateral proliferation of stepkin and in-laws.

Cohabitation

If the rise in divorce threatens to weaken these numerous kinship ties in the future, members of the more recent cohorts have been inventing new ways to strengthen them. One United States trend[7] that emanates from the pressures from oncoming cohorts to substitute new types of bonds for old ones is cohabitation (defined for census purposes as "an unmarried-couple household of two unrelated adults of the opposite sex with or without children under 15"). The increase of cohabiting couples has been striking: from a mere 400,000 in 1960 and 500,000 in 1970, up to 1 million or more in 1980 and to over 2.5 million by 1988 (U.S. Bureau of the Census, 1989a). Moreover, for 1987–1988 the National Survey of Families and Households shows that 40% of the cohabiting couple households include children (Bumpass, Sweet, & Cherlin, 1989, p. 19).

This pattern of cohabitation has been emerging primarily among adults in their 20s and 30s, with little cohabitation reported among older people, despite assertions about tax or Social Security advantage. When successive marriage cohorts are compared, the proportion of persons who cohabited before first marriage rose from 11% for marriages in 1965–1974 to 44% for marriages in 1980–1984, an increase that is even more pronounced among those in their second marriage. Viewed as cumulative experience in the lives of people reaching age 30 (or 35) today, almost half of those in this cohort have cohabited at some time; and the proportion is two thirds among separated or divorced persons (Bumpass & Sweet, 1989, pp. 6–7; see also London, 1991).

Although expressed norms may not yet have caught up with the prevalence of cohabitation (Sweet, 1989, p. 18), there is little sign that the rising trend is abating. As Bumpass et al. put it, "We must include cohabitation along with marriage if we are to understand family life in modern societies" (1989, p. 20). Thus new types of "kinship," including new intergenerational connections, seem to be taking shape.

Substitute Kin

In addition to cohabitation, numerous other forms of relationships are tending to replace many traditional consanguineous and affinal kin connections. These substitute forms include gay and lesbian couples, often with adopted children; adopted children for older people and foster parents for children; close quasi-familial connections within formal institutions, as with sympathetic aides in nursing homes and many others. In addition, types of "fictive kin" traditional among racial and ethnic minorities can become increasingly significant with the rising numbers and proportions of minorities in the United States population.

Adoption, whether or not legally or ritually affirmed, is one widespread form of "kinlike" connection. Much research has generally confirmed Ethel Shanas's "principle of substitution" (1979), i.e., when filial supports are not available, other types of relationships are substituted. One study of today's childless and unmarried older people (Johnson & Catalano, 1981) finds that they "adopt" not only distant and not-so-distant relatives, but also friends, neighbors, ministers, and even younger managers of housing. These childless unmarried persons engage in an anticipatory rehearsal for the future, establishing networks of relatives, friends, and neighbors as "a storehouse of resources . . . in preparation for the possibility of dependency" (p. 614).

Many historical and cross-cultural precedents attest to the importance of this form of substitute relationships. Judith Treas and Wei Wang, Chapter 5 in this volume, have noted the prevalence of substitute relationships in Shanghai. In the simple type of kinship structure (above), Brandes (1989) describes the adoption of "heirs" as the means of handling problems of property transfer and old-age care. An instructive example (Ericsson, 1990) comes from the experience of widows and spinsters in Sweden, which in the 19th century had a large unmarried population. Under such conditions (where cohabitation was also widespread), many unmarried women coped, even in old age, by earning their own living, often setting themselves up in retailing or handicrafts as independent entrepreneurs. Many of them then "created" their own family by taking in a foster child (sometimes an adult). This new family member served as a surrogate offspring—helping with the business, and presumably looking after the spinster in her old age and becoming heir to the business.

Substitute relationships can go both ways: There are foster parents for adult children, as well as foster children for older people. Victor Marshall, during discussions at the conference, took note of the current practice of the young of adopting parents because of their pensions, much as in the breakdown of the simple family in rural Spain and Portugal described by Brandes (1989).

Significant substitute relationships can extend into more formal societal arrangements. For example, though widely maligned, the "board and care homes" set up for indigent older people often encourage elderly residents to participate actively in family affairs as a grandparent might, creating interpersonal relationships similar to those in traditional family life (from a study in process by Kevin Eckert and Leslie M. Morgan).

Unlike substitutes chosen in cases of special need, fictive-kin arrangements have long been traditional in many cultures, including our own. As intensified in America by minority groups, the variety of such relationships is illustrated by a range of studies:

Among Mexican American families, in which numbers of uncles and aunts already abound, the baptismal ceremony establishes additional ties with godparents, thereby bringing two large families into a fictive-kinship relationship (U.S. Department of Health, Education, & Welfare, DHEW, 1979; Williams, 1990).

Among Asian Americans,

> friends are often a more important source of social support than kin, and friendships often take on the form of kinship. Thus, unrelated older individuals may be addressed as "aunt" or "uncle" or may play "mother" or "father" as a sign of close emotional ties and mutual obligation. (Liu & Yu, 1990, p. 22)

In the African American community, the kinship network is often extended through the creation of fictive kin (cf. the work by Johnson & Barer, 1990). As illustrated in one ethnographic study, "A woman who raises a sister's or a niece's or a cousin's child regards their offspring as much her grandchildren as children born of her own son and daughter" (Stack, 1974, p. 63). Further,

> as households shift, rights and responsibilities with regard to children are shared. These women and men who temporarily assume the kinship obligation to care for a child [come to foster] the child indefinitely, and thus acquire the major cluster of rights and duties ideally associated with "parenthood." (p. 92)

To what extent African Americans and other minorities in the future will retain their fictive extensions of the conventional family model will depend on both economic and sociocultural changes. Today's mounting numbers of single-parent families in need of surrogate relatives may extend such arrangements to the larger society. In the meantime, the large oncoming cohorts are clearly marked by a rich heritage of fictive-kin connections. These and many other types of substitute relationships can be negotiated and, as postulated in the latent matrix, are available for choice.

Persistent Traditional Ties

In the midst of all these changing patterns, and despite much dismal foreboding, many studies demonstrate that traditional kinship solidarity has certainly not disappeared. Recent research findings largely agree that family members continue to be the single greatest source of care for dependent older people. Sibling relationships are important ties that extend into older ages and are an alternative source of assistance for childless older people. On the whole, older people are themselves active participants in the kinship network, especially older black women who contribute significantly to their families, and to the extended community, by caring for children in the absence or work time of the mothers, many of whom are single.

In particular, recent studies begin to show the effects of extended longevity on husband-wife relationships and on exchanges of support between adult-child and parent generations (e.g., Rossi & Rossi, 1990; Uhlenberg & Cooney, 1990a). The demographic effects have been calculated by Watkins, Menken, and Bongaarts (1987), who simulate family changes for cohorts of women under the conditions existing in four widely spaced time periods (1880, 1900, 1960, and 1980). They demonstrate that, despite declining fertility and rising divorce rates, women in the 20th-century cohorts spent many more years than did their predecessors in marriage, and as parents, and as children of aged parents.

As these central family relationships are extended, they take on new forms and meanings. Consider *husbands and wives*, whose lives are inextricably tied to all kin members, including in-laws, stepkin, and others in the far-reaching latent matrix. A century ago, one or both members of married couples were likely to have died before the children were reared. Today, couples marrying at the customary ages can anticipate surviving together (apart from divorce) for at least 40 years on the average (Uhlenberg, 1980; Watkins et al., 1987). This extension of marital relationships provides continuing options to shape and alter them, or to end them. Reflecting the long-term changes in norms, the likelihood that marriages beginning in a given year will end in divorce has risen from 7% in 1860 to over 50% today (Sweet & Bumpass, 1987, p. 395).

For the latent-matrix model, the noteworthy point is this: As long as the marital pair survive, even if divorced, the potential linkages—in some form—persist. In unbroken marriages, the linkages provide the many shared family experiences of aging together from young adulthood to old age. The linkages provide an abiding meeting place for two individuals whose separate lives are also engrossed in extrafamilial roles—in work, continuing education, or retirement—roles that are also greatly extended by longevity. In couples separated by divorce, the remaining linkages may be purely ceremonial, financial, or instrumental, or (as time passes) they can bring renewed concern for one another's well-being. Thus even an ex-marriage affords a continuing potential for a close relationship that can be activated in manifold ways.

As lives are extended, *parent-offspring* relationships are similarly prolonged, and most take on new shapes that were only rarely conceivable for their shorter lived forebears. Differing in age, but moving in tandem across historical time, the typical mother-daughter pair now survive together for many decades. During most of these years they are no longer parent and little child: Both are adults, sharing many common experiences, though at different stages of their respective lives. As adults, they are equals in status, save for those elderly daughters taking responsibility for very old parents who have become so frail as to be dependent. Today the proportion of women at age 55 with a surviving parent is some 10 times greater than it was in 1800 (Watkins et al., 1987, p. 349).

Clearly, the nature of these prolonged parent-child relationships is open to choice (though unlike marriage they cannot be broken by divorce). There are many accounts in the literature of widespread reciprocal contributions of help and resources; of the closer bonds between women than between men; and of the heightened strains in small families without siblings to share in the care of an ailing parent (cf. Uhlenberg & Cooney, 1990a; also Bengtson, Chapter 1 in this volume). Alice Rossi and Peter Rossi (1990, p. 490) speak of the prolongation of parent-child relationships as a "great gift," rating their reciprocal "obligations" as extremely high. Of special interest are the ratings of "affective closeness," which show actual increases beyond adolescence with the age of the offspring, whether the quality of the relationship is rated by parents or by their children (pp. 277, 498).

For the future, the portents for filial relationships are shrouded in the ambiguities of current social trends, most especially the uncertain trends in basic values. At one extreme, Rossi and Rossi (1990) speculate that a high sense of obligation to kin, noted in the youngest cohort of their study, may result in a "delayed reciprocity" to their parents later in life—echoing a phenomenon noted by Foner (Chapter 6 in this volume) from a wide range of ethnographic reports. At another extreme, Goldscheider (1990) emphasizes the disadvantages to the older people of the future, because for the first time they must contend with children from that cohort in which substantial proportions have experienced mother-only families and the loss of paternal contact—even when the fathers are alive. (Some 25% of all births today are to single mothers—a phenomenon with still untold consequences for the future.) For the prolonged intergenerational relationships in America in the 21st century, will there be changes in values? Will oncoming cohorts with a heightened sense of obligation augur a shift away from the self-orientation and secularism of the 20th century?

Taken together, will these many intricate patterns of relationships today become institutionalized in the future, as such apparently disruptive patterns as divorce, remarriage, or cohabitation trigger new realities? Will they lead to the latent matrix of extensive relational choices?

All in all, there can be little doubt that the network of potentially significant relationships is becoming enlarged. The options are manifold. As David Schneider (1980) once put it, the American kinship system is permissive, "giving individuals great latitude to construct meaningful relations from a wide pool of potential kin." Among the more recent authors who share this view, Joan Aldous (1987) speaks of today's "young-old" as keeping their intergenerational ties voluntary rather than obligatory, just as their children do. She finds parents to be "selective in their attentions, concentrating them on those in greatest need" (p. 227). Far less clear for the future is what selections will become most frequent. Which of these many types of relationships will be sustained? How strong (or weak) will they become? Answers to such questions will depend mainly on trends in the larger society. But those young people today who later in their lives may influence these trends will certainly carry into the next century a varied array of kinship experiences.

Final Note: Intergenerational Connections

To the extent that key elements of the latent matrix may characterize the kinship structures of the future, what are the implications for the intergenerational contract that is addressed by Vern Bengtson in Chapter 1 in this volume? Unlike obligations to a spouse, where divorce permits new contracts to be negotiated, new norms have not been institutionalized to guide the patterns of rights, opportunities, responsibilities, and obligations in the filial relationship—the relationship that once bore the major burden of support for elderly parents.

Nevertheless, four major changes have been transforming the nature of the parent-child relationship:

1. The *power* balance has changed, now that for most of their lives parents and offspring are status equals.

2. *Property* and material resources are no longer the dominant base of the relationship, now that support from the state and other institutions enhances the independence of the old.

3. The heterogeneity of contemporary families in *age* (hence also in cohort membership) reduces the traditional "age gap" as a source of potential contention and conflict.

4. The many *alternative forms* of relationship available today diffuse the traditional primary focus on the intergenerational connection.

Watkins et al. (1987, p. 355) put it this way: family roles have become "blurred and redefined," as cohabitation "smudges" the distinction between married and unmarried, or divorce blurs the distinction between formerly married and never married.

Such changes foreshadow entirely new kinship forms. Though the larger society is still subject to age constraints—hence subject to possible age-based tensions and cleavages (but see Foner, 1974), the emergent kin connections examined in this chapter bid fair to transcend any such divisiveness. These new connections are optional rather than contractual or obligatory. And it is our view that they hold high promise of modulating, rather than exacerbating, whatever intergenerational strains, conflicts, or perceived inequalities the future may bring.

Acknowledgments

We appreciate many thoughtful comments from participants at the conference preceding this publication, especially those of the formal discussants, Lillian Troll and Mark Hayward, whose careful reading of the working manuscript pointed to several needs for clarification and substantiation. We are also grateful to other participants, some of whose works or comments we have cited, and to others, like Victor Marshall, who reacted to our revised version. Among the staff members at the National Institute on Aging who have assisted in searching the literature and preparing the manuscript are Karin Mack, Katrina Johnson, Ronald Abeles, and Jeannette Wilson.

Notes

1. These ideal types, though not the subsequent discussions of them, disregard the special complexities of kinship structure (such as "anchoring" and "asymmetry," as described in Hagestad, 1988).

2.   During the conference, Maris Vinovskis called attention to the frequent misinterpretation of increased longevity at birth, which confounds the extension of adult life with the decreases in neonatal mortality—an important topic for the future research agenda.

3.   The range of birth dates used to define a cohort is purely arbitrary, ranging—according to the research objective—from a 10-year interval to a matter of only months or even days.

4.   This simplified diagram (a modification of the Lexis diagram) cannot even suggest many aspects of the age stratification paradigm, such as the roles as well as the people involved, the dynamic interactions among cohort members, the dramatic differences in cohort size, the significant *asynchrony* between changing structures and changing lives, or even the unparalleled increases in longevity.

5.   Of course, there are dangers of "cohort-centrism" in reasoning from current lives about lives and structures in the future. Wars, depressions, or other unexpected events can occur; and past trends frequently reverse themselves (e.g., the current educational discrepancy between older and younger cohort members is expected to disappear). However, in Chapter 4 in this volume Richard Easterlin, Diane Macunovich, and Eileen Crimmins demonstrate that, contrary to expectations, the earlier cohort differences in income levels are being sustained.

6.   Despite slow declines in divorce rates that occurred in the 1980s, the numbers of divorced persons will continue to rise.

7.   Of course, cohabitation is by no means new. Long accepted in Sweden and other European countries, its prevalence in colonial America is illustrated by a diary that reports that unwed pregnancies constituted some 40% of the 106 first-time mothers in a rural Maine community some two centuries ago. There was widespread acceptance of sex before marriage, even among leading families. Most women married quickly after giving birth, and otherwise the community saw to it that the fathers bore responsibility (Ulrich, 1990).

10

Intergenerational Relations: Gender, Norms, and Behavior

Alice S. Rossi

Over the past 15 years there has been an exponential growth of research in the social sciences on sex and gender, reflecting the impact of the feminist movement in the years since its renascence in the mid-60s. Titles alerting us to this development crowd our library shelves, titles that suggest the wide array of disciplines involved, such as *Women and Health in America* (Leavitt, 1984), *Women and Evil* (Noddings, 1989), *Women's Ways of Knowing* (Belenky, Clinchy, Goldberger, & Tarule, 1986), *Women Changing Work* (Lunneborg, 1990), and *Women's Life Cycle and Economic Insecurity* (Ozawa, 1989). Books with titles that refer to gender rather than to women, such as *Gender and Power* (Connell, 1987) or *Gender and Stress* (Barnett, Biener, & Baruch, 1987), typically focus for the most part on women.

By comparison, research and policy publications on "intergenerational relations" or "intergenerational equity" rarely make reference to women or to gender. This applies to most of the chapters in this volume as well. Vern Bengtson (Chapter 1), a man with fine gender sensibility in his personal and professional relationships, rarely discusses the gender composition of contemporary versus future cohorts of the elderly, nor does he specify gender in any systematic way in analysis of the relationship between parents and adult children in the numerous essays based on data from his three-generation study. Fernando Torres-Gil (Chapter 12 in this volume) subtly alerts us to the fact that future cohorts of the elderly will be dependent on the wages of a work force of increasing ethnic and racial diversity, but says nothing about the implications of the fact that elderly cohorts will become increasingly female with the growth of the population over 75 years of age. Nor does he specify gender of the "seniors" who lobbied for the repeal of the Medicare Catastrophic Coverage Act (Torres-Gil, 1990), though one suspects they were largely male. Andrew Achenbaum (Chapter 2 in this volume) provides three very interesting historical examples of generational succession as a negotiation over the life course, almost entirely consisting of male historical figures, with no commentary about differences between women and men in negotiations between generations or across the life course (though in his conclusion he does suggest the need to think through the implications of aging societies becoming more female). Nor do the chapters by our other historian colleagues (Vinovskis, Chapter 3; Walker, Chapter 8; and Thomson, Chapter 11) pay any attention to the role of gender in the issues they deal with in this volume.

Were it the case that gender was not a significant axis in intergenerational relations, this neglect would not matter. But this is not the case, as this chapter will demonstrate. And how could it be otherwise, when age and sex are such fundamental attributes of any human creature, when the whole history of Western societies gives testimony to the very different positions held by women and men in almost every aspect of life, and when age and sex, together with ethnicity and race, are fundamental components of individual self-concepts? A social scientist must also assume that family and kindred (themselves rooted in reproductive sexual dimorphism) and ethnic and religious group membership are highly significant reference groups that frequently transcend even national identification, as shown in the persistence of ethnic loyalty and conflict in so many trouble spots on the globe, e.g., Ireland, India, Iraq, and the former Soviet Union.

The major research results to be reported in this chapter are drawn from a recent publication, *Of Human Bonding* (Rossi & Rossi, 1990). Of special relevance to the purposes of this volume on the contract between the generations is a discussion of the theoretical perspective on gender and a description of the design of the study, followed by a summary of some major findings on normative obligations to kin, and ending with a discussion of several issues that are important to our scientific understanding and public policy formation and warrant further research.

Theoretical Perspective on Gender

The infinite diversity of human taste and imagination is nowhere more apparent than in the ways in which cultures vary in the grooming of the human male and female, with almost no part of the body exempt from cultural prescription: from near-nudity to the fully upholstered Victorian lady, from shaven heads to hair below the waistline, from bare breasts to boned corsets. Beneath these exteriors of grooming differences, however, is the universal sexual dimorphism of the human species, rooted in mammalian reproduction, and elaborated and celebrated by means of cultural grooming patterns. We need to remind ourselves of the experience that underlies all intergenerational relations and family systems—the birth of a child—and the innate biological characteristics associated with birthing that differentiate male from female. In today's parlance, the distinction between "sex" and "gender" is relied upon to differentiate between those phenomena directly reflecting biological differences between male and female, to which we restrict the usage of *sex*, and those social and cultural characteristics that differentiate men from women, to which we now restrict the usage of *gender*. But when we are concerned with family life and the relations between the generations, the sex-gender distinction is murky at best. Families are formed, after all, through sexual coupling, conception, giving birth, and nurturing the young, and these behaviors draw upon biological sex differences, not merely socially constructed gender roles.

Human birthing also involves deep and seemingly irrational, intense feelings. Assuming "good-enough" socialization in their families of origin, most new parents feel a totally *irrational* attraction and love for their newborn. Here is this demanding, fragile, totally dependent 6- to 8-pound creature that disturbs our sleep, disrupts our plans, produces unpleasant odors, and turns red in the face and screams despite our care. Yet we submit to it, do without sleep, feed and clean it every few hours around the clock, and in a few weeks' time have fallen totally in love with it, satisfied with as small a reward as a fleeting smile long before such a smile could be intentional. The transition to parenthood may be a trial to many contemporary new parents because of competing desires and demands on them, but because of the intense feelings the experience evokes, it is also a powerful learning experience. As one woman put it, "children battle you into being more than you thought you were, into giving more than you thought you had in you to give. Those middle of the nights, you learn a lot about yourself" (McGoldrick, 1989, p. 211). Across cultures, the experience of pregnancy, birthing, and nursing gives women a biological edge in bonding with the neonate, quite apart from cultural rules differentiating the paternal from the maternal role in child care.

I stress reproductive sexual dimorphism and the irrational love for the newborn to emphasize an important respect in which I depart from the theoretical stance underlying a good deal of discussion on intergenera-

tional relations and intergenerational equity. In my judgment, there has
been an unfortunate encroachment, from population genetics and economics into sociology and psychology, of a rational-choice model of
human behavior, based on the calculus of self-interest, profit, and loss.
By this model, we give to others only on an expectation of getting
something back in return. There is little room in such thinking for altruism or irrational love, which I take to be of central importance in our
relations with our most intimate and significant others, surely including
spouses, parents, and children.[1] Robert Frank (1988), an economist who
broke with this tradition, suggests that researchers fear no greater hu-
miliation than calling some action altruistic, only to have a more sophisticated colleague later demonstrate that it was self-serving.

My major point here is that human behavior is as much determined by
our sexual physiology, emotions, norms, and the press of personal bi-
ography as by any rational calculation of self-interest, and to the extent
that sociologists and psychologists buy the economic model, they reduce the unique contribution they can make to our understanding of
intergenerational relations. It is highly doubtful that today's parents in
Western societies expect a full and fair return to them of their investment in parenting; rather, their parental expectations are fulfilled if their
children grow to a healthy, mature adulthood and invest in their own
children in turn. Indeed, far from expecting children to support them in
old age, data from a recent study by Paul Cleary and Mark Schlesinger
at the Harvard Medical School show that most older parents endorse the
view that parents should try to save money and property to pass on as
an inheritance to their children (P. Cleary, personal communication,
February 22, 1991). In sum, an exchange model, in my view, is inap-
propriate to an analysis of intimate relationships because satisfaction in
such relationships derives from an irrational love that prompts a partner
to want to do more for the other than the other partner gives.[2]

In approaching the design of our research on the relationship between
parents and adult children, gender held a central position as a major
predicted source of variation in the emotional quality and content of
interaction between the generations. The greatest intimacy, most frequent interaction, and most extensive pattern of reciprocal help were
predicted and were found in the same-sex dyad of mothers and daughters, and the least intimacy, interaction, and help exchange were predicted and were found between fathers and sons, with opposite-sex
dyads falling between the two same-sex dyads. A biosocial perspective
on gender draws upon the reproductive edge on attachment discussed
above, the persisting pattern of gender role division of parenting responsibility, and the greater stake women continue to have in family
relations than men have.

Counter to the view that family relationships have become more frag-ile and fragmented, it is my view that this does not apply to women nearly so much as to men. When Kingsley Davis reviewed trends in marital stability, fertility, and labor force participation of women, he concluded that marriage in Western societies was "falling out of fash-ion" (Davis & van den Oever, 1982, p. 507). Marriage and fertility rates have indeed fallen, while cohabitation and the divorce rate have in-creased, and there has been a marked increase in out-of-wedlock births. But it is probably also the case that men are more averse to long-term commitments than women. Whether a child is born inside or outside marriage, whether the marriage remains intact or is terminated by di-vorce, the relationship between mothers and children is not attenuated, though they may experience much stress and frequently impoverish-ment because the much lower pay scales of women often push divorced women and their children below the poverty line. By contrast, divorced men enjoy higher income following divorce (Hoffman & Duncan, 1988; Weitzman, 1985), typically renege on child support, and often fade as significant figures in their children's lives, with decreasing social contact over the years following divorce.[3]

Hence, several demographic trends in recent decades contribute to the tendency of women to have a greater developmental stake in main-taining close relations with their parents, siblings, and children than do men: More women than men remain unmarried to later ages; a higher proportion of women have children outside marriage; fewer women remarry following divorce; and widowhood often follows a serious re-duction in accumulated savings during periods of husbands' terminal illness. As a consequence, at all points of the adult life course, the probabilities are much higher that women will *need* the help and emo-tional support of family members than will men. It is probably also the case that women are aware that others will have need of *them*, as they observe their mothers' or their daughters' broken marriages, the strug-gle of divorced women friends rearing children alone, or their mothers' struggles to cope with ill husbands or reduced economic circumstances that go with widowhood. Hence women's developmental stake in fam-ily relationships is not a one-directional dependency, but rather an an-ticipated interdependence.

There are, of course, significant social changes taking place within American marriages, particularly those involving well-educated women with demanding jobs of their own. Many couples are coping with con-flicting demands from family and work, but there is no magical route to significant social change at the level of individual lives where that change must take place. As a consequence we are moving through a transitional era during which even husbands and wives who draw identical salaries do not necessarily show gender egalitarianism in family roles. Marriages in which women earn as much as their husbands, together with the smaller minority of marriages in which the wives earn more than their husbands, have higher rates of divorce than traditional marriages of higher earning husbands married to wives who are homemakers or employed part time (Benson-von der Ohe, 1987; Popenoe, 1988).

Consequently, whether as young unmarried women, or married women with husbands who cannot pull their weight as providers, or divorced women, or widows, women continue to have a greater probability of needing the financial, emotional, and social support of their kin than do men, and they can anticipate many occasions in life when they will be called on to meet the needs of other family members.[4]

Thus there were three factors that fed our expectation that gender continues to be a significant axis in the structure of intergenerational relations: First, women have a physiological edge in attachment to children, further intensified by parenting roles that still involve greater investment of time and energy on the part of mothers than of fathers. Second, a childhood of play and parental example perpetuates the socialization of girls to anticipate motherhood as a central role in adulthood to a much greater extent than childhood play or parental example encourages an emphasis on anticipated fatherhood for boys.[5] As a consequence, women acquire greater affiliative and relational attributes than men, as their mothers did before them. Third, the persistence of wage differences between men and women means that all the women in a family—mothers, sisters, daughters, and grandmothers—will experience many times of need and crisis during which the "latent matrix" of family relations (Riley, 1983) will come into play and women will provide help or be helped in turn.

Design of the Boston Kinship Study

The design implications of our approach to the study of relations between parents and adult children were these:

1. *Gender specification.* Implicit in the discussion above was the requirement that separate questions should be asked concerning mothers versus fathers or sons versus daughters of our major respondents, so that the four same-sex and cross-sex parent-child dyads could be compared.

2. *Life course focus.* We wished to chart how the parent-child rela-

tionship changes across the life course, so we designed a random probability sample with a representative age distribution of adults.

3. *Relationship focus.* We assumed the parent-child relationship might look very different, depending on which partner reported on it, much as Jessie Bernard (1972) has argued that every marriage is two marriages, a "his" and a "her" marriage. This led us to obtain access to the parents and adult children of our main sample respondents, yielding spin-off samples of some 600 parents and adult children of the respondents in the main sample.

4. *Personal biographies.* We assumed people live socially embedded lives with histories in the form of individual biographies. Nowhere is this more relevant than in a study of parent-child relations, since we carry the baggage of past experience and memory from early family life with us throughout our lives. We assumed that contemporary parent-child relationships show the mark of a shared past, and that recalled sentiment and family circumstances are as relevant as contemporary sentiment and needs in setting the parameters of interaction and obligation in the relationship. Hence we built into the design a number of variables dealing with experience in the family of origin. Combining data on the family of origin with identical measures on the family of procreation also permitted us to explore intergenerational continuity and transmission.

5. *Normative obligations within the kindred.* We wished to give special attention to how the parent-child relationship differs from other kin relations. How "special," in other words, are the obligations to parents and children compared to other kin or, indeed, to non-kin as well? To cover a wide array of kin types we used the factorial survey or vignette method, a technique developed by my husband and coauthor, Peter Rossi (Rossi & Nock, 1982), and described in greater detail below.

Hence, the overall data set we acquired consisted of a random probability sample in the Greater Boston area with personal interviews with 1,400 adults. At the end of the interview, respondents filled out a vignette booklet on normative obligations and a self-rating sheet on personal traits. With their cooperation, we obtained access to spin-off samples of 600 parents and adult children of these respondents, with whom telephone interviews were conducted, if they reside in the continental United States or Canada.

A Factorial Approach to Normative Obligations

A few words now on the design of the factorial approach to normative obligations. Social norms do not exist in a vacuum; they are embedded in highly specific ways in social life, with only a loose fit between actual behavior and the normative order. Much of the work of our legal system lies precisely in making discriminations about how legal norms apply to specific instances of behavior. The general principles are embedded in the statutes, but lawyers, judges, and juries have to fit specific instances of behavior into the meaning of those principles. We would thus expect much greater consensus when norms are stated in general terms, and much less consensus over how norms apply in specific behavioral contexts.

The implication of these assumptions is this: An understanding of the role of norms in affecting concrete kin relationships requires understanding how such general rules are interpreted in *specific* settings with *specific* kinpersons. Since there are so many potential applications to kin, the issue became how best to "sample" from among the many possible settings and the many different categories of kin to which the general norm may be applicable. Also implied is that our goal was to *infer* the general structure of obligations through the patterning of reactions to specific instances involving various kinpersons. We expect, for example, that most people would report higher obligations to a sibling than to a cousin, but we do not expect people to be able to articulate any general *principle* for why they feel this way.

The essence of the factorial method is to present respondents with a set of vignettes, each containing a short description of a specific kinperson in a common situation that might evoke a sense of obligation to make an appropriate gesture toward that person. We sampled social situations with four *crisis* occasions (unemployment, major surgery, a household fire, and a serious personal problem), and three *celebratory* occasions (having a birthday, winning an award, and moving into a new place). We sampled types of people with different degrees of relatedness to the respondent (74 relationships to kin, and to non-kin such as neighbors and good friends) and structured the relationships to distinguish between male and female, and between a married state and an unmarried or widowed state.

Gender was specified because we predicted that women kin would evoke greater obligation ratings than men kin, and marital status because unattached kin may evoke more obligation than married kin. Each respondent rated a set of 32 vignettes, *each set a separately and independently drawn probability-based sample of all possible vignettes,* of which there were about 1,600. Each vignette was rated by an 11- point 0-to-10 scale from "No obligation at all" to "Very strong obligation." In the case of crisis situations, the rating scales tapped either *expressive* help by providing "comfort or emotional support" or *instrumental* help by offering "some financial help." In the celebratory situations, the rating scales tapped either a gift by "giving something appropriate to the occasion" or a "visit" to the person described in the vignette. Some 1,200 respondents completed the vignette booklets, thus producing 36,000 vignettes for analysis.

Empirical Results of Normative Obligation Analysis

Symmetry of Normative Structure

The most important result of the aggregate level of analysis was the beautiful symmetry of the normative structure we found. Normative obligations to kin are highly structured and only modestly affected by variation in the situational stimuli. It mattered little whether the triggering circumstance was an impending birthday, major surgery, a household fire, or winning an award, nor whether the obligation was expressed in terms of emotional comfort, financial aid, a gift, or a visit. People are, however, more generous to a wider circle of kin in providing comfort than in giving money, which moves in a narrower circle of the kindred. What mattered most was the *degree of relatedness between ego and the kinperson in question*. Obligation ratings are more responsive to the number of connecting links than they are to the type of relative within a link category.

Thus, the primary kin ties to parents and children (with no connecting links) show the same average rating of obligation, 8.3 on the 0–10 scale. With *one* connecting link, we find roughly the same level of obligation to grandparents, siblings, and grandchildren, with an average hovering around 6 on the scale. Those connected by *two* links (nieces, nephews, aunts, and uncles) show an average of 4, and those with *three* connecting links (cousins) have an average of 3 on the 11 point scale. Ex-spouses, particularly if they remarried, evoke the lowest level of obligation of all, an average of 2 on the scale. Nor does it matter if respondents actually have a kinperson in their personal life to match the kin type in the vignette: The same rating level is given of obligation to, say, a brother, whether you in fact have a brother or not.

Unique Attribute of Parent-Child Obligations

A second major finding from the norm analysis is that the primary relationship both to parents and to adult children is relatively impervious to distinctions that matter in other kin relations. There is only a minor tendency to feel more obligation toward widowed mothers or unmarried daughters than to married parents or married children of either sex.

Significance of Gender in Normative Obligations

In all relationships other than the parent-child relationship, gender plays a significant role: Women kin evoke more obligation than men kin, e.g., grandmothers more than grandfathers. Gender of respondents plays a similar role, with women showing higher obligations to secondary and distant kin than men do.

Women are also important as *connecting links*, with significant increments to obligation level if the connecting link is a woman, especially a woman's mother, who is the connecting link to a maternal grandmother and a maternal aunt. When we asked, in another part of the interview, about which of the grandparents and which of the aunts or uncles had been particularly salient in childhood, as persons loved and admired in some special way, it was these same figures, the maternal aunt and maternal grandmother, who were most frequently cited. Thus the asymmetrical tilt to the maternal side of the family is found in all dimensions of the intergenerational relationship, whether affective closeness, frequency of social interaction, helping patterns, or normative obligations. When gender of both the respondent and the vignette kinperson is considered *jointly*, the female-female bond predominates in being associated with elevated obligation levels.

Norms and Behavior

There was considerable room for an analysis of the determinants of variation in the extent to which people felt obligated to others, because the standard deviation around the mean on the obligation ratings ranged between 2 and 4 points on the 11-point scale. That the past matters is clearly demonstrated in these data; we find that adult obligations to kin are rooted in early childhood experience. Using adjusted obligation indices (which measure by how much respondents expressed a stronger or weaker sense of obligation to kin than was *average* for the kin type rated), we found higher obligations to kin among those who grew up in intact families than among those whose families were broken by death or divorce, and in families in which high levels of parental affection and accessibility were reported than in families rated low in such parental affection and availability.

These findings were *independent* of a wide array of *current* characteristics such as age, gender, education, income, marital status, or ethnicity. Those whose parents had separated or divorced felt less obligation not only to parents but to children and other kin as well, underlining the important modeling the parent-child relationship represents, with ripple-out effects on obligations felt toward others in a kindred, and indeed even to current neighbors and friends. Parental absence in a child's experience, typically the absence of a father, may project the notion to a child that men have lower commitments to their children, a powerful lesson that may lower the child's sense of obligation to primary kin and other significant relatives as well.

Divorce has the effect on adults that broken homes have on children; both divorce and broken homes are related to lower levels of obligation to others, but it is divorced men (compared to married men) who show significantly weaker obligations to children, whereas divorced women do not differ from married women in this regard. Other analysis, on the impact of parental marital unhappiness, suggests that marital tension is associated with closer ties to mothers and maternal grandparents, and attenuated or strained relations with fathers and paternal grandparents. Divorce is not the beginning of the weakening of children's ties to fathers and paternal kin, but part of a process that began when the parental marriage became troubled.

Normative obligations are of intrinsic interest in their own right, but the story does not end there. They are implicated as significant predictors of the quality of current relations between parents and adult children. The average obligation rating of respondents was a significant predictor of interaction frequency and the level of help exchanged between the generations. Respondents who gave high obligation ratings also see their parents or adult children more frequently than those with low obligation levels, and more varied help is exchanged between the generations when obligation levels are high.

There are of course many predictors of interaction and help exchange rooted in the current circumstances in the lives of adults: Geographic proximity can facilitate or hinder interaction or patterns of help; poor health or stressed financial circumstances facing parents or adult children trigger more frequent contact and more extensive help. The point here is that over and above all such past and present predictors in our multivariate regression analysis, normative obligation level contributes a significant direct increment to the frequency of social interaction and the extent of help given or received between parents and adult children.

Gender and Expressivity

It will be recalled that following the personal interviews, respondents filled out a self-rating sheet on personal traits. These ratings provided three measures: *Expressivity, Dominance,* and *Drive.* The Expressivity scale is an abbreviated measure of femininity, the Dominance scale is a measure of masculinity, and the Drive scale taps traits more likely to reflect physiology, age, and metabolism, with the items "hard work-ing," "energetic," and "easily sexually aroused" loading on this factor.

The Expressivity scale was an important addition to the data analysis, because it provided an empirical handle on *why* gender is significant in so much of our research story. Tapping such qualities as being con-cerned to please others, eager to help others, affectionate, and able to express one's deepest feelings, the Expressivity scale consistently showed significant correlations in all the dimensions of the parent-child relationship we investigated. This was nowhere more apparent than in the normative analysis. Without the Expressivity measure in our regres-sion equations, gender of respondent was among the most significant predictors of obligation levels; with Expressivity *and* gender included as predictor variables, *only* Expressivity predicted obligation level. Men high on Expressivity, like women generally, showed higher obligation levels than men low on Expressivity.

By contrast, this pattern did not carry over to more directly behavioral measures on the parent-child relationship. For example, in the extent of help given to parents, Expressivity *and* gender are significant predictors. We take this to mean that many men and women respond to the needs of a parent even if such help goes against the grain of their personal inclination to be helpful and to please others. Custom and social expec-tations clearly play a strong role in the actual helping behavior, but any discrepancy between norm-driven behavior and personal inclination opens the door to elder neglect and abuse, as we are learning from a growing literature on elder abuse (e.g., Pillemer & Wolf, 1986).

Socialization and Kinship Norms

The finding that level of adult obligations to kin has its roots in early family life clearly implies that norms are learned at a very young age. An intriguing question remains: What is the socialization process that leads to the development of the highly structured symmetry of normative obligations? Clearly parents do not teach their children any rules of kin obligations in terms of the number of connecting links between children and various relatives they come to know. It seems likely that these norms are learned in much the way children learn to use language correctly, years before they have any knowledge of the rules of grammar. Just as the first kin words most children learn are terms for mother and father, so too the persons they first come to love and distinguish from all others are the parents, who remain the most significant "others" in the lives of children for many years. At the outer boundary of social encounters, the child also quickly learns to distinguish people either as trusted adults related to the children in some way or personally known by the parent or as strangers outside the family, toward whom parents alert children to be wary. At very young ages, children learn that the strange man their mother insists they kiss is an uncle met for the first time, whereas an equally strange man on Main Street is to be avoided.

Perhaps, as with language itself, it will never be possible to fully unravel exactly how children acquire an understanding of the rules of kinship. They acquire them through exposure to countless "examples" of kin types and appropriate behavior in interaction with them, much as they accumulate vocabulary and are able eventually to make synaptic leaps that produce grammatically correct whole phrases and sentences without learning the rules of grammar until fifth grade. So too, they may intuit from hundreds of discrete instances that more is owed to parents than to aunts, more to nieces than to cousins. In this respect, the normative structure of kinship is not different from other kinds of hierarchic structures, such as the prestige level of many different occupations, or the seriousness level of a wide array of different crimes, about which knowledge is acquired without ever being formally taught.

Nor should this surprise us. In a complex world, human rationality is bounded; we do not need to know just what the biochemical effects of cholesterol are on the body before we change our dietary habits. So too we do not need to know the rules of grammar to speak correctly, or the rules of kinship to behave correctly in relations with people in our kindred. Once learned in childhood, the distinctions among kin may provide a deep structure of learning that is highly durable, providing standards of behavior when new kin roles are occupied later in life. Having been a child, one knows something of what is expected of a parent; having been a nephew, one knows something of what is expected of an uncle, and so forth. By the same token, when early socialization is impaired, by a father's leaving home or a mother's inattention and distraction, there may be residual effects years later, indeed decades later, as we noted in the impact of parental divorce in childhood upon levels of obligation in adulthood.

Age and Normative Obligations

I have left for last an intriguing finding from our analysis of normative obligations: a negative relationship between age and level of normative obligations. The *older* the respondent, the *lower* the obligation level on all our norm measures. No matter what variables were introduced into multivariate analyses, age remained a highly significant predictor of obligation level, so this is a very robust finding. In hindsight, we wish we had measures not only of obligations respondents felt they *owed to others*, but obligations they felt were *owed to them*. We predict, but cannot demonstrate, that obligations owed to ego would show a similar negative correlation with age.[6]

What explains this life course pattern? Is there a progressive decline in normative obligations as actual obligations are fulfilled such that the elderly feel they have discharged their commitments? Is this a manifestation, in other words, of some general disengagement process? That hardly seems likely, since there is growing evidence that an appropriate model for what is taking place in old age is not so much *disengagement* as increased *selectivity* of activity and social interaction (Carstensen, 1987, 1991), with close kin and long-standing friends becoming of increasing subjective importance as adults age. Furthermore, the decline in obligation level is progressive across age groups, with no striking drop among the oldest adults. If actual fulfillment of obligations played any role, one would expect middle-aged adults to show higher obligations than the young or the old, but again, this is not the case; there is a steady linear decline across the life course.

Are cohort effects reflected here? But the age variable remains significant and negative when all the demographic variables that might tap such cohort effects are included in an analysis: Race, educational attainment, ethnicity, and family size do not reduce the negative effect of age on obligation level. In light of numerous complex secular trends, one might well have predicted cohort effects that would depress obligation levels among the *young*, not the old. For example, a wide array of theorists in historical demography, sociology, and political science have been writing for years about the secular trend in Western societies toward an increasing emphasis on autonomy and independence in child rearing (Alwin, 1988); privatization and utilitarian individualism (Bellah, Madsen, Sullivan, Swidler, & Tipton, 1985); and flexibility of attachment and detachment with individuals and groups (Dreitzel, 1984). Ron Lesthaeghe (1980, 1983) has argued that Western societies are undergoing a fundamental transformation from a child-centered culture to one that is self-centered, an orientation that gives priority to adults' own desires over the needs of others.

But were our data consistent with such secular trends, then one would expect that younger adults, who have lived their formative years as these shifts in values intensified, would feel much *less*, not *more* obligation toward others than older adults who grew up in more conformist times.

On the other hand, there are countertrends that are consistent with our research results. For one, parenting lasts for a much longer period of time: Eighty-six percent of Americans now graduate from high school, and one in five go on to higher education. For other young people, a poor labor market has also extended the years they remain at least partially dependent on parents. It is clear in our help exchange analysis that parents were providing high levels of help to their young adult children in their 20s and early 30s. The combined effect of these trends could press in the direction of recent cohorts of young adults feeling more obligation to parents than their counterparts felt in the past and, as a ripple-out effect, more obligation toward other kin than was the case for earlier cohorts.[7]

An even more interesting interpretation builds on James Coleman's point that life in dense urban areas and parental warnings to children to avoid contact with strangers weaken trust in the larger community beyond the boundaries of close kin that went with family life in small towns or in cohesive ethnic pockets of large cities in the past (Coleman, 1986). The trend toward finding people less trustworthy and the increase in crime that often makes living in urban communities a fearful experience may have the effect of psychological and social withdrawal into the known world of the safe and familiar. With parental concern for the safety of their children translated into repeated warnings to be suspicious of strangers approaching them, the response across cohorts of young people over the past several decades may be a narrowing of the "we" group to the world of family, kin, and friends, precisely because the "they" group has become a greater source of threat and fear.[8] The thinning of the social fabric noted by Bellah et al. (1985), Lesthaeghe (1980, 1983), Davis (1984), and others refers more to individuals' relationship to the larger community than it does to their relationship to the narrower world of kin and personal networks of known friends and co-workers. From this perspective, then, what seemed at first to be a conflict between our study results and larger secular trends may be consistent rather than contradictory.

Intergenerational Issues in the Future

More than 20 years ago, I made the point that adults can have ex-spouses but not ex-children (Rossi, 1968). If anything, that point applies more today than it did in the past, for the reason that it is the bonds between men and women that have weakened, whereas the bonds between women and children have not weakened to any great extent. In fact, with more children being reared by mothers alone, the mother-child bond may have intensified in recent years. Our Boston study has underlined the greater normative commitment of women toward kin, and of all adults to women kin, particularly if the connecting link is also a woman.

The triad of grandmother, daughter, and grandchildren, supplemented by female siblings and their children, provides not only open hearts, but open doors and open purses in times of need and trouble. These women represent not only latent resources in bad times, but ongoing social support in the good times as well. Women are indeed the "ministers of the interior," as Gunhild Hagestad (1986) put it, carrying much of the responsibility for family life and for intergenerational continuity. Sisters may become distant for some period in early adulthood as they establish their own families and work patterns, but later in life, particularly after the death of the mother who kept them informed about each other's lives, the sibling relationship takes on new significance. This may be particularly true in any cohort moving into old age that has had an elevated rate of childlessness, as today's elderly cohort has, and as many baby boomers will have when they in turn become elderly.[9]

Thus fluctuations in the fertility rate have important ramifications for the social support available to one cohort of elderly compared to another, but what changes may be the *composition* rather than the *size* or *availability* of kin support groups for the elderly. A clear implication is the need for family sociologists, gerontologists, and demographers to chart the likely characteristics of cohorts and the composition of their support networks as they move through the adult years into retirement.

There is another issue relevant to future fertility trends that is of importance to the intergenerational-equity debate: the assumption that low fertility is here to stay in Western societies. Indeed, a major reason for concern about Western societies' capacity to deal with the growing elderly population is the assumption that younger cohorts will continue to be very small in size compared to the baby boom cohort now entering middle age. Beneath many demographic projections, one finds a theoretical, rational, self-interest model borrowed from economics. Norman Ryder, for example, has recently argued that fertility will remain low because "parenthood is less rewarding, the ties between parent and child have weakened, and it matters less to a child's future what the parent does, and less to the parent's future what the child does" (1990, p. 448). Nothing in sociological research on status attainment supports such a proposition, nor does our research on the help exchange between the generations. It matters a great deal to children what their parents do for them as young adults, and as parents age their children remain emotionally salient and increasingly important to them.

What Ryder takes for granted in projecting a continuing low fertility rate is the human-capital argument that women's "time" is now too valuable to expend in home maintenance and child rearing, and hence is best used in labor with a monetary return. That same premise underlies the analysis of Richard Easterlin, Diane Macunovich, and Eileen Crimmins (Chapter 4 in this volume). Easterlin and his associates compare the financial well-being of today's baby boom cohort with that of comparable age cohorts in the 1960s and show that, despite worsening labor market conditions, the economic well-being of baby boomers has improved over their predecessors. They show, furthermore, that baby boomers are achieving this improvement largely through *demographic adaptations*, by postponing marriage, remaining childless or having fewer children, and high levels of spouse (read wife) employment.

I think it is quite possible that these demographic adaptations involve a frustration of personal desires for many adults in this cohort. In the depression years of the 1930s many young adults suppressed their desire for children simply in order to survive, yet changing economic and social circumstances following World War II led to an unexpected sharp rise in marriage and fertility rates, with many births to older couples still young enough to conceive the children they wished for but could not afford during the harsh times of the depression.

It should also be remembered that not all women now in the labor force are there by choice, and clearly many would prefer to work for fewer hours. Even among young married women with no children, Karen Seccombe (1991) has shown a strong preference for fewer hours of employment: The women in this youthful cohort actually worked on average 38 hours a week, but would prefer to work only 27 hours a week, 11 fewer hours. By comparison, the childless married men showed a preferred reduction of only 4 hours (40 actual versus 36 desired hours per week). In my own large classes of college students, there has been a growing gap over the past five years between the number of children students would "like" to have and the number of children they "expect" to have. Latent child hunger is no stranger in the land, and should economic circumstances change, many women would voluntarily withdraw from the labor force, reduce the hours they worked, postpone the return to employment following the birth of a child, or even go on to a third or fourth pregnancy as their mothers or grandmothers did before them.

Apart from the privileged stratum of American professional workers who are passionately committed to their occupations, there are millions who find that what they do on their jobs provides little intrinsic gratification, occasions much psychological stress, and often involves boredom to boot. Many women in their 30s are discovering what many men realize only in their 50s, that it is their personal lives away from the job that hold the greater meaning and more enduring significance. This surely plays a role in the growing proportion of men and women in their late 50s and early 60s who opt for early retirement.

One important shift of perspective is implicit in these comments: Those debating policy on intergenerational-equity issues might better look to the workplace, rather than to the family, for significant points of intervention through new public policies. Rather than encouraging research to explore how great the capacity or willingness is of families to absorb personal caregiving of the elderly and disabled, they might better focus on how to make the jobs people work at more rewarding, and the combination of job and family easier for young couples to manage. These efforts might even attract and hold older workers and hence reverse the trend toward early retirement.

It cannot be in the national interest for women to participate fully in workplaces structured for male employees with wives at home, at the expense of personal gratification in home and family, by not having children, limiting families to one child, or postponing childbearing to an age that entails risks of infertility or fetal defect. Nor is it in the interest of the nation, or the well-being of individual men and women, to diminish the time and energy invested in parenting; or to crowd out of their lives the time available to enjoy marital intimacy and quiet self-reflection, as so often demanded by busy work lives, with the result of stressed marriages, psychological depression, or cardiovascular disease.

In the past, economic insecurity was a social class issue, and the welfare state developed to narrow the *vertical* gap between rich and poor. In recent years, as Martha Ozawa points out (1989), the demographic changes that impact negatively on women create *horizontal* economic gaps based on gender rather than social class. The solutions to problems necessarily change as well. What is needed today is improvement in women's pay and job security; increased flexibility of working hours and family leaves; expanded child and elder care facilities and tax exemption levels; equalizing of the economic circumstances of couples with children and of those without children; provision of child and health care; development of new institutional devices to assure that men support the children they father; and empowerment of girls and women to take charge of their lives and value themselves for the qualities they have as women, whether or not they also take on the qualities associated with men. In other words, much of what concerns us today under the rubric of intergenerational issues could be solved by dealing with issues of gender inequity.

DeTocqueville long ago speculated that when the links between generations and the ties between blood and soil were finally broken, a certain carelessness about the future would appear, "with each man forever thrown back on himself alone, and there is a danger that he may be shut up in the solitude of his own heart" (1835/1969, p. 508). I suggest we should take him literally, that it is men he is speaking of. The tie between blood and soil has indeed been broken for most Americans, and there may well be greater isolation of adults from their contemporaries, but from the evidence we have on the parent-child relationship across the life course, the tie between the generations has not been broken, and it is women who have played and continue to play a critical role in assuring that it is not broken.

There may be wishful thinking involved here, but wishing can have real consequences if we put our minds and political energies to work. There is a half-forgotten language of generosity and community in America, as Mary Ann Glendon puts it, that gives rise to the hope that we might "still have the will, the charity, the vocabulary, and the vision to imagine a better way to live" (1987, pp. 141–142). Glendon speaks here as a comparative legal scholar with no reference to the fact that hers is a "female voice." Mine is also a female voice, and one that departs as Glendon does from the language of exchange theory and rational self-interest in preference for a language of caring and altruism.

Notes

1. Note sociologist Michael Hannan's comment in a review of Gary Becker's (1981) exchange theory on intimate relationships: "Becker's stark economic conception of actions cuts through the *romantic mist* that so often blinds social scientists" (1982, p. 68, italics added); and psychologist Daniel Goleman's summary of a similar trend in psychology: [I]n recent years, the mainstream of psychological research has looked at love almost as if it were a business transaction, a matter of profit and loss" (Goleman, 1985, cited in Frank, 1988, p. 186).

2. A study by Bernard Murstein, Mary Cerreto, and Marcia MacDonald (1977) explored whether the satisfaction couples report with their marriage is a function of the extent to which they are concerned with an equal contribution to the management of their households and leisure time use. They reported a *negative* correlation between indices of marital satisfaction and adherence to an exchange orientation, a flat contradiction of an exchange model prescription for a happy marriage. Note, too, that such results imply a rejection of what many feminists have espoused, marriage contracts that specify in detail what each partner expects from the other.

3. About 90% of never-divorced men over 60 years of age have weekly contact with children; by contrast fewer than half of ever-divorced men have this level of contact, and divorced remarried men's relations with stepchildren are as weak as their ties to their biological children (Goldscheider, 1990).

4. It is also the case that men have greater difficulty admitting it to themselves or actually seeking social support from others when they have genuine need for such help, a tendency no doubt rooted in male socialization pressures to be autonomous, independent, and self-reliant. This prompted Frances Goldscheider (1990) to argue that, in the decade ahead, it may be elderly *men* who will be at special risk, because family relations become more important in old age. Not only are men less willing to seek support, but it is unlikely that the children they fathered but abandoned, or the women who refused to marry them, will provide any caregiving to such men. While divorce and out-of-wedlock births leave women and their children at risk in early and middle adulthood, men will be at risk in old age, when employment-based resources are less important and family relations based on marriage and parenthood become more salient.

5. The experience of menstruation also contributes to an important sex difference in adolescence: Sex and reproduction are far more intimately linked in the minds of young females than they ever are for young males. I believe this sets the stage for greater sexual risk-taking by adolescent males than females, and low success rates in programs aimed at the adoption of effective contraceptive usage by teenager males. Ironically, fear of infection with the AIDS virus, a matter of direct personal concern to the young male, may stimulate far more consistent use of condoms than any urging of responsibility to avoid pregnancies has achieved in the past.

6. This would be the special mark of industrialized countries. Clearly in more traditional rural societies of the past or in predominantly peasant societies like mainland China, one would expect the elderly to feel more was owed to them than young adults feel was owed to themselves.

7. The prolongation of economic dependency on parents also raises serious questions about the traditional computation of "dependency ratios" in population research: Twenty rather than 15 years of age is more appropriate in industrialized societies for the cutoff definition of dependent young. So too, in light of longer and healthier lives in old age, the age of 65 as the cutoff for defining dependent elderly might more appropriately be extended to 70 or 75. Indeed, were this latter shift to occur gradually via extension of the age at retirement, the anticipated burden of an increasingly aging society would be greatly reduced. Using the Middle Series of census projections, the number (and percentage) of adults over 65 years of age in 1980 was 26 million (11% of the population), which will grow to 65 million by 2030 (21% of the population). But if 75 was the cutoff age, by 2030 there would be fewer then half as many dependent elderly, 30 million (or 10% of the population), not very different from the percentage over 65 fifty years earlier (in 1980). With 25 years remaining before the baby boom cohort retires, there is a long stretch of time for research, policy formation, and legislation to effect such a transition. (See Torres-Gil, Chapter 12 in this volume, for further discussion of this issue.)

8. Note, too, that our main sample was drawn in a highly urban area, the population-dense Boston Standard Metropolitan Statistical Area (SMSA). We do not know if the same negative relationship of obligation to age would be found in, say, a small midwestern town, or an isolated rural community in the Rockies.

9. In our research, we found siblings have special salience for childless elderly adults in an analysis of actual or intended written wills: The childless elderly were particularly prone to specify siblings, nieces, and nephews as beneficiaries—a lateral move that keeps funds and property "in the family," and shows the heightened salience of siblings and their descendants for childless adults (Rossi & Rossi, 1990, chap. 10).

PART V

The Politics and Polity of Age Groups and Generations

The chapters in Part V of this volume reinforce the importance placed on diversity, family, and sociohistorical context found in earlier chapters. But there is greater disagreement over critical issues and expected outcomes reflected in this part than in any other. Perhaps that is what is needed in a full discussion dealing with generational issues affecting policy issues in the 21st century. This is, after all, an era in which the politics of aging seem to be undergoing some notable transformations.

David Thomson, a social historian and sociologist from New Zealand and Cambridge University in England, suggests that the historical record provides contradictory messages to successive cohorts (Chapter 11). Rather than using cohort age as a basis for conceptual categorization, he audaciously employs the terms *selfish* and *unlucky* historical generations to describe the way some age groups play out their roles as taxpayers, workers, and beneficiaries. With the aging of the 20th-century welfare state experiment, there has occurred an inversion of emphasis within the electorate and among policymakers—a switch of the state's priorities from a focus on youth to a focus on the elderly over the past three and four decades of social policy development. Thomson predicts that generational relations will become increasingly strained in the future. In reflecting on the myth of a generational welfare contract, however, he acknowledges some shared generational experiences.

Fernando Torres-Gil, a policy scientist in public administration and social work, was a White House Fellow during the Carter years and staff director of a Congressional Committee on Aging during the Reagan presidency. He shares Thomson's views that those who advocate for today's elderly are often hamstrung by the success of their predecessors. Nonetheless, based on his firsthand experiences, Torres-Gil affirms the value of coalition politics—complete with its emphasis on reciprocity, intergenerational equity, and entitlements—as the political roles of the aged take new shape in the next century (Chapter 12).

The chapters by Thomson and Torres-Gil respectively play out the pessimistic and optimistic scenarios that Vern Bengtson set forth in his introductory chapter to this volume. The gap between them is so broad that even a commentator like Alan Walker, at once benign and prickly in his forecasts, fits plausibly in between. But *The Changing Contract Across Generations* holds no brief for relativism in policymaking circles. In the final chapter, by sociologist Jill Quadagno, historian Andrew Achenbaum, and social psychologist Vern Bengtson, proposals are made to use basic empirical research in confronting one of the thorniest policy dilemmas facing nations at the end of the 20th-century. What should we expect, in terms of the obviously changing demographic base of age groups in the next century? Will traditional bases for expectations and obligations among age groups be significantly altered in response to worldwide population aging? These are the challenges to future researchers and policymakers, as we move toward the 21st century of human experience.

11

A Lifetime of Privilege?
Aging and Generations at Century's End

David W. Thomson

To the outsider looking in, debates in the United States about *generation* are at once rich and chaotic, penetrating and shallow. They suggest both a populace and professions—gerontology in particular—bewildered by the changes now enveloping them. Much less of this is apparent elsewhere, not because others are more clearheaded but because their discussions of these matters have barely begun. In the United States, by contrast, the matter of generation has long been in the air, with depression children accredited special characteristics, baby boomers blamed for much else, and elderly and young pitted one against the other. Generation pervades political discourse and casual conversation, scholarly monograph and television chat show in ways without parallel abroad. I suspect this will change, and that all will soon have to grapple with generation: What might be learned from the example of the United States?

Most striking is the muddle. *Generation* means everything and nothing, for a host of concepts lurk behind the single word. It covers things as vague as a long sweep of time, a span of about 25 years, a particular point in the past, and all those alive at some moment. The most familiar, entangled notions are age groups, familial relations, and cohorts (groups defined by sharing a common experience, usually birth, in a particular decade) (Bengtson, 1989, and Chapter 1 in this volume; Marshall, 1984; Riley, 1992). Yet only in rare instances do we find consistency in an author, even after time is spent on definitions and exhortations for clarity. Few boundaries are set, generations-as-birth-cohorts slide into generations-as-age-groups and back again, and genealogical language abounds.

The generation debate betrays other problems. First, it is too narrowly focused on Social Security and the distribution of public expenditures. There is a very great deal more than these to relations between generations, however defined, even if our concern is just with interactions between generations and government. Second, the discussion is of a decidedly political bent. It is as though for many the only interest in generation is if it can help explain current politics, and if this fails the concept is rendered unimportant. This political bent, too, needs to be thrown out.

Third, the literature on age and generation (from gerontologists, other professionals, and political commentators) is marked by hesitancy, even timidity, with calls for decisive political vision and leadership on generational issues seldom being matched by parallel daring with research hypothesis or methodological initiative. Especially coy are the neoconservatives—self-styled hard men who rush to insist that nothing they may say is to touch the aged (Mead, 1986; Murray, 1984). This is understandable, yet unacceptable. To raise questions about generation is to bring in the elderly sooner rather than later, and political fortunes, research funding, and career success can hinge upon the display of a suitable solicitude toward the old. The pressures are real, but must be put firmly to one side.

A first step will be greater clarity of generational concepts, as many have insisted before. We lack, in the English language at any rate, a flexible or comprehensive vocabulary of generation, and this should ideally be remedied. Bengtson and his colleagues, like others, have urged that we reserve *generation* for familial relationships, and employ *cohort* to mean the group born in a common era (Bengtson, 1990). This is reasonable, but has met with little success, for several reasons. The proposal runs counter both to the major theoretical works on generation by Mannheim (1928/1952), and to the widespread current equation of generation with elderly and youthful age groups of the present moment.

In short, we do face definitional problems, but the complexities lie in more than semantics. It is the very evocative indefinability of *generation* that gives it a richness worth pursuing: Would *class* have captured the intellectual and emotional attention of so many for so long, if its meanings were clear-cut at the outset? We will have to live with and work through the confusions of generation for some time yet—each being specific in his or her own use of the term, and yet not expecting agreement on a single meaning. The chapters in this volume mark a step forward in this respect.

Generation here will mean a birth cohort to which history has given a distinctive character and unity. We are, in other words, concerned with Mannheim's classic *generation*—a group of people, linked by birth in a shared span of years, who as a consequence accumulate through life a common set of experiences that is peculiar to them and to no others born either earlier or later (Mannheim, 1928/1952). There is no suggestion in this that birth date alone matters in life, or that *cohort-cum-generation* enjoys a coherence or explanatory power that renders class, gender, race, and the like irrelevant. But it is to argue that, in certain crucial respects, history does seem to be giving some birth cohorts forceful, linked, and lasting experiences that transcend their many divides.

What follows is one social historian's assessment of the public significance of generation-as-cohort at the end of the 20th century. I suggest that generational tensions will increase in all societies, and that the "equity" debate will revive from its temporary torpor. However, it will not be the crude old-versus-young argument, which spluttered and faltered in the United States in the 1980s (Marshall, Chapter 7 this volume), but a more subtle and disturbing argument, rooted in the diverging life paths of the earlier born and later born. There were elements of this, articulated poorly and little acknowledged, in the first round of debate in the 1980s. These elements will become increasingly clear in the years ahead, with "lucky" or "selfish" generations—not age groups—well to the fore.

The reasons for this increasing tension have little to do with demographics, for like a number of others, I am not persuaded by either historical or contemporary evidence that there are any close, necessary, or automatic connections between demographic conditions and social or political decisions (Marshall, 1981; Walker, 1990a). Nor is the explanation in economics—it is not clear to me, for instance, that there is any unavoidable upper limit to the shares of national income that can be channeled to the aged, by either public or private means, before things start going badly wrong. Neither does the driving force lie in short-term crises—wars, recessions, business cycles, budget deficits, national debt, or the like. Instead, the potential for mounting generational conflict is structured into the modern state, though this was hidden during the first midcentury decades of large-scale collective action. My assessment will be pessimistic, perhaps unacceptably so to many in the United States for whom an upbeat ending still seems *de rigueur*. No easy options will be offered, for I can see none: A sharpening tension that is embedded in some of the most cherished values, institutions, and achievements of the last half-century presents no obvious remedies.

For years social scientists have been surveying the literature on generations, and asking that theory be left alone for a while in favor of empirical studies of generation in specific historical instances (e.g., Kertzer, 1983). Historians have not responded, or have done so only to conclude that generation cannot be made a significant variable in social history (Spitzer, 1973). My venture is different. Rather than posit that generation is a significant social force and seek evidence for this, I observe that history appears to be delivering contradictory experiences to successive cohorts, and speculate that this will lead to generation becoming an important dynamic. I go no further—a theory of generation is not on offer.

My concern will be with something more limited than the total experiences of generations. The guiding question is, How are successive generations affected by the modern state? Late-20th-century populations surrender large elements of individual resource and risk, as well as opportunity and freedom, to a common pool. In doing so they give to governments immense powers to direct the lifelong fortunes of individuals and generations. How has that power been exercised? The whole of the actions of the modern state are our interest—not just the effects of the familiar expenditures on social security, health, or education, but also the wider consequences of financial regulation, import control, interest rate setting, taxation demands, taxation exemptions, housing subsidies, inflation management, savings incentives, labor laws, and more.

The discussion in this chapter is of modern states in general, as a species. It draws heavily upon my own research in New Zealand, upon an early stage of my companion work on Australian, British, and United States data, and upon a wider reading of the comparative European literature (Thomson, 1989, 1991, in press). Through this research I detect a standard historical pattern that allows something to national peculiarities, but has more to do with the inherent dynamics of mass group action. Not all have moved along the same path at equal pace—New Zealand and the United States have perhaps gone furthest—but all are heading the same way. While others have much to learn from the long history of generational debates in the United States, so too could her scholars gain by looking abroad. Much of what has happened in the United States in recent decades has close—and not derivative—parallels elsewhere, and many current explanations that are tied to United States demography, constitution, politics, culture, or character fall apart when this is appreciated.

The Gamble on Youth

My focus is on historical trends, but their significance becomes clearer if we first recall what all have assumed would and must happen through time: The gulf between myth and reality is about to force a painful reassessment. The pooling of resource and risk through the mechanism of the nation-state, a process that began well before the present century but accelerated particularly rapidly in its middle decades, is underpinned by a number of unspoken yet crucial shared assumptions (Thomson, 1991, chap. 1). The less important of these have to do with immediate behaviors—who is to do or get what in the present moment—and it is to be regretted that these matters of *horizontal and vertical equity*, to employ the jargon of the trade, have captured all the attention.

More vital to individuals, generations, and the whole pooling enterprise are unexplored beliefs about the long term—matters of *temporal equity* we might call them. These matters were on the minds of politicians and scholars at midcentury, in contrast to their disappearance from debate after about 1960 (Burbidge, 1987). Integral to earlier discussions of social justice and security was a recognition that in establishing mass poolings, populations were playing with the assets and options of future persons in new ways. This created a vital trust between the adult voters of the moment and those who would come after.

An undefined compact was hinted at by many—the *implicit welfare contract between generations* I have called it, though it might be better to think of it in terms of a legal trust relationship, with the state as executor (Laslett, in press). The gamble and dangers for the later born were warned about, but in the face of pressing needs for reconstruction and revival following fertility decline, depression, and war, the demands of the moment took precedence over a more sober assessment of long-term risk.

Most of these assumptions about future behaviors are rather obvious. Everyone would have to belong to the pooling, and no generation could later decide to opt out; participation was not capricious or a matter of personal choice but governed by clear, agreed-upon, and enforceable rules; individuals, regardless of when they were born, could and must expect consistent treatment, and contributions drawn from and benefits paid to similar persons would be alike now and in the future; the whole exchange would continue indefinitely—no cutoff could be envisaged; all would retain faith in the wisdom of the pooling; and the demographic and other resources needed to run the exchanges through time would always be available, with the state using its powers to ensure this. In essence the assumptions are of continuity, consistency, and reciprocity, of a give-and-take that obligates all to act in similar and regular ways into an infinite future.

Such unvoiced notions and their significance may be made concrete by a simple test. Try imagining that such a compact or trust between earlier and later born does *not* exist. My personal participation in the modern state, costing me some millions of New Zealand dollars in compounded personal income that is lost to the taxes and other charges I must pay through life, is not unlike membership in an insurance scheme. A private insurer might offer me a policy whose terms read

> Your premiums will be $20,000 a year for life, but we have no idea what your returns will be, what form they might take, whether they will exceed or fall short of your payments, whether they will be greater or smaller than those of the earlier born, or even whether we will bother to make you a return at all.

I doubt that many would take up such an offer, and it can be no different with citizen and state. An assumed contract between generations has to exist to make the individual's gamble tolerable: Mass collective action in the absence of a contract is inconceivable.

This, then, is the issue for the historian: Have states behaved as they must, if the interests entrusted to them by all generations are to be protected and advanced? They have not, and there are no exceptions to this yet known to me. For most nations the day of reckoning with this fact seems to be arriving in the 1990s. Incessant changing of the rules of participation have produced the first "welfare generation," a birth cohort most of whose members, affluent and poor alike, have been treated uniquely generously through life by the modern state, relative to their successors. The boundaries of the welfare generation vary nation to nation, but in general encompass those born in the later 1920s, in the 1930s more particularly, and in the early 1940s. Its members were too young to experience the worst of depression or war directly, and have spent the whole of their adult lives in the most prosperous and expansionary era in known history. They reach old age bearing the assets and expectations of that experience, an experience not being repeated for their successors. And they will be the elderly of the 1990s and 2000s. The changing of the rules has also produced successors who have little reason to see the state in the same happy light, or indeed, for a great many as anything other than a persisting barrier to the advancement of themselves and their children.

The idea of *generation* in all its tangled nuances will be dragged powerfully and perhaps tragically into play. The rights and obligations of members of the welfare generation will have to be assessed in view of their lifelong interactions with others, and of what may increasingly be seen as their unsatisfactory history of exchange with those born both before and after them. But welfare generation individuals will then be old, and what is due the elderly, and due parents and grandparents, will be pressed with vigor and validity.

In the remainder of this chapter I want to explore just one question: How have incompatible generational experiences come about at the hands of the modern state? The matter of *why*, like so much else, must be passed over for now, except to note that I blame no persons or generations. Nor can I find satisfactory explanations in our standard "causes"—the ages or natures of populations, electorates, voters, politicians, or parties. Much of the change that concerns us here preceded any aging of the electorate, and companion changes have been introduced widely by varied populaces and political systems outside the United States. We must look instead to the system of exchange itself, and to the problems of sustainable, long-term management of a common resource (Thomson, 1991, chap. 6).

In simple outline, contrasting generational experiences have arisen from the inversion of emphasis and purpose that has overtaken all modern states in recent decades. This shift I shall call *political aging*, or the *aging of the welfare state*, to distinguish it from the secondary but not unrelated population aging with which all are more familiar. From the 1930s to the 1960s most expansion of government activity was for the benefit of young adults and their children, that is, for individuals in the early stages of the life cycle. The counterpart was a series of impositions upon the middle-aged and elderly, and this balance gave the vague *implicit welfare contract between generations* its substance and shape.

The citizen-taxpayer was to expect major benefits in the early adult years—through tax relief; housing assistance; veterans' programs; free or subsidized health and education services for children; employment protection through labor laws and currency and import controls; low interest rates; cash benefits (outside the United States) for children; and more. The costs were to be repaid in middle age and later, through heavy taxes, restrictions upon interest earnings, limited public services, and small old-age incomes.

But in the last two decades these priorities have been reordered toward the interests of the later stages of the life cycle, and that inversion threatens notions of continuity, consistency, and reciprocity. The switch from youth to elder priorities has been observed by many before me, although most have focused upon social security alone. But the implications for temporal equity have passed largely unremarked. For not only does the reversal challenge the fundamentals of an ongoing exchange. It also has occurred in a particular historical period, with specific generational consequences. Those who gained most from the "youth state" in turn benefit doubly by spending their middle and later years in a new "elder state" redesigned in step with their own aging. Nor is it intended or will it be possible to maintain an equivalent "elder state" for those who follow them into old age in the next century. The losses of those who follow are to compound through life, and it is this that gives generational debates an urgency at century's end.

The Citizen as Taxpayer

Although the shift of priorities from youth toward age has been apparent in many spheres, the assessment of lifelong generational fortunes remains little considered, and many of my examples must appear impressionistic and experimental. In offering them I hope others will be stirred or stung into extending the inquiry: At the least they will raise some of the questions for which we should prepare ourselves. One especially neglected area is taxation. Most people's income taxes are their immediate and visible contribution to the pool, their membership dues that earn entitlement to current and future returns. Yet despite this, research still centers upon taxation in the current moment only, and upon persons of different income levels but not different ages, life stages, or cohorts; and determinedly eschews issues of lifetime contribution.

Few people can be unaware that income tax has risen substantially over the past half-century, or that the worker of middle income in the 1970s and 1980s everywhere paid two or three times as large a fraction of earnings in income taxes as did a comparable worker in the 1940s, 1950s, or 1960s. (I treat as meaningless the fiction of a distinction between compulsory general taxes and compulsory social security contributions.) Few can remain unaware, too, that "real" or inflation-adjusted earnings and purchasing powers have not increased in the same order, or that in consequence the amount of lifelong taxes paid depends crucially upon when one is born.

The changes go a good deal further, however. During the past half-century, tax rates and exemptions have been restructured in a great many ways, with unequal effects upon various age groups and hence upon generations. High marginal-tax rates have come and gone, as have spouse and family allowances and rebates, mortgage interest deductibility, work-related exemptions, tax-free status for life insurance or superannuation payments, and more. These shifts have been neither random nor patternless. In general, midcentury governments used rates and exemptions, very deliberately, to lower taxes upon young adults and especially those with children, and to leave the financing of the modern state to the middle-aged, and to the elderly to a lesser extent.

This pattern has been reversed in the last 25 years, in unannounced, incremental, and yet unmistakable fashion. Tax allowances for dependent children existed in most nations from the 1940s to the early 1970s, but withered or disappeared soon thereafter (see, e.g., Central Statistical

Office, CSO, 1950–1990, on the United Kingdom; Levy, 1987, on the United States; Thomson, 1991, on New Zealand). Allowances for non-earning spouses went the same way (Britain is highly unusual in retaining a substantial "married man" tax allowance, or in continuing to call it that). Exemptions for life insurance premiums (in Britain, for instance) or employee pension and superannuation contributions (New Zealand and Australia, for example) have been cut or ended altogether, or retained only for the earlier born.

The age and generational implications of such moves are obvious, and other taxation trends reinforce them. In a number of nations the withdrawal of what might be called youth-favoring exemptions has been paralleled by the retention or introduction of elder-favoring ones. Britain's special tax allowances for the retired, for instance, were increased, while child allowances disappeared. Earned income, predominating in early life stages, was in general treated more favorably for tax purposes until the 1970s than was investment income, the preserve of those in later years of life. This was done through greater allowances for work-related expenses, and in some cases through deliberate earned-income exemptions, as happened in Britain. These allowances, too, have gone in the last 20 years—employees can make fewer and fewer deductions from taxable income, and the British penalties for unearned income ended in the mid-1970s. Death duties, a major source of direct taxation earlier in this century, have everywhere shrunk dramatically in the last two decades as affluence has spread, in consequence freeing the aging of the pressure to disperse assets and income.

Further, the universal move in the 1970s and 1980s toward fewer tax bands and lowered top-tax rates—toward less progressivity in short—was of maximal advantage to the welfare generation, then in middle age. All income statistics show that few of the highest incomes go to persons in their 20s or 30s, and most gains from these recent tax reforms were therefore gifts to those in their 40s and above. The concurrent massive decline in tax payments by the self-employed and by companies everywhere worked to the same end, since the holders of shares, like the self-employed, are predominantly in the second half of life (Page, 1983; Pechman, 1985). The steep rise in national insurance, social security, or payroll taxes, as general tax rates shrank, worked again to move taxation onto the working rather than the retirement years. New Zealand went even further: Tax exemptions for superannuation contributions have now been replaced by exemptions on payouts.

The cumulative effect has been a distinct shift in the burden of taxation onto the young, those formerly thought deserving of protection against such costs. There may be arguments for this, but the switch makes notions of generational consistency and reciprocity, or of long-

Table 1.   Income Tax Rates, 1945–1986

	New Zealand		United Kingdom	
	Single[a]	Family[b]	Single[c]	Family[d]
Year	(A)	(B)	(C)	(D)
	I. Income tax as a percentage of gross income			
1945	11	5		
1951	17	10	15	4
1956	15	9		
1961	15	10	19	9
1966	16	11		
1971	20	15	28	16
1976	25	21		
1981	27	23	30	26
1986	29	27	29	25
	II. Income tax less family benefits, as a percentage of gross income			
1945		−13		
1951		−3		1
1956		0		
1961		0		5
1966		3		
1971		10		16
1976		16		
1981		18		19
1986		18		19

Notes: [a] Taxes on median income for all New Zealand men aged 25–34, if only exemption claimed was the personal one.
[b] Taxes on median income for all New Zealand men aged 25–34, if only exemptions claimed were for the parent, spouse, and two children.
[c] Taxes (including national insurance contributions) on average earnings for all men in full-time manual manufacturing employment, if the only allowance claimed was the personal one.
[d] Taxes (including national insurance contributions) on average earnings for all men in full-time manual manufacturing employment, if the allowances claimed were for a married man and two children.
Sources: Thomson (1991, chaps. 2 and 3); CSO (1950–1990).

term security and justice, increasingly hard to sustain. Various ways of analyzing the consequences are possible, and I offer the New Zealand and United Kingdom experiences as instances of what this might show; nothing I have yet seen indicates that the results would be very different elsewhere. (The analyses that follow are from Thomson, 1991.)

A first analysis is of income tax rates faced by identical individuals or tax units at various points in time, as summarized in Table 1. In the New Zealand calculations gross income is the median income for all men aged 25 to 34, as reported by them at the 5-year national censuses. British data are less specific, and here I indicate the tax treatment of men who had the median gross earnings for all full-time manual workers in manufacturing industries, regardless of age; this method unfortunately downplays the worsening tax position of young men over time. Column A shows income taxes as a percentage of gross earnings if the men had all been single, Column B if they had been married with two small children and a spouse without earnings of her own. Columns C and D are the British counterparts to A and B, and compulsory National Insurance (social security) contributions are included in taxes.

The estimate of taxes is made in two stages. Step I indicates the rates if we assume that the only tax exemptions available were the standard personal and dependents ones. The assessment thus overestimates probable tax payment in the earlier decades, though less so in the later decades, given the availability, then disappearance, of many work-related tax allowances. But even so, the shift over time is striking. The "price of participation," in simple income tax terms, has doubled and trebled. Consistent treatment for similar persons born in different times is not in evidence, and this remains true as the exercise extends away from the median. Step II takes account of the cash benefits paid automatically since the mid-1940s on the basis of children. For many families in New Zealand the substantial family benefits were larger than the total, maximized income taxes being assessed against them, even if children were as few as two, and the result was the negative effective tax rates shown. Better age-specific income data for Britain would in all likelihood return a similar result.

The table makes clear that rates of contribution in the form of income taxes depend vitally upon date of birth. Effective rates of sacrifice, as we might call them, are now for many 10 and more times as great, as a fraction of income, as for similar persons born two or three decades earlier. Nor should we be confused about nominal and real incomes here. In the New Zealand case, for instance, as in the United States, real purchasing power after adjustment for inflation was about 15% lower by 1986 than in the 1960s for persons under about age 40. That is, the new tax impositions are on smaller real incomes. Moreover, actual tax payments for large portions of younger adults in the 1950s and 1960s were well below the theoretical maximums indicated by the table. Not all tax exemptions are being counted; the half who had less than median earnings paid fewer taxes still; and most adults received more than two child benefits (the average family size for the cohort was closer to three in Britain, closer to four in New Zealand). In 1951 only about one quarter of all New Zealand men aged 25–34 faced a positive effective tax rate, as calculated in this way. By 1986 almost all of that age did so (and few of them faced a tax rate less than about 15%).

A second analysis takes account of the changing composition of co-horts—of the numbers of men and women in paid employment, married and single, total numbers of children, and receipt of social security or welfare payments of all types. This analysis explores what might have been the overall cohort income and income taxes, at various points in time. I estimate that the effective income tax rate for all persons aged 25–34 in New Zealand was 6% around 1951, 4% in 1961, and at least 12 and 16% in 1971 and 1981. The much-publicized mushrooming of un-employment, single-parent, sickness, and other payments to young adults, a development apparent in all states in the 1970s and 1980s, should be seen in this light.

A third analysis is more speculative, both philosophically and techni-cally, though central to any serious generational study. What might an individual's or a cohort's lifetime taxes total—and by extension, what relation do these taxes bear to gains? Estimates in terms of dollars are straightforward enough, but since the real purchasing power of popu-lations changes over time, it makes little sense to count the few dollars paid in taxes in 1950 in the same way as the thousands of dollars paid by the same or similar persons in 1990, even when inflation adjusted. Each represents a different fraction of gross income and hence a varying degree of personal sacrifice, and a flexible *unit of sacrifice* is needed to account for this. In this instance I assess income taxes as a fraction of average gross earnings in the years in which they were paid, and so derive one measure of relative sacrifice. So long as all generations are treated consistently the method should serve our limited comparative purposes. For the Earlys—a "typical couple" born in 1930, with median income, and average on other characteristics for their cohort throughout life—income tax will sum to about 6 years of average pay, 6 units of sacrifice, between leaving school and retirement. (Postretirement taxa-tion is treated separately for all cohorts in this analysis.)

Similar assessments for later cohorts proceed along parallel lines, though they necessarily involve guesses about future tax trends. Gov-ernments seek to assure us that income taxes will not rise again; de-mographers and economists insist that they must, if we are to maintain even part of the public spending to which we have grown accustomed. I assume here, very conservatively, that overall tax rates neither rise nor fall in the coming decades. If this is so, then it will leave the Lates—born in 1955 and otherwise similar to the Earlys—paying at least 15 units of sacrifice by age 60, more if tax rates rise or retirement age is raised, as most now anticipate. In other words, their most visible of contributions to the collective pooling will cost them about three times as much per-sonal sacrifice, relative to income, as their identical predecessors.

The analysis was then repeated for those with income above and below the median, and it was striking to find how common have been mounting exactions from the later born. For individuals and for families, at well above and well below median income, or with smaller and larger than average numbers of children, effective tax rates multiplied much as they did in the median case reported here. In view of this, I hold it valid to speak of some shared generational experiences that transcend the more obvious divisions.

It is, of course, reasonable to insist that contributions take many forms other than income taxes, even if these are perhaps the most politically sensitive contributions. People of all birth dates pay indirect taxes or user charges for public services, and they make large unpaid inputs by rearing children, maintaining homes, assisting relatives, raising funds for schools, and so on. But it is not clear that these are as generation specific as income taxes appear to be, or are distributed in contrary patterns in generational terms. For instance, the recently introduced health service charges in the once-free public systems of New Zealand and Britain have predominated in areas of medical care used by young adults and children rather than by the aged. Or again, most government planners assume that those who will be middle-aged and elderly in the next century will have to do more informal caring for relatives than is the case for current cohorts in that life stage. In other words, throwing things other than income taxes onto the generational scales does not work at once to right the imbalances suggested above, and may perhaps accentuate them still further.

The Citizen as Worker

What of generational returns, of benefits drawn from the pool? These take perhaps even more forms than do inputs, and will prove more troublesome to pin down. But as with contributions, some generational patterns are becoming clear—the prizes, too, are being rationed by date of birth. This results from a range of government actions and inactions, perhaps the most significant of which have little to do with social security or public spending. The postwar states, as many have observed before me, were concerned first and foremost with securing employment, and with the well-being that would flow from employment to workers and their families. Social security, health, public education, and the like were adjuncts, or means of assisting the majority to get and hold jobs, and of providing a modest protection and living to those unable to work.

In support of the goal of secure employment, governments regulated their economies heavily, in the belief that the market would always fail to deliver secure employment and good earnings if left to itself—the 1920s and 1930s had taught them that. Policies varied from nation to nation, and between large and small economies, but much was pursued in common. These policies included foreign exchange controls to protect local production; import quotas, bans, and duties to shelter home industries and employments; subsidies, grants, and low-interest loans to new businesses; large-scale development of infrastructure using public money; direct tax-funded investment in nationalized or semipublic enterprises; labor laws to improve work conditions and boost remuneration; superannuation incentives to stabilize work forces and reward current employees out of future production; soldier rehabilitation schemes to ease young men into jobs, families, and homes; education and training programs to promote the young into the work force; rent controls to hold down costs for businesses and young families; and mortgage and interest regulations forcing older lenders to make advances to governments and to younger borrowers at rates favorable to borrower rather than to lender.

The impacts of these policies can be debated. No one doubts that a surge occurred in investment, full employment, and real earnings from the time governments adopted these priorities. What is questioned is how much of the uplift was coincidental and would have happened anyway. But in considering generational experiences this distinction is perhaps not too crucial, for few can perceive it. Younger adults enjoyed fast-rising incomes, job security, promotions, low-interest loans, and the like; and the avowed purpose of governments was to provide these very things, if necessary at the expense of the earlier born. The middle-aged and elderly faced, in consequence, incomes and consumption held back in order to assist in nation building, population growth, and investment for the future. All this gave added meaning and substance to the compact between generations—an implicit employment contract was to complement the welfare contract.

Little of this use of government power now remains. In the last 25 years, central functions of the modern state—employment protection, lifelong income enhancement, long-term investment in human and capital goods—have been abandoned, with highly unequal impact upon earlier born and later born. The break came most noticeably in the early 1970s, and has accelerated since.

Exchange controls have been eased or removed altogether, and with that the deliberate attempt to protect local employment has ended. Import restrictions and duties have been lowered or abolished, to similar effect. Expansion and even maintenance of infrastructure has slowed sharply. Interest rate controls have been reduced and inverted, with governments now manipulating them to maximize gains for persons in later life. Subsidies for new businesses, for research, or for training of younger workers are still talked about, if little in evidence, while spending on redundancy, disability, early retirement, and other measures to ease the financial status of older workers has been expanded many times over. Formal contracts and informal understandings on tenure or job security have been replaced by a growing "casualization" of the work force, under which the later born enjoy fewer of the leave entitlements, superannuation packages, promotion ladders, or health insurance available to predecessors doing the same job. Deficit financing has replaced balanced budgets, pushing up interest rates and internal and external borrowing, to the immediate profit of older lenders and to the lasting cost to the later born, who face repayment of the collective debt.

The most obvious manifestations in private lives of these macrolevel policy changes are perhaps seen in employment and earnings; the effects upon incomes I shall note presently. Levels vary, but across many nations around one half of the high unemployment of the 1970s and 1980s was borne by those under age 30. Historical comparisons indicate that there is nothing natural or inevitable about this—until the 1970s it was always the middle-aged who bore most of the unemployment. It is true that those past about age 55 have been leaving work forces in growing numbers, but while some describe this as "unemployment," most studies show it to be in large part a voluntary response to the enhanced income and leisure that now go with aging (e.g., Cribier, 1989, on France; Johnson, 1988, on Britain; Merrilees, 1986, on Australia; Wadensjo, 1990, on Sweden; Wolfson, 1986, on Canada).

Meanwhile, the earnings of the young who do secure full-time employment have everywhere been falling, relative to those of older employees. In Britain in 1975, for example, the median gross earnings for all men aged 21–24 in full-time employment were 79% of those for men aged 40–49, but just 67% by 1988. For those aged 25–29 the fall was from 92 to 82% (CSO, 1950–1990). In New Zealand, Australia, and the United States the data are similar in scale, even before taxation changes and their unequal age effects are added into the account (Denison, 1985; Easterlin, 1987; Easterlin, Macunovich, & Crimmins, Chapter 4 in this volume; Radner, 1985; Thomson, 1991).

Less quantifiable is the decline for the later born in what we might call lifetime remuneration. Some aspects are immediate—the loss of sick pay, leave allowances, or redundancy protection that goes with casualization. More significant yet may be the shrinkage in superannuation coverage now being reported in some states, and the increasingly parlous condition of employee pension trusts in many others. Various additional fringe benefits granted during the heady days of economic growth are also being curtailed, creating what Martin Rein (1981) has called an insider-outsider effect, pitting those (earlier born) with stable employment against those (later born) without. In general this rationing is in effect occurring on the basis of birth dates, with fringe benefits being retained for those who already have them but denied to those coming later. The popular term for this—"grandparenting"—is immensely significant, and potent, in a generational study.

Many structural or market force reasons are advanced to explain these shifts, the most noted perhaps by Easterlin: Young workers of the 1970s and 1980s had the misfortune to be too numerous (Easterlin, 1980, 1987). This argument has force so far as it goes, but can be challenged. Countries with baby booms of different timing and scale—the United States, Britain, Sweden, and New Zealand, for instance—nevertheless all gave young adults declining relative incomes and less secure employment in the last 20 years. Governments may not have been in full and conscious control of events—they never are. But the later born have experienced governments that not only failed to counteract cyclical and structural forces harmful to their interests, but that also declared through their policies that their sympathies lay with others. Predecessors had not been expected to accept such governments.

The Citizen as Beneficiary

The final area of political aging I want to consider is public expenditure. Given the greater attention addressed to this in all countries, the literature is more extensive and the trends even less in doubt. An expansion and redirection of social security expenditure is reported widely, as one instance of the shift. Everywhere pensions to the elderly were kept modest in the early postwar decades, with the elderly commonly receiving around one quarter or one fifth of the average wage. The real innovations of midcentury lay elsewhere, for in many nations old-age pensions had been in existence for several decades already. What was new and distinctive in midcentury were family allowances, with veterans' assistance, sickness, and other benefits giving additional income support. The United States was something of an exception and should be viewed as such: In Europe, where fears of population decline ran deep, family policy was seen widely, along with employment security, as the foundation of the new welfare state (Girod, de Laubier, & Gladstone, 1985; Glass, 1940; Kalvemark, 1980; Spengler, 1979; Teitelbaum & Winter, 1985).

Many countries brought in cash allowances for families in the 1930s and 1940s, some on a universal basis and a few more selectively, and individual payments could be substantial (Kamerman & Kahn, 1978). New Zealand may have stood at one extreme, with weekly grants for every child equivalent to about 6 hours of average male wages or a third of an old-age pension, but significant financial assistance was widespread in other countries. Around 1950 family benefits in New Zealand absorbed almost as large a fraction of national income as did old-age pensions—in France they took rather more.

Little changed through the 1950s and early 1960s. Old-age pensions remained static relative to earnings, and eligibility conditions were eased only slightly. Family allowances continued, though in some instances they were allowed to erode in worth. But from the later 1960s much altered, as social security treatments of old and young moved in opposite directions. Preston's important 1984 article alerting Americans to this phenomenon has drawn much criticism for its implication that rising benefits for the aged have been bought with funds taken from children. It is true that the trade-off is not so simple or crude, but it is not unreasonable to juxtapose things in this way, at least in countries other than the United States. For several decades modern societies had run major benefit programs for just two groups selected by age alone. Each program was integral to the ongoing exchange between earlier and later born, and their diverging paths since about 1970 are both central to and symbolic of a wider revision of collective purpose (Preston, 1984a).

In all developed nations provision for the aged was enhanced from the late 1960s or early 1970s (see, e.g., Fogarty, 1982, on the United Kingdom; Ginsburg, 1983, on Sweden; Patterson, 1981, on the United States; Saunders, 1987, on Australia; Shiratori, 1985, on Japan). (One partial exception has perhaps been Britain, where the aged were granted relatively few new rights or higher benefits in this period—and where this much-condemned "miserliness" may yet, rather ironically, slow the buildup of generational tensions.) In each case the extensions went beyond those entitlements already built into social security plans at the outset. Contracts were broken and informal understandings ignored, as ages for full assistance fell, means and assets testing were eased or abolished, residency requirements were waived, and benefit levels rose both in real terms and relative to the incomes of younger persons. A doubling and better in benefit values has been reported, and in a number of nations replacement ratios (measuring postretirement income as a fraction of preretirement income) have gone near or past 100%.

At the same time, family allowances were curtailed or ended altogether, through a mixture of neglect and arguments that turned assistance to children into wasteful expenditure, a spur to immorality or irresponsibility, a cause of overpopulation, or a motherhood trap. In

Britain family allowances, like old-age pensions, had long been more meager than in many other places, and in the 1970s and 1980s they retained much of their former value while other benefits shrank. But even there provision for young families eroded (Field, 1980; Lister, 1982). Elsewhere governments toyed with new or revised family programs, but neither stopped the slide nor enacted anything comparable to the assistance of earlier decades. An extreme perhaps is New Zealand: Universal family benefit had been worth about 30% of an old-age pension per child in the late 1940s, just 3% by the mid-1980s, and the scheme ended altogether in 1991.

Other public expenditures have been reshaped similarly. Some public spendings have shrunk markedly, and housing is the most striking major example. A central plank of the midcentury "youth state" was the use of taxpayer funds to help young adults acquire housing. Assistance took many forms worldwide. For young owner-occupiers there were direct grants, low-interest government loans, tax deductibility on mortgage interest, interest rate controls, and an absence of capital gains taxes or of subsequent mortgage revisions. For young renters there were rent controls and tenancy protection, subsidies to private landlords, and more especially heavy construction programs in subsidized public rental housing. Together these direct public expenditures often equaled or exceeded the total cost of old-age pensions or public health provisions.

But since the late 1960s all governments have lost interest in supporting the young through housing, and direct public expenditures for housing are now routinely one third to one fifth, or even less, of what they were 20 years ago, relative to national income (Flora, 1986; OECD, annual). The loss, from the point of view of the later born, is rather greater than this. For one thing, young adults in the 1970s and 1980s formed much larger fractions of the total population than previously; a shrinking portion of national income was thus rationed ever more thinly across a swelling section of the population.

Moreover, these data cover only the most direct of government expenditures, and state powers, as we have seen, had formerly been used more widely. My own modeling exercises consider the cumulative impact of all these changes—young adult earnings, taxes, house prices, interest rates, government assistance schemes, social security benefits—upon the costs of identical houses for identical first-time buyers in New Zealand. These analyses indicate a three- to fivefold increase in the true costs of housing in the last 20 years. A house that in the 1950s or 1960s took 15% of net income in interest repayments (for a median-income, single-earner family with two children) now absorbs at least 60% of total income. I anticipate that comparable studies elsewhere will reach similar conclusions—and add weight to the "shrinking middle class" argument.

Other public expenditures have undergone parallel if less radical revision. Public education spending in most nations has fallen since the early 1970s, relative to national income, although the numbers of children and youths have not so declined. Health expenditures have grown meanwhile, often by 30 to 50% when measured as a fraction of national income, and within that, spending has tilted toward the middle-aged and elderly. In Britain, for instance, those of retirement age accounted for about one fifth of health costs in the 1950s, one quarter in the early 1970s, and more than 40% just a dozen years later (CSO, 1973–1990). Population age structure changed much less.

Little has been done by economists to assess the compounding effects of all this for the individual or for generations, other than to note that the current elderly gain more from social security than they have contributed, or than their successors will receive in turn. I have experimented more ambitiously with the New Zealand data in at least two ways. First, I have sought to divide the main public welfare expenditures—social security, education, health, and housing—into the shares going to those over age 60 and to those under age 40 (little goes to the middle-aged). Certain contestable working assumptions have to be made, for example, that all public expenditure on education is for the full and sole benefit of those under 40. However, these assumptions cause few problems as long as the same assumptions are made at all times, for all cohorts. When divided in this way, total net public expenditure upon those over 60 absorbed around 4% of the GNP throughout the 1950s and 1960s, but 10 to 12% in the 1980s. Spending upon those under 40 has remained close to 10% of the GNP for the last half-century, and the fractions of the total population in each group have not altered (Thomson, 1991).

Second, I have reconsidered the experiences of the Earlys (born 1930) and Lates (born 1955), this time assessing their gains through life. For the Earlys, lifetime benefits from the pool—counting cash allowances and use of all public services, including shares in services like defense and justice—will sum to a minimum of 37 units of average pay. Their income taxes will total 6 units at most, and their indirect charges will total anything up to an unlikely theoretical maximum of 14. For their identical successors, benefits will reach perhaps 25 units, if current levels of public expenditure and of old-age provision per head are retained for the next 50 years. This will not happen, and a final tally somewhat less than 20 units seems more plausible. Their lifelong taxes will be considerably greater than 20, with income taxes alone not less than 15 units, and their total lifetime incomes (personal cash incomes, plus services, less taxes) will be perhaps two thirds of those of the Earlys.

Some of the consequences are already with us, although most lie hidden in the futures of the later born. Among the immediate indicators are the affluence of large fractions of the middle-aged and elderly, the rapid removal of the aged from poverty, the growing proportions of the young sinking into poverty, mounting youth homelessness, and stalled and declining health and education levels of children and young adults.

Other immediate effects are revealed through income studies. Everywhere—I know of no exceptions—the net cash or personal income of the middle-aged and elderly has advanced faster in the 1970s and 1980s than that of younger adults and families, often bypassing them on average (see, e.g., Bradbury, Doyle, & Whiteford, 1990, on Australia; Easterlin, MacDonald, & Macunovich, 1990a, and Levy, 1987, on the United States; Erikson & Aberg, 1987, and Vogel, Andersson, Davidsson, & Häll, 1988, on Sweden; Keller, ten Cate, Handepool, & van de Stadt, 1987, on the Netherlands; Thomson, 1991, on New Zealand). In the cases of the United States and New Zealand, at least, there has occurred an absolute decline in real incomes, for the population under about age 40 of around 10 to 20% in the last two decades, and in the Netherlands of a little less. In those same places real incomes of the middle-aged and elderly have meanwhile risen by at least as much. Savings behaviors appear to be shifting similarly, with possibly profound implications for individuals, families, and national economies in the long run. The aged of the 1980s did not dissave, as conventional life cycle theory says they should, but expected to build further assets and went on to do so, while investments by younger persons shrank (Danziger, van derSaag, Smolensky, & Taussig, 1983; Torrey & Taeuber, 1986).

There are, at every turn, a range of particular explanations for each one of these developments, and I cannot address them here. What is of interest, however, is how much our existing measures of resources, such as some of those employed above, mask the true decline in the fortunes of the later born and the lasting, deepening, and ineradicable consequences of these declines, come what may. Easterlin et al. (Chapter 4 in this volume) and Rossi (Chapter 10 in this volume) hint at this when noting that, while earnings of young adults have undoubtedly shrunk, those people have responded with various adaptations that help to restore their real and relative purchasing powers of the moment. In other words, had the young not adapted, by no longer seeking the things once available to people like them but now too expensive (marriage, children, housing), they would have shown up in our conventional statistics as even poorer than they did.

Furthermore, the things that young adults are economizing upon are investments. The result probably will be that continuing declines of purchasing power confront them through life, as they in turn look for support to the much smaller generations following them, just when those shrunken cohorts also face infrastructure replacement, debt redemption, and more that did not take place in the last quarter of the 20th century. How we might model total lifetime real incomes, or declining current incomes combined with shrinking future prospects, I do not yet know. But my impression in the New Zealand case is that the underlying collapse in the economic fortunes of those born after about 1950 may have been of the order of 30 to 40% between 1970 and 1990.

Comment

Where might all this lead? Like most historians I am wary of prediction, and certainly do not suggest that reshaping of age priorities and generational experiences is all there has been to the last few decades. Nevertheless, I do sense, as I live and move in a number of countries, that a loss of faith in the ability of the state to deliver the expected lasting security and comfort is now well advanced. At this stage the responses are bewilderment, withdrawal, and incipient anger, but are not feeding into connected argument, cohort politics, or new ideas about the social order. I anticipate that these will come, but I may be overinfluenced by my New Zealand experiences, as researcher and as citizen, and I am aware of counterarguments.

Many point, for instance, to continuing high support for social security and similar programs, when expressed by all ages in social surveys, as evidence that no deep disenchantment is yet surfacing (Cook, 1990; Walker, Chapter 8 in this volume). This may be true, though it is notoriously easy to produce contrary results in such exercises by rephrasing and reordering questions.

At the minimum, we are likely to find ourselves debating age, history, responsibility, and the future in ways not heard of late. The process will be unpleasant and wrenching, at once debilitating and invigorating: Let us not flinch from it, as some cautious colleagues and "friends of the elderly" urge. In closing I want to pick out, in no particular order, a sample of the issues that I am especially keen to see addressed head-on in the next decade.

First, what is a "right" to comfort or security, dignity or self-esteem in old age—is "right" at century's end more than "want" in fancy garb? The rights of the elderly of A.D. 2000 will look increasingly flimsy on most of the familiar grounds, especially that of participation in ongoing collective action: What lasting substance can they be given? Can the aged of the 1990s have a right to things not given by them to their predecessors, or intended or possible for their successors? Might rights be peculiar to certain cohorts, and yet remain rights rather than something else? Do successors have an obligation to observe such rights, and if so, on what grounds? Is not their obligation equally strong to the rights of their own future selves and of their children? No agreement on these should be presupposed, for successive generations will hear the questions differently: To those born after World War II the message throughout will be "Few of these rights are for you."

A second cluster of queries awaits demographers, who are urged to leave population projections and dependency ratios alone for a time, to give long-run cohort experiences greater attention, to focus on the individual and family rather than on population aggregates, and to speculate upon large issues. How are demographics, policy, and cohort experiences interacting? Easterlin (1980, 1987) has addressed some of these questions, but too few others have followed, and the consensus still seems to be that demographics is an historical independent or rogue elephant, something outside the control of societies. That is, fertility, marriage, mortality, or migration move this way and that through time, for reasons little understood and beyond the play of deliberate policy. But this must be open to doubt. Cohort studies such as that introduced here suggest close links, with demographics moving in step with economic fortunes when these last are viewed more comprehensively than simply current cash in hand. In other words, societies may be getting the demographics they choose, rather than those inflicted upon them by an unknown agency. This is an unfashionable suggestion in a rapidly aging world, since to acknowledge it is to raise tricky matters of individual and collective motive, emotion, and responsibility. It needs to be researched even so.

Third, the economists have a central part to play—when do they not? Some questions for them are obvious. What needs and desires, strengths and limitations, might aged rather than youthful work forces have? Does economic growth solve distributional issues for an aging population? At present this is the panacea grasped at by most, politicians in particular, but I for one cannot understand it. The experience of the past half-century has not been that successive cohorts of the aging will accept modest increases in real income along with falling social position—they have wanted increased pieces of an increasing cake. There has been no sign of an acceptance of a decline in relative standing for the aged—of smaller pieces from whatever the cake may be—and yet that is the basic premise behind all arguments of the "growth will solve it all" category. Why will it work?

Beyond lie larger matters upon which we need the economists' reflections. What has been the connection between massive population growth and the elaboration of capitalist culture and society through the last two centuries or so? Is economic growth likely for aged populations, given their possible propensity for consumption over investment, or high-interest returns over low? And what of savings? How can individuals or cohorts save as a population ages? Through past centuries, and especially in the present, much "saving" has amounted to little more than being bailed out later by more numerous and prosperous successors. What happens when the generational flow is reversed, and the prospect of being subsidized by successors shrinks? Are "public" and "private"—social insurance and private insurance—alternatives in such circumstances? Much current planning, by both governments and individuals, hinges upon the faith that they are alternatives, and that resources that cannot be drawn from depleted cohorts of successors by taxes can somehow be taken through superannuation, returns on property, interest, and the like. Is this realistic?

The study of aging is moving well beyond the detail of retirement program or health care and to the intellectual heart of modern society: There could be no more exciting era to be involved in this subject.

12

Interest Group Politics:
Generational Changes in the Politics of Aging

Fernando M. Torres-Gil

Generational relationships have a singularly political quality about them. Relations between age cohorts are affected by the interest group nature of politics in the United States and the unique development of a politics of aging. Organizations representing various constituencies attempt to influence a pluralistic political system in order to gain power. Old-age groups are one of the more visible interest groups in American politics.

Analysts tend to view the politics of aging, however, as homogeneous, as an interplay among mainly white, English-speaking, relatively well educated, and active older persons and their families. In turn, scholarly discourse about the meaning of generational relations assumes a sameness about the populations under study.

The older population is, however, an increasingly diverse group with differences of ethnicity, race, gender, income, and economic and educational status, and those differences will significantly alter the relationships between age cohorts in the population. This chapter posits that diversity is a critical variable in exploring relationships between generations, and suggests that the analysis of interest group politics needs to go beyond intercohort relationships to the possibility of intracohort tensions. Diversity may have the potential to polarize both an expanding older population and an aging society, or it may force the political process to identify the common ground upon which all groups, regardless of age, should tread. In short, we may see a changing political contract, from one where the body politic views older persons as a monolithic force, whose political legitimacy has garnered public entitlement, to one that is fragmented and engenders resistance in pressing its demands.

How might diversity affect the political nature of generational relationships? What are the implications of inter- and intracohort politics for our understanding of societal responses to generational politics? Responses to those questions require an examination of the historical context of the politics of aging and the interest group nature of American politics. Diversity can then be factored in as a variable in assessing the potential outcomes of inter- and intracohort politics.

Politics and Age

The politics of aging is a fundamental aspect of examining the political implications of generational issues. The growth of old-age politics, where older persons develop an identification with old-age issues and advocate on behalf of themselves and other senior citizens, is a manifestation of cohort-based politics. The politics of aging has become a crucial factor in American politics, because persons age 60 and over register and vote in high numbers and because they increasingly have shared concerns. This phenomenon fascinates elected and appointed officials, researchers, and the public. In recent years, interest in the politics of aging has generated debate about generational relationships and about the potential conflict between old and young. Generational equity is viewed as an issue of competition for scarce public resources, creating both a backlash against the political influence of the elderly and also tension between competing age groups.

Why have generational equity and conflict between age groups become political issues in the United States? Ironically, old-age interest groups may be victims of their own success. Their ability to preserve and, in some cases, to expand their entitlement programs contrasts with the inability of other groups, particularly the poor, minorities, and children, to maintain programs and benefits. Some of the public have begun to perceive the elderly as too powerful and somewhat selfish, rather than as a group effectively exercising the democratic process.

Herein lies the dilemma facing the politics of aging in the United States: The political contract is changing. During the first 60 years of the politics of aging, advocacy groups for the elderly were successful in promoting an image of older persons as a group with legitimate needs. Decision-makers and the public sympathized with the political agenda of old-age groups. That view is giving way to the overgeneralized view that older persons are doing well and receive too many public benefits. Old-age groups today are forced to justify their political demands and compete with other interest groups for public support.

Diversity and intracohort politics will be the hallmarks of this modified political contract. The diversity of the elderly population will increasingly affect the ability of old-age groups to maintain a common agenda. Intracohort politics—competition within an age cohort—is likely to be one outcome of this diversity, with groups of older persons developing alliances with nonelderly groups who share common concerns (e.g., poor elderly working with welfare beneficiaries for health care coverage). In addition, the growing income disparity among older persons, with many more doing well, and many doing poorly, will exacerbate the effects of diversity and intracohort politics. Politically sophisticated interest groups of more affluent aged will have greater political leverage. In turn that may polarize the older population by creating fragmentation among old-age groups that had heretofore seemed to agree on key policy issues (e.g., Social Security, Medicare, and long-term care). The emerging schism of the elderly electorate will have profound implications for public policy and generational relationships.

This chapter examines the politics of aging in light of this set of circumstances. Contemporary political realities may alter our views about the political role of older persons—as individuals and as organized constituents—in interest group politics. Social and ethnic diversity, inter- and intracohort politics, ideology and economics, as well as the uniqueness of the United States political system, are factors in understanding changes in the political contract among generations.

Interest group politics, a key aspect of American politics, serves as a basis for exploring those issues. The questions asked are: What is the nature of generational conflict and competition between old-age interest groups when diversity becomes a major factor in the politics of aging? What conceptual issues arise in assessing the future of the politics of aging in the United States and other nations?

The United States is not alone in facing these issues. Other nations are also experiencing demographic changes, including an increase in the number of older persons. They face growing expenditures for their elderly populations, especially for pension and health care programs. Canada, Great Britain, Australia, and New Zealand have political values and ideologies similar to those of the United States and face the pressures of diverse populations that are growing older. At present, however, no other nation appears to be experiencing the mix of generational competition, old-age politics, and diversity among age groups found in the United States. On the other hand, these countries may in fact begin to face similar tensions in coming years.

Interest Group Politics

Interest group politics has become an important element in decision-making in the United States. Those who understand the system of making laws and influencing appointed and elected officials, who know how to organize and how to use the media, and who can raise and use money for such purposes usually have a disproportionate amount of influence. Some groups, such as the National Rifle Association and banking and real estate interests, effectively influence the legislative and executive branches. Others, such as environmentalists and minority groups, struggle to expand their influence.

The high level of interest group politics in the United States is unique. This is primarily due to the pluralistic nature of its political system, a permeable system that lends itself to many ways of influencing policy decisions. Access to appointed and elected officials gives lobbyists and interest groups opportunities to influence regulations, executive decisions, and implementation of programs. The needs of legislators to raise large sums of money and to maintain ties to voters with a high propensity to vote (e.g., elderly persons), and their desire to stay in office, allow advocates, lobbyists, and interest groups to maintain pressure and leverage over elected officials and their staffs. This interest group political influence is not matched in Great Britain, Canada, Australia, and New Zealand, which have parliamentary forms of government, loyalty to the political party in power, and in some cases publicly financed elections.

Legislators and appointed officials in the United States are influenced by public opinion, particularly the opinion of those most likely to vote. The ideological stance of those voters has important bearing on political decisions. The United States lacks the public consensus that exists in Great Britain and Canada about the central government's responsibility toward the social needs (such as health care and family allowances) of disadvantaged populations; and taxpayers there are more willing to pay higher taxes. A greater ideological diversity exists in the United States. In fact, much of the electorate supports self-reliance, a reduced public role, and fewer taxes, and that diversity is reflected in the political activity of interest groups.

Interest group activity in the United States is currently under scrutiny for its supposed narrow and selfish agenda. The gun control lobby, abortion rights groups, farmers receiving subsidies, and senior-citizen groups have been criticized for placing their own concerns above the needs of society. Some would even view organized interest groups as less politically effective than in the past. Predicting the demise of interest group activity in the United States, however, is premature. Experience in recent years demonstrates not so much a loss of political influence by interest groups, but rather a shift in ideology. During the Reagan-Bush years, interest groups favored by liberals (e.g., groups representing women, minorities, the elderly, the poor, and consumers) lost access to government and influence because of government's conservative shift toward other interest groups (e.g., business, real estate, banking, savings and loans, and defense). Thus, given the pluralistic nature of our political system, a high level of interest group activity will probably remain; only the cast of characters will change.

Among organized interest groups, groups of older persons are perceived as a prominent political force both at national and state levels. More than 20 organizations purport to represent the elderly in Washington, D.C. In contrast, the elderly play a limited role in Canada and Great Britain. According to Walker (1986b), there have been few signs "of heightened political awareness on the part of either politicians or elderly people themselves of the potential power of older citizens in the political arena." Advocacy groups for the aged developed in Scotland and England during the 1930s, primarily to promote old-age pensions, but in recent decades no such groups have arisen, nor have any participants in advocacy for the aged enjoyed the level of visibility experienced by senior-citizen groups in the United States. Marshall, Cook, and Marshall (Chapter 7 in this volume) maintain that senior power is much less developed in Canada than in the United States, with Canadian seniors more likely to seek power and influence through organizations not specifically age based.

The use by the elderly in the United States of their political influence is under scrutiny. Have they become a selfish, narrow-interest group concerned with preserving their own benefits at the expense of generational competition? Will diversity and inter- and intracohort politics raise the specter of a schism among older voters? Are they a monolithic political force with the ability to promote a unified agenda?

To answer such questions, we must examine the evolution of the politics of aging in the United States and consider why it occurred as it did here. As we shall see, during the last 60 years older persons have evolved into an effective advocacy and political force. Yet today the impact of diversity on the politics of aging raises important questions in our analysis of generational relationships.

The Rise of Old-Age Politics

With its organized interest groups, the politics of aging reflects a storied history. As Day says, the "amorphous senior movement of the

early 20th century has developed into an array of established and institutionalized political organizations" (1990, p. 15). The politics of aging
began in the 1920s with the formation of several groups advocating
old-age pensions—the American Association for Old Age Security
(AAOAS), the American Association for Labor Legislation (AALL), and
the Fraternal Order of the Eagles. The Great Depression resulted in
several mass social movements of older persons, such as the Ham and
Eggs Group, formed by Robert Nobel, and End Poverty in California,
organized by Upton Sinclair. The Townsend Movement, the best known
of the time, was organized by Dr. Francis Townsend and eventually
represented more than 2 million older persons. Each movement supported some income maintenance program for older persons, in much
the same way as the advocates for the aging in Great Britain and
Canada.

The overall effect on public policy was mixed. These early groups gave
impetus to passage of the Social Security Act, but were given no credit
for its formulation or implementation. Their greatest contribution was
furnishing the elderly with a collective voice and identity.

Organized interest groups representing the elderly did not reemerge
until the 1950s and 1960s. Representative of today's institutionalized
interest groups are organizations such as the American Association of
Retired Persons (AARP), the National Association of Retired Federal
Employees (NARFE), the National Council of Senior Citizens (NCSC),
the National Council on Aging (NCOA), and the National Committee to
Preserve Social Security and Medicare (NCPSSM).

Why have such groups proliferated and flourished? Reasons vary, but
most such organizations involve a large, educated, active, and middle-
class older membership; sophisticated leadership and staff; and shared
concerns (income security, health care, and social services). Primary is a
common agenda dedicated to the preservation of current age-based entitlement. After 60 years of advocacy and legislation, older persons enjoy a vast array of public benefits and programs predicated on age. They
have a stake in maintaining Social Security benefits, the Supplemental
Security Income (SSI) program, health care coverage under Medicare,
social programs under the Older Americans Act (OAA), protections
accorded by Disability Insurance, and civil-rights safeguards of the age
discrimination laws.

How effective have old-age groups been in expanding and preserving
such benefits? Opinions vary. Throughout the 1960s and 1970s, age-
based groups actively participated in the passage of Medicare, Medicaid,
SSI, and the OAA. They were integral to events such as the White
House Conferences on Aging. Some scholars (Binstock, 1981; Lammers,
1983; Pratt, 1976; Williamson, Evans, & Powell, 1982), however, would

draw no direct correlation between the support of these groups for major policies and the passage of legislation. At best, these groups are credited with increasing public awareness, with providing some measure of credibility to legislation introduced, and with the expansion of benefits. Interest groups representing labor, civil-rights interests, and business, along with sympathetic national administrations and legislators, are more often considered responsible for passage of certain old-age policies (Binstock, 1987; Heclo, 1988).

Opinions on who has had the most political influence are changing, however. Scholars and other observers (Day, 1990; Light, 1981; Longman, 1985b; Rauch, 1987) increasingly view the elderly as one of Washington's most effective lobbying groups. The ability of some old-age groups to build memberships, to provide sophisticated policy analysis, to marshal grass roots support, and to utilize direct mail and political-action committees has created the impression that if they cannot effect the passage of legislation, they can at least block changes in existing policies. The repeal of the Medicare Catastrophic Coverage Act in 1989, a law expanding benefits but requiring affluent older persons to pay higher taxes, was tied exclusively to opposition by senior citizens. AARP, NCPSSM, and the Families, USA advocacy group are regarded as integral players in national policymaking. As Day observed, "Aging-based interest groups are at the pinnacle of their organizational success and have achieved Washington insider status" (1990, p. 33).

As political participants, older persons are seen as more active in electoral politics than other age groups. Their voter registration and voting rates are higher (Hudson & Strate, 1984). For example, between the 1964 and the 1988 presidential elections the percentage of those 65 and over who voted increased from 66 to 69%, while those aged 18–24 who voted dropped from 51 to 36%. Those aged 25–44 who voted also decreased, from 69 to 54%. This imbalance also holds for congressional elections from 1974 to 1986, with the percentage of elderly who voted increasing, and the percentage of those aged 18–44 who voted decreasing (U.S. Bureau of the Census, 1989c). Given the growing proportion of persons 65 and older, one might assume that older persons will increase their collective electoral muscle.

Ideology and Agendas

What are the concerns of the old-age groups and whom do they represent? The priority issue concerning the elderly in Great Britain, Canada, Australia, New Zealand, and many other social democracies involves pensions, or retirement income, as well as health care coverage. To the extent older persons feel a need to organize, such issues have provided a common agenda.

In the United States, too, this has been the case, but Social Security, more than private pensions, has been the issue galvanizing older persons into a political block of advocates and voters. Demands for income security in retirement gave rise to old-age groups in the United States, and threats to the Social Security system inspire new recruits today. Medicare, the Older Americans Act, and other age-based entitlement programs reinforce age as a political tool.

The extent to which a unity of concern will hold among older persons is in question, however. What if the eligibility age for Social Security and Medicare were raised, thus excluding younger, more politically active elders? What if such programs were means tested (requiring that individuals meet a maximum income or asset test to qualify), thus benefiting poor older persons? The unity of purpose enjoyed by old-age groups could conceivably crumble. Divisiveness among older persons over legislative priorities, and competition over public benefits, would alter their political influence. On the other hand, previously underrepresented groups of older persons (minority elderly, older women, and senior citizens in rural areas) might have the opportunity to have an impact on public policy, assuming that they were able to establish effective interest groups or alliances with nonaging groups. Such scenarios will be discussed later. A more salient issue concerns the divisive or unifying effect of ideology and the effect of what Walker (Chapter 8 in this volume) terms a "restructuring of the welfare state" on old-age constituencies.

Thomson and Walker (Chapter 11 and Chapter 8 in this volume, respectively) contend that their countries, New Zealand and Great Britain, respectively, have undergone a retrenchment of the welfare state. During the 1980s, the Roger administration in New Zealand and the Thatcher government in Great Britain echoed Reagan's approach, scaling back benefits to families, to young persons, and to the poor, and holding the line on programs for the aged. This reflected a shift in what had heretofore been a consensus in New Zealand and Great Britain, and to a lesser extent in the United States, that government is responsible for such constituencies and that the public should willingly pay for benefits. This ideological shift is creating tensions among constituencies (e.g., unions, the poor, and health care workers) and is threatening the programs older persons have enjoyed. Unlike in the United States, elders in New Zealand and Great Britain do not have organized groups to protect their interests.

Through the 1980s, older persons in the United States faced a similar retrenchment in government support for their programs. The ideological shift away from a progressive, New Deal-oriented government created a less inviting, less receptive political environment. The election in 1980 of a Republican president who was committed to downsizing government and to reducing social programs signaled an end to the insider status aging organizations enjoyed through the 1970s (Torres-Gil, 1981). Efforts by the administration to reduce Social Security and health benefits prompted interest groups to return to political basics: grass roots organizing and direct mail. Extraordinary mobilization efforts throughout the 1980s positioned senior-citizen organizations to resist cuts in benefits, as noted above.

Generational Conflict

Success has not come without cost, however. The elderly's growing share of the federal budget, cutbacks in programs for other groups, and greater public visibility of aging as a major domestic issue have placed seniors in a vulnerable position. Public sentiment is shifting. The elderly are no longer viewed strictly as a needy, disadvantaged minority, but rather as a too-powerful, selfish interest group concerned only with preserving its own benefits. Ironically, the dissemination of data detailing the elderly's socioeconomic status provided the ammunition for this new stereotype.

The generational-equity debate in the United States began in 1984 with a presentation by Samuel Preston, who analyzed poverty rates among young and old, and public expenditures on behalf of the elderly. The message delivered was that the elderly were thriving at the expense of children, and that the federal government was spending too much on the aged. The attention given this presentation, and its subsequent publication in national forums (*Demography*, 1984; *Scientific American*, 1984) generated tremendous interest in the subject of generational equity (Fairlie, 1988; Jones, 1988b; Lamm, 1985). The formation of Americans for Generational Equity (AGE), which later merged with the American Association of Boomers (AAB), provided a forum for policymakers, elected officials, and those who felt the situation was unfair. Congress held hearings and used generational-equity arguments to support or oppose legislation affecting older and younger persons. Academics, editorialists, and advocates passionately debated the subject. Groups such as Generations United formed to counter AGE and AAB and to promote an intergenerational perspective.

The discussions, however, painted a simplistic picture of generational conflict, which became a convenient ploy to justify the retrenchment and restructuring of social programs and a shift of responsibility to the individual, to the private sector, and to local government. These changes and a widening chasm between the affluent and poor made the debate even more timely. The success of the elderly in protecting their benefits—and the unwillingness of the public and the political system to respond to the needs of low-income and minority elderly, children, and the poor—encouraged simplistic conclusions about where to place the blame for perceived inequities. Old-age advocates were partially to blame, though, for portraying all the elderly as poor and needy when arguing for expanded public benefits, while promoting them as productive, healthy, and well-off when extolling their consumer and market potential.

The generational-conflict thesis gave momentum to the developing image of older persons competing with younger groups for scarce public resources. Policymaking reflected the debate. Legislators increasingly took budget-neutral approaches, where additional benefits for the elderly would be offset by taxing seniors or by shifting the cost to them. Imposition of a premium surcharge on older persons in 1988 signaled a loosening in the apparent control of the elderly over the purse strings. Hereafter, older persons would have to justify the need for additional benefits; if trade-offs were necessary, other groups, such as the poor, minorities, and medically uninsured, would be given the benefit of the doubt.

This short- and long-term set of developments has placed the politics of aging at a crucial crossroads. The success of older persons as a political interest group is in question. In part, this is because public and elected officials are more astute in recognizing that older persons are neither all poor nor all well-off. The politics of aging must now confront the diversification of the older electorate and the increasing ability of disadvantaged older persons to play the interest group game. Generational-equity debates serve as an indicator, pretext, and symbol that older persons in the United States may be stripped of the social and political legitimacy they once enjoyed and that the political role of the elderly will be more complex.

Past and Future Politics of Aging

A useful framework for understanding changes in the politics of aging in the United States is to view the political role of older persons as an evolving process distinguished by several periods: pre-1930 (Young Aging), 1930–1990 (Modern Aging), and post-1990 (New Aging).

The Young Aging Period

Prior to the 1930s, the United States had few social programs for the elderly. Beyond federal pensions and limited health care coverage for Civil War and World War I veterans and certain classes of government employees (civil service), government provided the aged little. If they required assistance, family, community, charity organizations, and local government (e.g., county work farms) were expected to respond. As a young nation, the United States reflected an orientation toward youth and away from the "old" nations of Europe. Westward expansion, the rapid growth of cities and industry, democracy, constant change, social and economic mobility, and low life expectancy diverted attention from older persons. This Young Aging period saw little need for developing old-age policies, although governments in Germany and other European countries had introduced them.

The Modern Aging Period

In the Modern Aging period, the role of the elderly and society's approach to addressing their needs changed dramatically. During this 60-year period, American ideology allowed government a central role in citizens' social, economic, and personal lives. This included providing for the elderly through various programs, agencies, and benefits, and adopting age as one of several criteria for defining eligibility and for identifying the deserving and needy. Age 65 became the age for receiving full Social Security benefits (age 62 for partial benefits) and Medicare. Age 60 was the benchmark for receipt of OAA services. At 55, one could participate in employment programs for older persons. Age segregation in the Modern Aging period also included the establishment of senior-citizen interest groups and an "aging enterprise," comprised of service providers and professionals, to serve a growing elderly population.

The net outgrowth of this period was an implied political contract; individuals grew up expecting to receive certain benefits based on their age rather than on their income or need. Their willingness to be taxed during their working years and to pay into Social Security was based on their belief that they were entitled to such benefits. Public appreciation for the accomplishments of old-age cohorts during this period contributed to this sense of entitlement. Overcoming the depression of the 1930s, winning a world war, warding off Communism, and contributing to the nation's prosperity during their youth gave older persons a political and public legitimacy that enabled them to press for additional benefits. The intergenerational transfer aspect of Social Security and

Medicare (with the work force supporting older persons at the time, rather than building a reserve for their own retirement) was viewed as reasonable during the Modern Aging period.

This era represents America's initial attempt at responding to population aging; large-scale programs and services were created to provide an extensive and expensive system benefiting senior citizens. Old-age groups were viewed as relatively homogeneous: white, English-speaking, and middle-class. It is this system, a product of our view of old age and the elderly then, upon which the aged and their families now depend.

The New Aging Period

The Modern Aging period is giving way to a New Aging period where changes in the political contract and diversification may alter our view of the elderly and the manner in which government and society provide for them. In the 1990s, the schism in the political agenda of old-age interest groups may result in a restructuring of programs developed during the Modern Aging period. The effects of longevity, generational relationships, diversity, and interest group politics may add discord to the interrelationships of senior-citizen advocacy groups, but may also add a new political dimension of alliances with nonaged interest groups.

Longevity.   Life expectancy has dramatically increased (from 48 years at the turn of the century to around 75 today); morbidity rates have also declined (Taeuber, 1990). This means simply that we will live longer and be active at later ages. More persons see themselves as retirees and elders, and thus recognize their stake in social policies geared toward seniors. Longevity will complicate social and political relationships. Families will witness four-generation households and the associated dilemmas they pose (caretaking, long-term care, and women's views of their roles in society).

Generational relationships.   During the Modern Aging period certain generations became distinct. They included age cohorts (ranging from 5 to 20 years) with particular historical and ideological perspectives. Best known of these is the baby boom cohort, the large post-World War II population born between 1946 and 1964. Prior to the baby boomers was the New Deal generation, those who were born in the early part of this century, who experienced the Great Depression of the 1930s and World War II, and who benefited from postwar economic expansion. That generation includes today's very old (70 years of age and over), who have the greatest stake in Social Security, Medicare, and other old-age benefits. The younger-old (55–69 years of age), fewer in number, have benefited from the prosperity of the 1950s and 1960s. Following the baby boomers will be a relatively small "baby bust generation" (born between 1965 and 1979), and a somewhat larger "baby boomlet."

The Modern Aging period marked the development of age consciousness (identification with contemporaries and with public policies benefiting one's age group). The political credibility of old-age interest group politics during this period was based on promoting age consciousness. Witness the development of old-age lobbying groups and the creation of large-scale entitlement programs for older persons (e.g., OAA and Medicare).

Age consciousness is expected to increase during the New Aging period, although that does not necessarily equate with unanimity for a political agenda. Day sees several "contemporary conditions likely to enhance the relevance of old age to political attitudes" (1990, p. 9): institutionalization of old-age government benefits, political mobilization in defense of existing programs, and increased group consciousness among incoming cohorts of elders threatened with the loss of such benefits and programs. Ironically, the political backlash developing toward old-age programs may forge a tighter common agenda within old-age cohorts.

If age consciousness increases and we continue a policy of age-based benefits, we may see contradictory feelings on the part of younger cohorts: expectations that they will not need old-age benefits but then a realization, as they age, that they are in fact dependent on old-age benefits. Today's age cohorts, particularly younger groups such as baby boomers and baby busters, see public benefits and services for older persons as the norm, and expect them for their elders and parents. They expect less for themselves, imagining perhaps that they can avoid the exigencies of old age (dependency, illness, and poverty). Many also feel that programs such as Social Security and Medicare may be inaccessible when they retire, either because of insolvency or changes in eligibility requirements.

The reality is that if they are unable to save sufficiently for their retirement throughout a longer life expectancy, if budget cuts limit public benefits after the turn of the century, or if we fail to adopt universal and social insurance policies (e.g., a national health care system) covering everyone regardless of age or income, today's middle-aged and younger cohorts may need old-age benefits far more than their grandparents or parents ever did.

In the politics of the New Aging period, age consciousness, age-segregated benefits, and the cumulative effects of failed expectations and growing dependency may combine to create deep divisions between and within age cohorts.

Diversity. Political analysis has failed to address sufficiently the effect of relationships within cohorts as opposed to relationships between cohorts. Intracohort competition and tensions may affect the politics of aging more than conflicts between cohorts. This will be the next major issue in the politics of the New Aging period. Differences within the older population will become more glaring, and subgroups of the poor, minorities, older women, and persons living alone may join political alliances that compete with groups of more affluent elders. This diversity and varying levels of political effectiveness among subgroups of the old age cohort will be the basis of such competition.

Differences will be based on gender, race, and socioeconomic status. Those differences have always been evident in the older population. The critical change in the New Aging period is that old-age organizations will be less able to maintain a primarily middle-class, nonminority agenda, and groups of disadvantaged elders may establish their own political agendas separate from the mainstream senior-citizen advocacy groups. Income will be a key factor in intracohort politics. When Social Security was adopted, approximately 75% of persons 65 and over were poor (Smolensky, Danziger, & Gottschalk, 1988). This figure dropped to 35% in 1959, 24% in 1970, and 12% in 1986 (Preston, 1984a; U.S. Senate, 1988; Villers Foundation, 1987). Thus, through the 1970s, establishing a common agenda for entitlement programs and developing non-mean-tested eligibility criteria were easy.

Today, discrepancies between the affluent and poor elderly are as apparent as those between the economic haves and have-nots in society as a whole. Many more elders are educated, economically secure, and healthy. Large numbers, however, are poor or marginally poor and depend on public benefits such as SSI, disability insurance, Medicaid, and nutrition centers for survival. Many live near the poverty level, buoyed only by Social Security. For example, while women constitute 59% of the total elderly population, they account for 72% of the elderly poor. Older blacks are nearly three times as likely to be poor as older whites (Villers Foundation, 1987).

Ethnic and racial diversity is dramatically altering the demographic profile of the United States and specifically the demographic profile of the elderly. The 1990 census projections will show approximately 14% of the white population to be 65 years or older, compared to 8% for the black population and 6% for the Hispanic population. By 2030 about 23% of the white, 18% of the black, and 13% of the Hispanic population could be 65 and older (Taeuber, 1990). Older members of ethnic and racial groups may have more in common with minority-based politics (e.g., language and poverty issues) than with the politics of middle- and upper-income older persons (e.g., issues of preretirement planning and leisure activities).

Interest group politics. The combination of diversification and interest group politics will widen this divide among the elderly and will fragment the political influence of established aging organizations. It will be more apparent that old-age organizations reflect middle- and upper-income older persons rather than politically disadvantaged groups of elders. Studies show that interest group politics favors narrow, privileged groups (Bachrach, 1967; Schattschneider, 1960), and that most interest groups representing the aged tend to favor middle- and upper-income elderly (Binstock, 1983; Heclo, 1988; Longman, 1987b). Given that politics rewards those who play the game best, interest groups proficient in fund-raising, direct mail, media manipulation, and constituency-based politics will have an edge over those less proficient.

The question in the interest group politics of the New Aging period, with its greater diversity, is: To what extent will inter- and intracohort politics create a schism in the politics of aging? Evidence strongly suggests that most interest groups represent the more articulate and educated elders, and not the poor, the sick, or minorities. Furthermore, interest groups that effectively use the tools essential to modern politics tend to focus on constituents who are able to contribute financially and otherwise. The controversy over the Medicare Castrophic Coverage Act in 1989 and the budget debates of the 1990s graphically illustrated that, with few exceptions, aging groups fought hardest to protect middle-income, not poor, elders. The rapid increase in minority and ethnic elderly, whose life expectancy is increasing, will aggravate this schism, since they have traditionally played the interest group politics game ineffectively. (Organizations such as the National Hispanic Council on Aging, National Caucus and Center on Black Aged, and the National Indian Council on Aging were created to address the political inequities facing minority elderly.)

The central issue related to the diversity in the New Aging period is not that the numbers of disadvantaged older persons will increase or that the proportions of the well-off and the poor are changing, although both are happening to a great extent. The relevant issue is that sub-groups of older persons may become more politically organized, with political agendas different from most of today's senior organizations. In addition, younger cohorts from those populations, as they age, will acquire an age identification as older persons, but with a greater diversity of political goals and organizations. Thus, we cannot assume a simple dichotomy of one generation versus another generation nor can we examine relationships between age cohorts unless we understand inter- and intracohort dynamics. Some tensions between young and old will remain if we continue the present pattern of age-segregated policies, but the more likely outcome will be a diversified politics of aging.

Among older persons we will see greater diversity of opinions about political issues, and between age cohorts we will see more links based on political priorities rather than on age. Such inter- and intracohort politics will affect social and family relationships and create opportunities for intergenerational programs and activities, but they will also lessen the overall political influence of older voters and their advocacy groups. The ideological politics of the 1980s and early 1990s, whereby conservative national administrations favored affluent and private-sector interests to the detriment of the poor and politically powerless, exacerbated divisions between and within age cohorts. Some aging lobbies played into this kind of politics by protecting the interests of middle- and upper-income elderly at the expense of the poor elderly and other needy groups. The implications of diversity and inter- and intracohort relationships for the politics of aging will affect policy choices and political alliances.

Implications

Although elders and their interest groups will continue to have a collective voice on specific issues, such as preserving Social Security benefits, differences among subpopulations of the elderly, and interest group politics, will create competition among the elderly on many other issues, such as means testing and higher eligibility ages, especially in the face of budget deficits. Increased age consciousness, coupled with inter- and intracohort relationships, will increase the potential for divisiveness and conflict, since the neediest, regardless of age, will be at a disadvantage; well organized, relatively well-off elderly carry more weight, are more age conscious, and can play the political game.

This is not to imply that the role and importance of age-based organizations will decline. A larger older population, with an increased number of educated and healthy elders, will boost seniors' political visibility—although it does not guarantee enhanced political influence (McKenzie, 1991). Old-age groups will have to work harder, and will have to compete more on the basis of "power" than on the basis of the public's sympathy. To the extent that party identification continues to decline and individuals remain highly mobile, senior-citizen groups may continue as the prime vehicle for expressing concerns and demands. Cutler notes that "tomorrow's elderly are already being socialized to the potential politics of age" (1981, p. 151). Old-age organizations will be able to vie for new recruits. Some will become more powerful as they effectively exercise the tools of modern politics. The groups with the greatest influence will be characterized by effective use of direct mail; fund-raising; a focus on "red-flag" issues such as cutbacks in Social Security benefits; direct services to members; use of the media; and lobbying at federal and state levels.

However, intracohort politics will increase the disparity and diversity of political agendas. Lower income elderly will support certain public-policy approaches that middle-class elderly may not support. Some groups will endorse means-tested entitlement programs, while others will argue against them. Those who favor congregate meal services in a time of cutbacks may clash with those supporting increased funding for home-delivered meals. Intercohort and intracohort politics may see younger groups and the affluent elders advocate expanded nursing-home and long-term care. Inner-city minority elders may demand increased housing and transportation subsidies, while nonminority elders in affluent retirement locales will be concerned with protecting their pension and retirement benefits.

Already we see policy dilemmas arise in responding to the concerns of the elderly as a whole while meeting the needs of disadvantaged older persons. The OAA, for example, designed to provide a host of social and supportive services to all persons 60 years and over, is unable because of limited funds to respond to all persons wishing services. Thus, the federal government and its state counterparts utilize a "targeting" scheme that avoids direct means testing of the program but gives preferences to those elderly with the greatest social and economic needs, with an emphasis on low-income and minority elderly. This risky approach may erode political support among affluent elders who oppose what they see as "welfare" programs, while at the same time the poor and isolated elders demand more services. On a broader scale, the health care debate in the United States fosters divisions between those groups who seek health care coverage for the medically uninsured (primarily working adults and children), and interest groups who want to expand long-term care for older persons.

We are witnessing a rewriting of the political contract that sustained old-age politics in the United States during the Modern Aging period. Old-age groups may no longer be able to demand expanded benefits or the public support to frighten politicians away from imposing tax burdens. Disadvantaged groups will not be satisfied with representation by established old-age organizations nor with public policies that assume a homogeneous population of retirees. Group competition and justification of demands on a cost-benefit basis rather than as a moral obligation may become the norm. Senior-citizen organizations may find themselves developing alliances with other groups, such as the poor elderly, older women, organizations representing children, and minorities. Generations United, for example, has established a coalition of consumer, labor, children, and senior groups, and AARP is establishing networks with minority populations.

The politics of aging in the United States has the potential to influence other countries that are facing a restructuring of their welfare states and that are hence putting elders in a precarious situation. Elders in nations such as Great Britain and Canada, countries that have yet to see generational conflicts or a politics of aging, may find themselves emulating the interest group politics of the United States. The trend toward privatization and diminution of government responsibility for universal entitlement has been problematic for older persons in those countries. According to Walker (1986b), the political commitment to provide a minimal pension level and other benefits to the elderly was whittled away during the Thatcher years with poverty affecting more older persons. If this were to happen in Canada, New Zealand, and Australia (with their legacies of welfare state support for disadvantaged populations), we might see a trend of old-age groups in those countries developing alliances with other disadvantaged groups.

Despite its detractors, the interest group nature of the United States politics of aging actually gives it its strength. Here older persons and disadvantaged populations do not depend entirely on the public and on political parties to represent their interests. Even during the Reagan administration's most intense efforts to reduce the Medicare budget drastically and to scale back Social Security, elder interest groups triumphed. We can expect old-age groups, and their allies, to exercise political activism during the 1990s, when pressure to reform social policies will increase. Great Britain and other nations may find their older persons taking notes from interest groups in the United States.

Senior citizens in these other countries may become politically active, and at the same time a more complex politics of aging will occur in the United States during the 1990s. Intercohort and intracohort politics mixed with a more diverse political agenda among old-age groups will be the norm. This will be the case as subsequent generations become elders.

Tremendous diversity—in education, income, and employment—is evident in the baby boom population of 75 million born between 1946 and 1964. This group represents several distinct age cohorts varying widely in political attitudes. The oldest (those now in their 40s) tend to be more liberal and activist, the youngest more conservative. Many are financially comfortable; many are not. As this population develops an age consciousness and begins to identify with aging concerns, its members will join no single organization. They will gravitate toward different organizations representing their particular circumstances and issues. Diverse organizations and political positions will proliferate.

Conclusion

The generational nature of the politics of aging provides a rich arena for investigation and analysis. There is much to understand about the changes occurring in organized efforts of old-age groups and in the effects that diversity, longevity, and generational relationships will have on the political agendas of the elderly. Focusing on the dynamics of generations relating to or competing with each other ignores the more complex interplay of competition within and between age cohorts. The future politics of older and younger persons may see linkages based on political agendas and public policy objectives rather than on age alone. The increasing involvement of heretofore neglected populations—older women, the poor elderly, and minority and ethnic elders—will have a great impact on the political cohesiveness of old-age organizations and on how the public and political system view the demands of older persons.

On the other hand, those newly empowered groups of older persons present opportunities for alliances that are more intergenerational. An important area for study will be the degree of competition and cooperation between those groups. The point at which diversity creates more division than social gains will require analysis, as will a delineation of what constitutes common concerns among diverse groups.

The interest group model for examining political activity and the formulation of public policy must account for diversity and newly empowered groups. The extent to which older persons and their organizations adapt to the new political contract will say much about their political influence in the coming years. Any study of generational relationships should consider how the political nature of those relations will ultimately affect the provision of benefits and services to individuals and to families.

13

Setting the Agenda for Research on Cohorts and Generations: Theoretical, Political, and Policy Implications

Jill Quadagno, W. Andrew Achenbaum, and Vern L. Bengtson

The theme of this volume has been that the prevailing social compact regarding the expectations, obligations, and succession of age groups may be undergoing change. As we move from the 20th to the 21st century, we are beginning to experience the consequences of trends in population aging that began decades earlier. The contributors to this volume—a distinguished cast of social scientists who have been examining various aspects of age, age groups, and social structure—have approached this phenomenon in a variety of ways, reflecting its multidisciplinary dimensions.

In this concluding chapter we attempt to summarize some of the emergent themes from the preceding chapters, relating them to the theoretical, political, and policy research issues that are likely to engage scholars in the future. First we describe another recently published volume on "generations" in history (Strauss & Howe, 1991) and second we discuss how the contributors to *The Changing Contract Across Generations* have treated the issues quite differently from Strauss and Howe. Third we explore the "micro-macro" linkages between cohorts and generations, as reflected by the contributors to this volume. Fourth we review the nature of the social contract between and among age groups in the context of chapter contributors' arguments. Fifth we ask: What are policymakers to conclude from the emerging generational debate?

Cycles of Generations

By coincidence, shortly after the contributors to this volume met at the University of Southern California to discuss the first drafts of their chapters, *Generations: The History of America's Future, 1584–2069* was published by William Strauss and Neil Howe (1991). The publisher describes *Generations* as "the book that changes forever your view of our national legacy . . . and our destiny." In 538 pages (including more than 100 pages of tables, notes, appendixes, and glossary), Strauss and Howe purport to describe and explain developments in our national experience through a succession of 18 generations. "What a panorama!" exults a dust jacket blurb from David Stockman. Senator Albert Gore, Jr., declares that "*Generations* is the most stimulating book on American history I have ever read." Father Theodore Hesburgh is no less enthusiastic: *Generations,* he claims, "will attract a lot of attention because it appears at a time when a sense of lost direction prevails." Harvard political scientist Richard Neustadt predicts that "it will start a lot of arguments—all to the good!" Why do these readers find *Generations* so engaging? We suspect it is because Strauss and Howe developed an ingenious thesis, seemingly bolstered by considerable historical evidence.

Strauss and Howe begin their view of generational cycles with a simple premise: People born in a particular set of years perceive historical events and react to new opportunities and challenges differently from those who are older or younger than they. Generations, Strauss and Howe hypothesize, interact in "a recurring cycle of four distinct types of peer personalities, arriving in the same repeating sequence" (p. 33). A dominant *idealist* generation is followed by a recessive *reactive* generation, in turn by a dominant *civic* generation and then by a recessive *adaptive* generation (p. 376). This cycle repeats itself. "Constellational eras and generational lifestyles follow predictable patterns, within which each generation has a limited choice of scripts . . . their social behavior is governed by a well-defined and relatively unchanging life cycle" (p. 441).

The authors' understanding of *generation* differs from the ways contributors to this volume use the term. According to Strauss and Howe, "a generation is a cohort-group whose length approximates the span of a phase of life and whose boundaries are fixed by peer personality" (p. 60). The authors claim that the "basic phase of life" has manifested itself in 22-year segments during three centuries of United States history (p. 34). For each cohort group, roles change over the life course. Youth (up to age 21) perennially has been a period of dependence. Activity and increasing leadership have characterized rising adulthood (ages 22–43) and midlife (44–65). Elderhood (ages 66–87) always has been a time for stewardship. Strauss and Howe assume that biomarkers in the human life cycle have a timeless quality. In addition, "basic social roles also follow a relatively fixed age schedule" (p. 47).

The engine that drives Strauss and Howe's *Generations* is powered by the ways that particular "cohort-groups," situated in their specific historical settings, respond to "social moments" that disrupt the prevailing order as they mature over time. Alternating between outward "secular crises" and inward "spiritual awakenings," these social moments "normally arrive in time intervals roughly separated by two phases of life (approximately forty to forty-five years)" (p. 71). The authors' four types of cohort groups—*idealist, reactive, civic,* and *adaptive*—are at different stages of development when a particular secular crisis or spiritual awakening occurs. Differences in the ways these four generational types respond to the same social moment reflect the divergent manner in which they were nurtured and provided nurturing.

How people in *Generations* adapt to change also highlights peer preoccupations as well as others' perceptions of a particular cohort group's negative and positive attributes. At the interstices of generational, societal, and historical time, Strauss and Howe note yet another regularity: "Each generation develops a lifelong endowment agenda pointing toward the endowment activity that society neglected or reversed during its youth" (p. 373). Whether one accepts the authors' interpretation of recent trends depends on whether one believes that their model makes it possible to predict future developments in generational relations.

Back to Basics About Age, Aging, and Social Change

Contributors to this volume could be expected to raise a host of objections to the thesis presented in *Generations*. Consider some of the conclusions in *The Changing Contract Across Generations*. Although Strauss and Howe cite Matilda White Riley, they do not grasp fully the logic of her age stratification model (1985), which their construct only superficially resembles. Nor do they seem to appreciate a favorite theme of the Rileys: Due to increases in life expectancy at every stage of life, there are bound to be structural and cultural lags as humans rework societal norms and expectations to take advantage of these added years. Alice Rossi's chapter surely challenges the representativeness of the predominantly male biographies limned in *Generations*. Strauss and Howe minimize gender-specific variations; they apparently discount the possibility that over time differences between men and women have increased in some realms and diminished in others.

Chapters in this volume that focus on trends in the United States raise issues about politics, economics, and ideas not mentioned in *Generations*. Maris Vinovskis (Chapter 3) reports that older Americans have long recognized their stake in investing in quality education for youth, even though they have sometimes been less supportive of taxes for measures that appear to be in their immediate self-interest. His chapter suggests that any given cohort group might simultaneously manifest civic and reactive traits, in the vocabulary of Strauss and Howe. Victor Marshall, Fay Lomax Cook, and Joanne Gard Marshall (Chapter 7) corroborate this point by noting that the "crisis" rhetoric over Social Security in the United States (but not in Canada) has scarcely eroded remarkably solid transgenerational support for this domestic program. Does their evidence suggest that Strauss and Howe might exaggerate the extent of discontinuity from generation to generation?

Reviewing trends in the economic status of younger and older workers during the past 25 years, Richard Easterlin, Diane Macunovich, and Eileen Crimmins (Chapter 4) find that the former group has made sacrifices in terms of leisure, privacy, and bearing children to maintain their *relative* economic status. Their measures provide criteria for making such discriminations, which are unavailable in *Generations*. Fernando Torres-Gil's analysis (Chapter 12) of interest group politics underscores the importance of recent developments in American pluralism difficult to convey in a generational model that stresses "normal," modal patterns. He takes race and ethnicity more seriously than Strauss and Howe.

Cross-cultural comparisons reveal just how parochial a bias exists in the interpretation of United States history set forth in *Generations*. In different ways Nancy Foner (Chapter 6) and Judith Treas and Wei Wang (Chapter 5) demonstrate that tensions within cohort boundaries often are as salient as those across birth cohort lines. It is hard to imagine how David Thomson's analysis (Chapter 11) of the unique concatenation of demographically based politics, policy innovation, and unexpected economic circumstances in New Zealand could be superimposed on the American experience. Yet the factors Thomson invokes are universal ones, which surprisingly get little play in *Generations*. The important debate in this volume between David Thomson and Alan Walker, moreover, reminds us that, depending on the historical problem in question, *generation* may or may not be the best prism for understanding the structure and dynamics of advanced industrial societies.

Ironically, given their biocultural definition of *generation*, Strauss and Howe cannot account for contradictions and paradoxes in the ways that state policies concerning family welfare have evolved. The theoretical model presented in *Generations*, in other words, does not help us to understand the political context in which the changing contract across generations is being negotiated. This volume, in contrast, attempts to bridge the realms of basic and applied research.

The Micro-Macro Link: A Crucial But Unappreciated Issue

Until about the mid-1960s, most research in social gerontology focused on the individual experiences of aging people. "Up to the present time most of the attention of research workers and of practitioners has been focused on the aging of the organism and on alterations in the circumstances of older people," declared Clark Tibbitts three decades ago in the *Handbook of Social Gerontology* (1960, p. 6). He went on to say that "more recently there has been a rising interest in personality changes and adjustment in response to the underlying processes and to the situational changes." Much emphasis thus was placed upon psychological and microsocial aspects of the aging process.

A new "sociology of age" gained prominence when Matilda White Riley and several of her collaborators (1968) began to stress the importance of concepts such as *stratification* and *structure* in research on aging. Other researchers, such as Leonard Cain (1964), had done the critical spadework, suggesting ways in which age was a crucial dimension in social organization and behavior. But it was the Russell Sage projects, which culminated in the three-volume set, *Aging and Society*, that influenced a rising generation of gerontologists. In illustrating how society was stratified on the basis of age, Riley identified age cohorts (that is, individuals born in the same period of time) and the historical time through which these cohorts moved as the primary components of an age stratification system. The succession of cohorts is a source of social change because "their particular historical experiences make unique contributions to social structures" (Riley, Foner, & Waring, 1988, p. 243).

Theoretically, a sociology of age stratification focuses inherently on the macrosocial level, since the unit of analysis is society. Yet, because much of the research generated by this model focused on social psychological processes, the tradition became identified with primarily microlevel issues. In Chapter 9, Matilda White Riley and John Riley link cohorts both to the macroconcept of a stratification system as well as to the microunit of the family. The elegant model they refine in *The Changing Contract Across Generations* provides a theoretical framework by linking individuals to structures and thus micro to macro.

Among the new theories of the sociology of age being developed was a bold "political economy of aging" (Myles, 1989; Quadagno, 1982; Walker, 1986d). The transformation of the position of the elderly within most Western industrialized democracies has given increased salience to an approach that locates the understandings and realities of aging within political and economic institutions. Adherents of this new political economy of aging contend that the "social and economic status of elderly people is defined not by biological age but by the institutions organized wholly or partly on production" (Walker, 1986d, p. 149). Many experiences affecting older people, it is argued, are "a product of a particular division of labor and structure of inequality rather than a natural concomitant of the ageing process" (Fennel, Phillipson, & Ever, 1988, p. 53). Furthermore, understanding the relationship between the state and the elderly means understanding the operations of the modern welfare state, for as John Myles (1989) notes, the modern welfare state is, first and foremost, "a welfare state for the elderly." Clearly this view of the recent past diverges radically from the deterministic model of generations presented by Strauss and Howe. It is a commonplace among social scientists to differentiate between the public and private spheres and between the individual and the state. *The Changing Contract Across Generations* posits another research perspective. No chapter in this volume bridges the micro-macro link on an empirical and theoretical level more clearly than that by Alan Walker (Chapter 8). Walker argues that the idea of a distinct separation between social policies as a macroissue and caring relationships within the family as a microissue creates a false dichotomy, one that not only separates the public from the private domain, but also obscures how state policies affect family relationships. For example, as the state attempts to minimize its financial commitment to the family, it increases the burden on the family in general, and on women in particular, who subsequently assume responsibility for care. Thus, what appears to be a macrolevel issue, the decline of the welfare state, has direct effects on the more intimate interpersonal relationships within the family.

The Nature of the Social Contract

The idea of a social contract is at least as old as the work of Thomas Hobbes, who in 1651 envisaged it as a covenant by which individuals renounce their own wills and submit to the higher authority of the state. The contract as a covenant of subjection, in Hobbes's ideal state, was the first transition from a "natural" to a "civil state," which depended for its preservation on the individual's bending his or her will to the contract (Cassirer, 1964, p. 256). The chapters in this volume provide several perspectives on the nature of the intergenerational contract, ranging from a set of informal norms and sanctions inherent in society to formal policies set by the state. Although no consensus on particulars emerges from these chapters, each suggests in its own way that a new contract between the generations is in the making.

In nonindustrial societies the social contract between generations represents an informal, socially sanctioned set of rules regarding reciprocity between generations. In this milieu, as Nancy Foner demonstrates in Chapter 6, the social contract between generations is often clearly defined and state intervention plays no role. In many such nonindustrial societies the informal contract with the elderly is readily fulfilled. Children, kin, and neighbors care for physically incapacitated elderly until the end. What sustains the contract is a variety of factors—bonds of affection, a sense of reciprocity over the lifetime, powerful economic inducements or negative sanctions, and broad cultural values.

Yet, under some conditions the contract fails. Under some circumstances, having no children (in particular, no sons) makes older people vulnerable in old age. In societies where rights to property ownership exist, a lack of property may lead to neglect. But from a Western perspective, what may appear to be neglect or abandonment may instead be a fulfillment of the societal contract within a given cultural context.

Another cross-cultural look at the intergenerational contract—this time in contemporary Shanghai—appears in Chapter 5 by Judith Treas and Wei Wang. Treas and Wang trace the historical transition that has occurred in this contract in response to the enormous macrosocial change of the past few decades. Historically, children (especially sons) were, and still often are, the mainstay of support for the elderly in Shanghai. But the recent one-child policy legislated by the government has reduced the likelihood that older people will have sons to provide care in old age and thus has increased their insecurity. While pensions are becoming more common, at least among industrial workers, the state has yet to fill in the gap that is created by a decreasing family size by providing a stable public pension system.

Changing fertility patterns and such concomitants of modernization as housing shortages have also undermined the normative base of the intergenerational contract, making it more difficult for children to fulfill their traditional filial obligations. While some older people still believe that children should support their elderly parents, others espouse a more individualistic philosophy. Thus, the contract in China may soon appear more similar to that of Western industrialized nations, where the contract is between the individual and the state rather than between parent and child.

The new political economy perspective depicts the welfare state as an intergenerational contract, an arrangement negotiated between the working and the retired over the quality of life in old age. Political theorists differ, however, on how this intergenerational contract is constituted and on what impact it has on independence in old age. Broadly speaking, the relationship between the elderly and the state has been characterized in two dominant ways. One theory defines the intergenerational contract as a mechanism of labor market management, in which social policies result from the needs of capital to control the labor supply (Quadagno, 1990). Implicit in this argument is the view that, by restricting their access to the labor market, social welfare policies have increased the dependence of older people on the state. A second perspective defines the intergenerational contract as a product of class struggle, which has resulted in what has been termed a *citizen's wage* (Myles, 1989).

The core element of the citizen's wage is the idea that individuals can earn the right to benefits. Rather than representing a transfer of income between generations or from one age cohort to another, the citizen's wage represents a transfer of wages across the life course, from one's working life to one's old age.

In the past 10 years, challenges have arisen to the idea that retired persons have earned the right to the benefits they receive. Implicit in this view are the assumptions that (a) there is a finite amount of resources available for social spending; (b) conflict between the generations will inevitably increase as competition for scarce economic resources increases; and (c) unless present levels of entitlements for the elderly (public pensions and medical care) are substantially reduced, the demographic imperative of the aging population will place an intolerable economic burden on the state. Conventional wisdom holds that pensions represent little more than a transfer of resources from the working population to the aged.

The ideological basis of this view derives from the construction of the *dependency ratio,* a measure frequently used by demographers to describe the demands likely to affect the political and economic arrangements of the market and state as a result of population aging. Dependency ratios "indicate the contribution of the age composition of a population to society's problem of economic dependency" (Siegel & Taeuber, 1986, p. 81). As Fernando Torres-Gil suggests in Chapter 12, these issues have sometimes been framed in the United States in terms of generational equity. Yet, according to W. Andrew Achenbaum in Chapter 2, generational tensions do not ineluctably escalate into war between age groups. In the depths of the Great Depression, for example, the current needs of the elderly were pitted against the future interests of youth and the middle-aged. But there was less stereotypic rhetoric and less overt age-based polarities in the 1930s than are expressed in popular and scholarly media today. Apparently more than demographic configurations shape the political economy and culture of aging.

Experts disagree also about the reconstruction of the nature of the intergenerational contract. Have the elderly as a group benefited in recent years disproportionately in terms of social spending when compared to other age groups? Have gains to the elderly come at the expense of other age groups? Do the elderly have the power to make the decisions that privilege them, and to permit this advantage to continue? Do they deliberately set out to redistribute resources for their own benefit?

Although no contributor to the *Changing Contract Across Generations* is willing to suggest that age wars will erupt in the next decades, the consensus among most authors in this volume is that a basis for conflict between generations does exist. Where authors differ is in how they define the nature of that conflict. Maris Vinovskis (Chapter 3) suggests that generational conflict in the United States can be located in willingness to spend, particularly in regard to paying taxes for education. His data show that while support for spending on education has increased among older people, they are still less likely than other age groups to spend. Overall, age is the best predictor of support for increased federal funding either of public schools or of college students. Whether an age effect or a cohort effect is operating, the aged are more fiscally conservative than younger people. Given the increasingly small proportion of households with school age children and the reluctance of some voters to provide more than minimal levels of education for other people's children, Vinovskis's findings raise serious questions about whether we can generate the political will to spend for our future educational needs, which are important both to our children and to keeping our economy competitive.

According to David Thomson in Chapter 11, an even more fundamental source of conflict among generations exists. Thomson argues that the elderly today have fared well in terms of benefits but the next generation, which will likely see their benefits reduced, will fare poorly. By Thomson's definition, taxes and redistribution—the state's contribution to the generational contract—have increasingly come to favor the elderly. Further, the earnings of the young are falling while their rates of unemployment rise. Because today's aged are treated more generously than the aged of the next generation are likely to be, conflict will increase. Thus, for Thomson the fundamental source of generational conflict is the unequal distribution of resources.

A contrary view is provided by Richard Easterlin, Diane Macunovich, and Eileen Crimmins in Chapter 4. Undeniably, trends in individual earnings patterns in the United States since the 1960s have favored older ages, a finding that seemingly confirms the view that inequality between young and old is increasing. Yet overall there has been a remarkable similarity in the rate of increase in average income among age groups. This trend toward equality results from several decisions that have leveled out the differences noted above.

Easterlin, Macunovich, and Crimmins argue that rational choices that both young and old have made have reduced the degree of inequality stemming from differences in job opportunities and in benefits provided by the state. These choices include a decline in the average number of children per household, an increase in the number of working adults per household, and a tendency to share households as children remain in the homes of their parents at later ages. A predicted labor shortage also indicates that lifetime earnings between young and old will converge. Thus, the existing tensions between generations are not a permanent problem but rather a transient phenomenon linked to the demographic strain caused by the baby boom. In the future, any tensions that exist are likely to be ameliorated by the tendency toward convergence of resources.

By contrast, Alan Walker (Chapter 8) argues that the idea of a demographic squeeze on societal resources is a false issue, manufactured by those wishing to restructure welfare states and cut back social programs. In his view, the entire generational-equity debate is a sociopolitical construct. Thus, the prospect of conflict between generations is largely a matter of social and economic policy rather than inherent in any properties of age cohorts.

Have the particular dimensions of this conflict become manifested yet in any measurable way? Victor Marshall, Fay Cook, and Joanne Gard Marshall (Chapter 7) find considerable evidence that it has developed in the United States over the particular issue of the allocation of resources; surprisingly, it has not developed in Canada, which is comparable to the United States in terms of the proportion of the population that is elderly, the relative degree of poverty of young and old, public support for programs for older people, and the quality of the social security program. Thus, whereas Thomson highlights the universal features of the problem, Marshall, Cook, and Marshall stress the importance of aspects of resource allocation that are peculiar to the United States.

Marshall, Cook, and Marshall attribute the difference between Canada and the United States to several factors. One concerns the distribution of societal resources. The greater emphasis in Canada on universality and the greater balance of benefits in Canada between the young and the old have been partially responsible for a lower level of rhetoric about generational equity. A second factor concerns differences in the political structure between the two countries. Interest group lobbying is relatively unimportant in Canada compared to the United States, which makes the elderly lobby less organized and less visible there. This thesis supports the argument implicit in Vinovskis's suggestion that a politically self-conscious elderly population is capable of blocking cuts in benefits to themselves and of mobilizing against expenditures to other age groups. The implication of both chapters is that some intergenerational tensions have been generated by the powerful presence of the old-age lobby in the United States.

What Are Policymakers to Conclude?

In the United States in the 1980s, several political leaders gained national visibility by probing the extent of antipathy among age groups and questioning the distribution of limited national resources at both ends of the life cycle. Americans for Generational Equity (AGE), founded in 1984 by David Durenberger, a first-term Republican senator from Minnesota, attracted a distinguished board of directors and consultants before its founder's financial problems forced AGE out of business. Richard Lamm probably will be remembered more for urging senior citizens to consider their duty to die economically than for his accomplishments as governor of Colorado. George Bush is likely to be the last United States president to have served in World War II; Bill Clinton is a baby boomer. Most of the serious Democratic presidential hopefuls of 1992 did not come of age until the 1950s. All of this suggests that the transfer of political power from one age group to another is under way. How this succession is negotiated may well effectuate the changing contract across generations.

It seems clear, however, that United States citizens in general, and lawmakers in particular, do not yet understand what stake any generation has in policymaking. The plea for "generational equity" seems to be a politically correct slogan. Groups such as the American Association for Retired Persons (AARP) and organizations that imitate it, such as the new American Association of Boomers (AAB), tend to develop marketing tools designed to bolster their membership by invoking points of divergence across generational interests. As Bernice and Dail Neugarten point out, such emphasis on generational inequity is at best paradoxical:

> Despite the fact that age is becoming a less relevant basis for assessing age competencies and needs, and even as traditional age norms and conceptions of age groups are becoming blurred, we are witnessing a proliferation of public and private policy decisions in which the basis for defining target groups is age. (1986, pp. 45–46)

Preferential tax treatments for people over 55, commitments to ending age discrimination in the marketplace, and age-based entitlements in Social Security are well-intentioned federal initiatives. They may, however, fail to address deeper inequities in the contemporary United States political economy.

To be blunt, racial and gender-based inequalities have been more enduring and pernicious hallmarks of American society than have historic differences across age or generational lines. Since the colonial period, white, middle-class, native-born males generally have been able to acquire a home and accumulate some other possessions through dint of hard work; in later years, a majority of this segment of the population have been able to liquidate assets so as to maintain a living independent of work. And with the possible exception of the present cohort of baby boomer men, most adult, male, white children could expect to do better than their fathers. The same generalization simply cannot be made about other groups in the United States population. Despite significant progress since the 1960s, low-income minorities generally have been disadvantaged from conception, and have remained so over the course of their lives. Women constitute a majority of the United States population, but in the courts, marketplace, and households of this country, theirs is not the dominant voice.

To focus on such age-based questions as whether the so-called "notch babies" are getting slightly smaller Social Security benefits than those born before 1917 and after 1921 utterly ignores bigger policy conundra. How can this "blip" compare to the fact that nearly 40 million Americans lack *any* health care insurance? Tragically, those with the least financial wherewithal are the most vulnerable. The elimination of catastrophic care coverage for senior citizens, moreover, poses a significant financial risk on the very old and their children. Differentiating between federal health care policies for the old (Medicare) and for the poor (Medicaid) no longer makes sense in an aging society (Achenbaum, 1986). Policymakers in the United States must decide how much longer this country can afford to ignore the inequities wrought in an expensive, inadequate patchwork of private and publicly financed health care delivery programs. One might come to the debate with generational interests in mind, but it would be more astute to begin with other criteria (income, race, and gender) and then see how they interact with age (Quadagno, 1990).

It is at this point that two items on any future research agenda of relevance to policymakers become most evident. On the one hand, it is important to recognize that *age group*, *cohort*, and *generation* are not equivalent terms, as Bengtson emphasizes in Chapter 1. But it is even more critical to comprehend the dynamics of race, gender, and class from a gerontologic perspective. As long as gerontology depicts the "problems" of the elderly as primarily age based, the field forecloses its opportunity to explicate discontinuities in the ways that various segments of the population form alliances and compete for resources over time. On the other hand, policymakers need to take account of the temporal dimensions of any contract between generations. And this entails grappling with historical time and societal aging amidst generational negotiations.

To resolve present-day disputes, United States politicians have adopted the expedient of shifting costs to the future. To "save" Social Security in 1983, for instance, they raised (ever so gradually) the retirement age in the 21st century. This tack satisfied the accountants. It gave everybody ample time to adjust to a new set of rules that would affect working lives. Objections were raised, to be sure. Liberals worried that the policy change would penalize the disabled. Conservatives wanted to go even further in altering retirement rules. Some wanted to index the retirement age so that it would rise automatically, as do monthly benefits. Others hoped to establish a retirement age baseline comparable to the life expectancy that beneficiaries enjoyed when the original legislation was enacted in 1935.

Missing in all of this contractual negotiation across generational lines was a sense that "risks" were asymmetrical at the micro- and macrolevels. To the extent that Social Security was to be viewed as part of an individual worker's "citizen wage," then raising the retirement age meant that people who retired after 2007 would get less than they might otherwise have expected before the rules were changed. And yet, if Social Security were viewed as "social insurance," then another interpretation was plausible: To the extent that Social Security collectively pools the risks of old-age dependency with the limited resources at its disposal, then making this slight bureaucratic adjustment seemed more palatable than allowing the program to dissolve because it had exceeded its resources. *Which* image of the future should guide policymakers in sorting out people's stake in the commonweal: one that gives priority to individual luck, or one that acknowledges that, in times of scarcity, something is better than nothing?

Conclusion

From the perspective of a United States cultural historian, "we have clearly entered a period in which the intergenerational compact underlying Social Security is being renegotiated" (Cole, 1989, p. 382). Most of the contributors to this volume would agree with this statement, but they would take Thomas Cole's argument a step further. To accommodate the challenges and capitalize on the opportunities of an aging society will require making significant changes in our political economy, social roles, and cultural norms. The "conversation between generations" (Laslett, 1979) that will ensue is bound to be fractious if it ultimately is to prove fruitful.

This is why the changing contract across generations requires a fundamental review of our conceptual theories, a reconsideration of the politics of age and aging, and a rethinking of policies designed to strengthen people's ability to maintain their independence and to make contributions to the well-being of others. We hope that the ideas in this volume will stimulate future research in this critical area.

Acknowledgment

The authors thank John M. Cornman for his help in thinking through some of the broader issues discussed in this chapter.

References

Achenbaum, W. A. (1978). *Old age in the new land.* Baltimore: The Johns Hopkins University Press.

Achenbaum, W. A. (1986). *Social Security.* New York: Cambridge University Press.

Achenbaum, W. A. (1989a). Politics, power, and problems. *Journal of Policy History, 2,* 206–229.

Achenbaum, W. A. (1989b). Public pensions as intergenerational transfers in the United States. In P. Johnson, C. Conrad, & D. Thomson (Eds.), *Workers versus pensioners: Intergenerational justice in an ageing world* (pp. 113–135). Manchester: Manchester University Press.

Achenbaum, W. A. (1990). The V.A. by the numbers. *The Aging Connection, 11,* 3.

Achenbaum, W. A. (in press). The politics of aging: The geriatric imperative of the Department of Veterans Affairs. *Journal of Aging and Social Policy.*

Ahrons, C. R., & Rogers, R. H. (1987). *Divorced families: A multidisciplinary developmental view.* New York: W. W. Norton.

Aldous, J. (1987). New views on the family life of the elderly and the near-elderly. *Journal of Marriage and the Family, 49,* 227–234.

Alwin, D. F. (1988). From obedience to autonomy: Changes in traits desired in children 1924–1978. *Public Opinion Quarterly, 52*(1), 33–52.

America is at war with its children. (1989, October 12). *San Francisco Chronicle,* p. 35.

Americans for Generational Equity. (1990). *Annual report.* Washington, DC: Author.

Amoss, P., & Harrell, S. (1981). Introduction: An anthropological perspective on aging. In P. Amoss & S. Harrell (Eds.), *Other ways of growing old* (pp. 1–24). Stanford: Stanford University Press.

Anderson, M. (1977). The impact on the family relationship of the elderly of changes since Victorian times in governmental income maintenance. In E. Shanas & M. Sussman (Eds.), *Family bureaucracy and the elderly* (pp. 36–59). Durham, NC: Duke University Press.

Arensberg, C. M., & Kimball, S. T. (1961). *Family and community in Ireland.* Gloucester, MA: Smith. (Original work published 1940)

273

Argyle, A. W. (1963). *The Gospel according to Matthew.* Cambridge: Cambridge University Press.

Auer, L. (1987). Canadian hospital costs and productivity. In *Appendix A: Aging with limited health resources: Proceedings of a Colloquium on Health Care* (pp. 179–185). Ottawa: Economic Council of Canada.

Axtell, J. (1974). *The school upon a hill: Education and society in colonial New England.* New Haven, CT: Yale University Press.

Bachrach, P. (1967). *The theory of democratic elitism: A critique.* Boston: Little, Brown.

Bailyn, B. (1960). *Education in the forming of American society.* Chapel Hill: University of North Carolina Press.

Baltes, P. B., & Smith, J. (1990). Toward a psychology of wisdom and its onto-genesis. In R. J. Sternberg (Ed.), *Wisdom: Its nature, origins, and development* (pp. 87–120). New York: Cambridge University Press.

Banting, K. G. (1987). *The welfare state and Canadian federalism.* Kingston: McGill-Queen's University Press.

Barker, J. C. (1990). Between humans and ghosts: The decrepit elderly in Polynesian society. In J. Sokolovsky (Ed.), *The cultural context of aging* (pp. 295–314). New York: Bergin & Garvey.

Barnett, R. C., Biener, L., & Baruch, G. K. (1987). *Gender and stress.* New York: Free Press.

Barrett, M. (1980). *Women's oppression today.* London: Verso Books.

Barrett, M., & McIntosh, M. (1982). *The anti-social family.* London: Verso Books.

Barzun, J. (1961). *Classic, romantic and modern* (2nd rev. ed.). Garden City, NY: Doubleday.

Becker, G. (1981). *A treatise on the family.* Cambridge, MA: Harvard University Press.

Belenky, M. F., Clinchy, B. M., Goldberger, N. R., & Tarule, J. M. (1986). *Women's ways of knowing: The development of self, voice, and mind.* New York: Basic.

Bellah, R. N., Madsen, R., Sullivan, W. M., Swidler, A., & Tipton, S. M. (1985). *Habits of the heart: Individualism and commitment in American life.* Los Angeles: University of California Press.

Bengtson, V. L. (1989). The problem of generations: Age group contrasts, continuities, and social change. In V. L. Bengtson & K. W. Schaie (Eds.), *The course of later life: Research and reflections* (pp. 25–54). New York: Springer.

Bengtson, V. L. (1990, November). *Generations and aging: Continuities, conflicts and reciprocities.* Presidential Address to the meeting of the Gerontological Society of America, Boston.

Bengtson, V. L., Cutler, N. E., Mangen, D. J., & Marshall, V. W. (1985). Generations, cohorts, and relations between age groups. In R. Binstock & E. Shanas (Eds.), *Handbook of aging and the social sciences* (2nd ed., pp. 304–338). New York: Van Nostrand Reinhold.

Bengtson, V. L., & Dannefer, D. (1987). Families, work and aging: Implications of disordered cohort flow for the 21st century. In R. A. Ward & S. S. Tobin (Eds.), *Health in aging: Sociological issues and policy directions* (pp. 256–289). New York: Springer.

Bengtson, V. L., & Kuypers, J. A. (1971). Generational differences and the "developmental stake." *Aging and Human Development, 2,* 249–260.

Bengtson, V. L., Marti, G., & Roberts, R. E. L. (1991). Age group relations: Generational equity and inequity. In K. Pillemer & K. McCartney (Eds.), *Parent-child relations across the lifespan* (pp. 253–278). Hillsdale, NJ: Lawrence Erlbaum Associates.

Bengtson, V. L., & Murray, T. M. (in press). Justice across generations (and cohorts): Sociological perspectives on the life course and reciprocities over time. In L. Cohen (Ed.), *Justice across generations: What does it mean?* Washington, DC: American Association of Retired Persons.

Bengtson, V. L., & Robertson, J. F. (Eds.). (1985). *Grandparenthood*. Beverly Hills: Sage.

Bengtson, V. L., Rosenthal, C., & Burton, L. (1990). Families and aging: Diversity and heterogeneity. In R. H. Binstock & L. George (Eds.), *Handbook of aging and social sciences* (3rd ed., pp. 263–287). San Diego: Academic Press.

Bengtson, V. L., & Schutze, Y. (1992). Altern und Generationenbeziehungen: Assichten für das kommende Jahrhundert. In P. B. Baltes & J. Mittelstrasse (Eds.), *Zukunft des Alterns und gesellschaftliche Entwicklung* (pp. 492–517). Berlin: Walter de Gruyter.

Benson, C. S., & O'Halloran, K. (1987). The economic history of school finance in the United States. *Journal of Education Finance, 12*(4), 495–515.

Benson, S. P., Brier, S., & Rosenzweig, R. (1986). *Presenting the past*. Philadelphia: Temple University Press.

Benson-von der Ohe, E. (1987). *First and second marriages*. New York: Praeger.

Berger, M. C. (1989). Demographic cycles, cohort size, and earnings. *Demography, 26*, 311–321.

Bernard, J. (1972). *The future of marriage*. Beverly Hills: Sage.

Beveridge, W. (1942). *Social insurance and allied services*. London: HMSO.

Bible. (1962). *Revised standard version*. New York: Oxford University Press.

Binney, E. A., & Estes, C. L. (1988). The retreat of the state and its transfer of responsibility: The intergenerational war. *International Journal of Health Services, 18*(1), 83–96.

Binstock, R. H. (1981). The politics of aging interest groups: Interest group liberalism and the politics of aging. In R. Hudson (Ed.), *The aging in politics* (pp. 47–73). Springfield, IL: Charles C. Thomas.

Binstock, R. H. (1983). The aged as a scapegoat. *Gerontologist, 23*, 136–143.

Binstock, R. H. (1987, September). *The implications of population aging for American politics*. Paper delivered before the annual meeting of the American Political Science Association, Chicago.

Binstock, R. H. (in press). Transcending intergenerational equity. In V. L. Greene, T. R. Marmor, & T. M. Smeeding (Eds.), *Economic security, intergenerational justice, and the North American elderly*. Washington, DC: Urban Institute Press.

Bonior, D. E., Champlin, S. M., & Kolly, T. S. (1984). *The Vietnam veteran*. New York: Praeger.

Booth, C. (1984). *The aged poor in England and Wales*. London: Macmillan.

Bould, S., Sanborn, B., & Reif, L. (1989). *Eighty five plus: The oldest old*. Belmont, CA: Wadsworth.

Bowles, S., & Gintis, H. (1976). *Schooling in capitalist America: Educational reform and the contradictions of economic life.* New York: Basic Books.

Bradbury, B., Doyle, J., & Whiteford, P. (1990). *Trends in disposable income: Incomes of Australian families, 1982/3 to 1989/90.* Sydney: University of New South Wales Press.

Brandes, S. (1989, November). *Kinship and care of the aged in traditional rural Iberia.* Paper presented at the Meeting of the Social Science History Association, Washington, D.C.

Brody, E. M. (1985). Parent care as a normative family stress. *Gerontologist, 25,* 19–29.

Brym, R. J., with Fox, B. (1989). *From culture to power: The sociology of English Canada.* Toronto: Oxford University Press.

Bumpass, L., & Sweet, J. (1989). *National estimates of cohabitation: Cohort levels and union stability* (Working Paper No. 2). Madison: University of Wisconsin.

Bumpass, L., Sweet, J., & Cherlin, A. (1989). *The role of cohabitation in declining rates of marriage* (Working Paper No. 5). Madison: University of Wisconsin.

Burbidge, J. (1987). *Social Security in Canada: An economic appraisal.* Ottawa: Canadian Tax Foundation.

Burgess, E. W. (1948). The family in a changing society. *American Journal of Sociology, 53,* 417–21.

Burton, L., & Bengtson, V. L. (1985). Black grandmothers: Issues of timing and continuity of roles. In V. L. Bengtson & J. Robertson (Eds.), *Grandparenthood* (pp. 304–338). Beverly Hills: Sage.

Button, J. W., & Rosenbaum, W. A. (1989). Seeing gray: School bond issues and the aging in Florida. *Research on Aging, 11*(2), 158–173.

Cain, L. (1964). Life course and social structure. In R. E. L. Faris (Ed.), *Handbook of modern sociology* (pp. 272–309). Chicago: Rand McNally.

Caldwell, J. C. (1982). *A theory of fertility decline.* New York: Academic Press.

Callahan, D. (1987). *Setting limits: Medical goals in an aging society.* New York: Simon & Schuster.

Carstensen, L. L. (1987). Age-related changes in social activity. In L. L. Carstensen & B. A. Edelstein (Eds.), *Handbook of clinical gerontology* (pp. 221–237). New York: Pergamon Press.

Carstensen, L. L. (1991). Selectivity theory: Social activity in life-span context. In W. Schaie (Ed.), *Annual review of geriatrics and gerontology* (pp. 195–215). New York: Springer.

Cassirer, E. (1964). *The philosophy of the enlightenment.* Boston: Beacon.

Cattell, M. (1990). Models of old age among the Samia of Kenya: Family support of the elderly. *Journal of Cross-Cultural Gerontology, 5,* 375–394.

Central Statistical Office. (1950–1990). *Annual abstract of statistics of the United Kingdom.* London: Author.

Central Statistical Office. (1973–1990). *Social trends.* London: Author.

Chakravarty, S. (1988, November). Cry baby: The intergenerational transfer of wealth. *Forbes,* pp. 222ff.

Checkland, S. G., & Checkland, E. O. (Eds.). (1974). *The poor law report of 1834.* Harmondsworth: Penguin Books.

Christian, P. B. (1989). Nonfamily households and housing among young adults. In F. K. Goldscheider & C. Goldscheider (Eds.), *Ethnicity and the new family economy: Living arrangements and intergenerational financial flows* (pp. 57–73). Boulder, CO: Westview Press.

Chudacoff, H. (1990). *How old are you?* Princeton, NJ: Princeton University Press.

Clark, M. (1973). Contributions of cultural anthropology to the study of the aged. In L. Nader & T. Maretzki (Eds.), *Cultural illness and health* (pp. 78–88). Washington, DC: American Anthropological Association.

Clark, R., & Spengler, J. (1980). *The economics of individual and population ageing.* Cambridge: Cambridge University Press.

Cohen, J., Segal, J. R., & Temme, L. V. (1986). Service was an educational disadvantage to Vietnam-era personnel. *Sociology and Social Research, 70,* 206–208.

Cole, T. R. (1989). Generational equity in America. *Social Science Medicine, 29,* 377–383.

Coleman, J. (1986). Norms as social capital. In G. Radnitzky & P. Bernholtz (Eds.), *Economic imperialism* (pp. 130–142). New York: Paragon House.

Colson, E., & Scudder, T. (1981). Old age in Gwembe District, Zambia. In P. Amoss & S. Harrell (Eds.), *Other ways of growing old* (pp. 125–154). Stanford: Stanford University Press.

Connell, R. W. (1987). *Gender and power: Society, the person, and sexual politics.* Stanford: Stanford University Press.

Cook, F. L. (1990). Congress and the public: Convergent and divergent opinions on Social Security. In H. J. Aaron (Ed.), *Social security and the budget* (pp. 77–107). New York: University Press of America.

Cook, F. L., Marshall, V. W., Marshall, J. G., & Kaufman, J. E. (1991, May). *Intergenerational equity and the politics of income security for the old.* Paper presented at the Donner Foundation Conference, Economic Security of Elderly Persons in Canada and the United States, Yale University, New Haven, CT.

Cooney, T., & Uhlenberg P. (1990). The role of divorce in men's relations with their adult children after mid-life. *Journal of Marriage and the Family, 52,* 677–688.

Cowan, R. (1988). Senate OKs cabinet status, judicial review for vets. *Congressional Quarterly, 46,* 1977–1980.

Cox, F. M., & Mberia, N. (1977). *Aging in a changing village society: A Kenyan experience.* Washington, DC: International Federation on Ageing.

Cremin, L. A. (1970). *American education: The colonial experience, 1607–1783.* New York: Harper and Row.

Cremin, L. A. (1980). *American education: The national experience, 1783–1876.* New York: Harper and Row.

Cribier, F. (1989). Changes in life course and retirement in recent years: The example of two cohorts of Parisians. In P. Johnson, C. Conrad, & D. Thomson (Eds.), *Workers versus pensioners: Intergenerational justice in an ageing world* (pp. 181–201). Manchester: Manchester University Press.

Crimmins, E. M. (1985). The social impact of recent and prospective mortality declines among older Americans. *Social Science Review, 70,* 192–198.

Cutler, N. E. (1981). Political characteristics of elderly cohorts in the twenty-first century. In S. B. Kiesler, J. N. Morgan, & V. K. Oppenheimer (Eds.), *Aging: Social Change* (pp. 127–157). New York: Academic Press.

Dalley, G. (1988). *Ideologies of caring.* London: Macmillan.

Damon, A. L. (1976). Veterans' benefits. *American Heritage, 27,* 49–53.

Daniels, N. (1988). *Am I my parents' keeper?* New York: Oxford University Press.

Dannefer, D. (1988). What's in a name? An account of the neglect of variability in the study of aging. In J. E. Birren & V. L. Bengtson (Eds.), *Emergent theories of aging* (pp. 356–384). New York: Springer.

Danziger, S., van derSaag, J., Smolensky, J., & Taussig, M. (1983). The life-cycle hypothesis and the consumption behaviour of the elderly. *Journal of Post-Keynesian Economics, 5,* 208–227.

Davis, J. A. (1986). British and American attitudes: Similarities and contrasts. In R. Jowell, S. Witherspoon, & L. Brook (Eds.), *British social attitudes* (pp. 89–114). Aldershot: Gower.

Davis, K. (1984). Wives and work: Consequences of the sex role revolution. *Population and Development Review, 10,* 397–418.

Davis, K., & van den Oever, P. (1982). Demographic foundations of new sex roles. *Population and Development Review, 8,* 495–511.

Davis-Friedmann, D. (1983). *Long lives: Chinese elderly and the communist revolution.* Cambridge, MA: Harvard University Press.

Davis-Friedmann, D. (1985). Intergenerational equities and the Chinese revolution. *Modern China, 11*(2), 177–201.

Day, C. (1990). *What older Americans think: Interest groups and aging policy.* Princeton, NJ: Princeton University Press.

Demkovitch, L. (1984, June). When a booming population of old vets checks in for V.A. health care, look out. *National Journal, 16,* 1091–1093.

Denison, E. (1985). *Trends in American economic growth, 1929-82.* Washington, DC: Brookings Institute.

Denton, F. T., Li, S. N., & Spencer, B. G. (1987). How will population aging affect the future costs of maintaining health-care standards? In V. W. Marshall (Ed.), *Aging in Canada: Social perspectives* (2nd ed., pp. 553–568). Markham: Fitzhenry and Whiteside.

Department of Health and Social Services. (1985a). *Reform of Social Security,* CMND 9517. London: HMSO.

Department of Health and Social Services. (1985b). *Reform of Social Security-Programme for change.* London: HMSO.

DePauw, L. G. (1985). Harris survey provides data on women veterans. *Minerva, 3,* 25–29.

deTocqueville, A. (1969). *Democracy in America.* Garden City, NY: Doubleday Anchor. (Original work published 1835)

Donzelot, J. (1979). *The policing of families.* London: Hutchinson.

Dowd, J. J. (1984). Beneficence and the aged. *Journal of Gerontology, 39,* 102–108.

Dreitzel, H. P. (1984). Generational conflict from the point of view of civilization today. In V. Garms-Homolova, E. M. Hoerning, & D. Schaeffer (Eds.), *Intergenerational relations* (pp. 17–26). Lewiston, NY: G. J. Hogrefe.

Duesenberry, J. S. (1966). *Income, saving, and the theory of consumer behavior.* Cambridge, MA: Harvard University Press.

Duncan, O. D. (1966). Methodological issues in the analysis of social mobility. In N. J. Smelser & S. M. Lipset (Eds.), *Social structure and mobility in economic development* (pp. 51–97). Chicago: Aldine.

Durenberger, D. (1989). Education and the contract between the generations. *Generational Journal, 2,*(1), 5–8.

Durkheim, E. (1951). *Suicide.* New York: Free Press.

Easterlin, R. A. (1980). *Birth and fortune: The impact of numbers upon personal welfare.* London: Grant McIntyre.

Easterlin, R. A. (1987). The new age structure of poverty in America: Permanent or transient? *Population and Development Review, 13*(2), 195–208.

Easterlin, R. A., Macdonald, C., & Macunovich, D. J. (1990a). How have American Baby Boomers fared? Earnings and economic well-being of young adults, 1964–87. *Journal of Population Economics, 3,* 277–290.

Easterlin, R. A., Macdonald, C., & Macunovich, D. J. (1990b). Retirement prospects of the baby-boom generation: A different perspective. *Gerontologist, 30,* 776–783.

Economic Council of Canada. (1989). *Legacies: Twenty-sixth annual review.* Ottawa: Economic Council of Canada.

Eichler, M. (1983). *Families in Canada today: Recent changes and their policy implications.* Toronto: Gage.

Elam, S. (1989). *The Gallup/Phi Delta Kappa polls of attitudes toward the public schools, 1969–88.* Bloomington, IN: Phi Delta Kappa Educational Foundation.

Elkins, S., & McKitrick, E. (1962). *The founding fathers: Young men of the Revolution.* Washington, DC: American Historical Association.

Ericsson, T. (1990, June). *Widows and spinsters: The demography of small business women in late nineteenth century Sweden.* Paper presented at Conference on the Historical Demography of Aging, Bowdoin College, Brunswick, ME.

Erikson, R., & Aberg, R. (Eds.). (1987). *Welfare in transition: A survey of living conditions in Sweden, 1968–81.* Oxford: Clarendon Press.

Estes, C. (1986). The politics of ageing in America. *Ageing and Society, 6,* 122–134.

Estes, C. L., Swan, J., & Gerard, L. (1982). Dominant and competing paradigms in gerontology: Towards a political economy of ageing. *Ageing and Society, 2*(2), 169–85.

Evans, R. G. (1985). Illusions of necessity: Evading responsibility for choice in health care. *Journal of Health Politics, Policy and Law, 10,* 439–467.

Fackelmann, K. A. (1986). The V.A.'s blueprint for the future. *Medicine & Health Perspectives,* (September 15) pp. 36–45.

Fairlie, H. (1988, March 28). Talkin' bout my generation. *New Republic,* pp. 19–22.

Fedyk, F. C. (1990, October). *Federal/provincial/municipal jurisdictional issues: Their impact on seniors in Canada.* Paper presented at the meeting of the Canadian Association on Gerontology, Victoria, B.C.

Fennel, G., Phillipson, C., & Ever, H. (Eds.). (1988). The *sociology of old age.* Philadelphia: Open University Press.

Fessler, P. (1984, June 2). Tactics of new elderly lobby ruffle congressional feath-
ers. *Congressional Quarterly Weekly Report*, pp. 1310–1313.

Feuer, L. (1969). *The conflict of generations*. New York: Basic Books.

Field, F. (1980). *Fair shares for families*. London: Study Commission on the Family.

Fields, G. S., & Mitchell, O. S. (1984). *Retirement, pensions, and Social Security*.
Cambridge, MA: MIT Press.

Finch, J., & Groves, D. (Eds.). (1983). *A labour of love*. London: Routledge.

Fischer, D. H. (1965). *The revolution of American conservatism*. New York: Harper
& Row.

Fischer, D. H. (1970). *Historians' fallacies*. New York: Harper & Row.

Fischer, D. H. (1977). *Growing old in America*. New York: Oxford University Press.

Fisher, R., & Ury, W. (1983). *Getting to yes*. New York: Penguin Books.

Fishlow, A. (1966). The American common school revival: Fact or fancy? In H.
Rosovsky (Ed.), *Industrialization in two systems: Essays in honor of Alexander
Gershenkron* (pp. 40–67). New York: Wiley.

Flora, P. (Ed.). (1986). *Growth to limits: The European welfare states since World War
Two*. Berlin: de Gruyter.

Fogarty, M. (Ed.). (1982). *Retirement policy: The next fifty years*. London: Heine-
mann.

Foner, A. (1974). Age stratification and age conflict in political life. *American
Sociological Review, 39*, 187–196.

Foner, N. (1984a). *Ages in conflict: A cross-cultural perspective on inequality between
old and young*. New York: Columbia University Press.

Foner, N. (1984b). Age and social change. In D. Rertzer & J. Keith (Eds.), *Age and
anthropological theory* (pp. 195–216). Ithaca, NY: Cornell University Press.

Foner, N. (1985). Old and frail and everywhere unequal. *Hastings Center Report,
15*, 27–37.

Foot, D. K. (1984). The demographic future of fiscal federalism in Canada. *Canadian Public Policy, 10*, 406–414.

Fortes, M. (1949). *The web of kinship among the Tallensi*. London: Oxford University
Press.

Fortes, M. (1970). Pietas in ancestor worship. In M. Fortes (Ed.), *Time and social
structure and other essays* (pp. 164–200). London: Athlone Press.

Fowler, L., & Shaiko, R. (1987, September). *The graying of the constituency: Active
seniors in congressional district politics*. Paper presented before the annual
meeting of the American Political Science Association, Chicago.

Frank, R. H. (1988). *Passions within reason: The strategic role of the emotions*. New
York: W. W. Norton.

Friedman, M., & Friedman, R. (1980). *Free to choose*. Harmondsworth: Penguin.

Fuchs, V. (1986). Sex differences in economic well-being. *Science, 232*, 459–464.

Furstenberg, F. F., Jr. (1990). Divorce and the American family. *Annual Review of
Sociology, 16*, 379–403.

Garfield, E. (1985). The 100 most-cited papers ever and how we select "citation
classics." In E. Garfield, *Essays of an information scientist: 1984* (p. 176). Philadelphia: ISI Press.

Garms, W. I., Guthrie, J. W., & Pierce, L. C. (1978). *School finance: The economics
and politics of public education*. Englewood Cliffs, NJ: Prentice-Hall.

Gatz, M., Bengtson, V. L., & Blum, M. J. (1990). Caregiving families. In J. E. Birren & K. W. Schaie (Eds.), *Handbook of the psychology of aging* (3rd ed., pp. 404–426). San Diego: Academic Press.

Geertz, C. (1966). Religion as a cultural system. In M. Banton (Ed.), *Anthropological approaches to the study of religion* (pp. 1–46). London: Tavistock.

Gifford, C. G. (1990). *Canada's fighting seniors*. Toronto: James Lorimer.

Ginsburg, H. (1983). *Full employment and public policy: The United States and Sweden*. Lexington, MA: Lexington Books.

Girod, R., de Laubier, P., & Gladstone, A. (Eds.). (1985). *Social policy in western Europe and the United States, 1950–80*. London: Macmillan.

Glascock, A. (1990). By any other name, it is still killing: A comparison of the treatment of the elderly in America and other societies. In J. Sokolovsky (Ed.), *The cultural context of aging* (pp. 43–56). New York: Bergin and Garvey.

Glass, D. (1940). *Population policies and movements in Europe*. London: Oxford University Press.

Glasson, W. H. (1918). *Federal military pensions*. New York: Oxford University Press.

Glendon, M. A. (1987). *Abortion and divorce in western law*. Cambridge, MA: Harvard University Press.

Glenn, C. L., Jr. (1988). *The myth of the common school*. Amherst: University of Massachusetts Press.

Goldscheider, F. K. (1990). The aging of the gender revolution. *Research on Aging, 12*, 531–545.

Goldscheider, F. K., & Goldscheider, C. (Eds.). (1989). *Ethnicity and the new family economy: Living arrangements and intergenerational financial flows*. Boulder: Westview Press.

Goldstein, M. C., Ku, Y., & Ikels, C. (1990). Household composition of the elderly in two rural villages in the People's Republic of China. *Journal of Cross Cultural Gerontology, 5*, 119–130.

Goleman, D. (1985). *Vital lies, simple truths*. New York: Simon & Schuster.

Goodman, E. (1988, May 22). Time to call in bridge builders for the warring generations. *Chicago Tribune*, Section 5, p. 2.

Goodwin, G. (1942). *The social organization of the Western Apache*. Chicago: University of Chicago Press.

Goody, E. (1973). *Contexts of kinship*. Cambridge: Cambridge University Press.

Goody, J. (1976). Aging in nonindustrial societies. In R. H. Binstock & E. Shanas (Eds.), *Handbook of aging and the social sciences* (pp. 117–129). New York: Van Nostrand Reinhold.

Gould, S. G., & Palmer, J. L. (1988). Outcomes, interpretations, and policy implications. In J. L. Palmer, T. Smeeding, & B. B. Torrey (Eds.), *The vulnerable* (pp. 413–442). Washington, DC: Urban Institute Press.

Gouldner, A. W. (1960). The norm of reciprocity. *American Sociological Review, 25*, 161–178.

Government of Canada. (1982). *Better pensions for Canadians*. Ottawa: Government of Canada, Minister of Supply and Services Canada, Catalogue No. CP 45–48/1982E.

Graebner, W. (1980). *A History of retirement*. New Haven, CT: Yale University Press.

Gronvall, J. (1989, January). V.A. cabinet status more than gesture. *United States Medicine*, 12–15.

Guemple, L. (1977). The dilemma of the aging Eskimo. In C. Beattie & S. Crysdale (Eds.), *Sociology Canada: Readings* (pp. 194–203). Toronto: Butterworth.

Guemple, L. (1983). Growing old in Inuit society. In J. Soklovsky (Ed.), *Growing old in different societies* (pp. 24–28). Belmont, CA: Wadsworth.

Gui, S. X., & Associates. (1987). Status and needs of the elderly in urban Shanghai: Analysis of some preliminary statistics. *Journal of Cross-Cultural Gerontology, 2*, 171–186.

Guillemard, A. M. (1980). *La vieillesse et l'etat*. Paris: Presses Universitaires de France.

Hagestad, G. O. (1982). *Older women in intergenerational relations*. Paper for the Physical and Mental Health of Aged Women Conference, Case Western Reserve University, Cleveland, OH.

Hagestad, G. O. (1986). The family: Women and grandparents as kinkeepers. In A. Pifer & L. Bronte (Eds.), *Our aging society* (pp. 141–160). New York: W. W. Norton.

Hagestad, G. O. (1987). Parent-child relations in later life: Trends and gaps in past research. In J. B. Lancaster, J. Altmann, A. S. Rossi, & L. R. Sherrod (Eds.), *Parenting across the life span* (pp. 405–434). Hawthorne, NY: Aldine de Gruyter.

Hagestad, G. O. (1988). Demographic change and the life course: Some emerging trends in the family realm. *Family Relations, 37*, 405–410.

Hagestad, G. O. (1990). Social perspectives on the life course. In R. H. Binstock & L. K. George (Eds.), *Handbook of aging and the social sciences* (3rd ed., pp. 151–168). San Diego, CA: Academic Press.

Hamilton, H. D., & Cohen, S. H. (1974). *Policy making by plebiscite: School referenda*. Lexington, MA: Lexington Books.

Hannan, M. (1982). Families, markets and social structures: An essay on Becker's treatise on the family. *Journal of Economic Literature, 20*, 65–72.

Hareven, T. (1982). *Industrial time and family time*. Cambridge: Cambridge University Press.

Hareven, T. (1987). Reflections on family research in the People's Republic of China. *Social Research, 54*, 663–689.

Hareven, T., & Adams, K. (1989, November). *The second generation: A cohort comparison in assistance to aging parents in the United States*. Paper presented at the meetings of the Social Science History Association, Washington, D.C.

Heclo, H. (1988). Generational politics. In J. L. Palmer, T. Smeeding, & B. B. Torrey (Eds.), *The vulnerable* (pp. 381–411). Washington, DC: Urban Institute Press.

Hernandez, L. L. (1989). Nonfamily living arrangements among black and Hispanic Americans. In F. K. Goldscheider & C. Goldscheider (Eds.), *Ethnicity and the new family economy: Living arrangements and intergenerational financial flows* (pp. 17–37). Boulder, CO: Westview Press.

Hewitt, P., & Howe, N. (1988). Generational equity and the future of generational politics. *Generations, 12*(3), 10–13.

Hill, R. (1970). *Family development in three generations*. Cambridge, MA: Schenkman.

Hinricks, K. (in press). Insecurity regarding social security: Public pensions and demographic change in Germany. In J. Guillemin & I. Horowitz (Eds.), *Inter-generational rivalries*. New York: Transaction Books.

Ho, D. Y. F. (1989). Continuity and variation in Chinese patterns of socialization. *Journal of Marriage and the Family, 51*(1), 149–163.

Hoffman, S. D., & Duncan, G. J. (1988). What are the economic consequences of divorce? *Demography, 25*, 641–645.

Holmes, A. E. (1990). "Such is the price we pay": American widows and civil war pensions. In M. A. Vinovskis (Ed.), *Toward a social history of the American civil war* (pp. 171–196). New York: Cambridge University Press.

House of Commons. (1983). *Report of the parliamentary task force on pension reform*. Ottawa: Queen's Printer for Canada.

Hudson, R., & Strate, J. (1984). Aging and political systems. In R. H. Binstock & E. Shanas (Eds.), *The handbook of aging and the social sciences* (2nd ed., pp. 554–588). New York: Van Nostrand Reinhold.

Hutton, W. R. (1987, April 8). The old and young aren't foes. *New York Times*, p. A27.

Imhof, A. (1986). Life-course patterns of women and their husbands: 16th to 20th century. In A. B. Sorensen, F. E. Weinert, & L. R. Sherrod (Eds.), *Human development and the life course: Multidisciplinary perspectives* (pp. 247–270). Hillsdale, NJ: Lawrence Erlbaum.

Jacobs, J. B., & McNamara, R. J. (1986). Vietnam veterans and the agent orange controversy. *Armed Forces & Society, 13*, 57–79.

Jefferson, G., & Petri, P. A. (1986). Financial retirement in China: Theoretical and empirical perspectives. In J. H. Schultz & D. Davis-Friedmann (Eds.), *Aging China: Family, economic, and government policies in transition* (pp. 213–242). Washington, DC: Gerontological Society of America.

Johnson, C. L., & Barer, B. M. (1990). Families and networks among older inner-city blacks. *Gerontologist, 30*, 726–734.

Johnson, C. L., & Catalano, D. J. (1981). Childless elderly and their family supports. *Gerontologist, 21*, 610–618.

Johnson, M. D. (1969). *The purpose of the Biblical genealogies*. Cambridge: Cambridge University Press.

Johnson, P. (1988). *The labour force participation of older men in Britain, 1951–81*. London: Centre for Economic Policy Research.

Johnson, P., Conrad, C., & Thomson, D. (Eds.). (1989). *Workers versus pensioners: Intergenerational justice in an ageing world*. Manchester: Manchester University Press.

Johnson, P., & Falkingham, J. (1988). *Intergenerational transfers and public expenditure on the elderly in modern Britain*. London: Centre for Economic Policy Research.

Jones, J. (1988a, June). *Ageing and generational equity: An American perspective.*

Paper presented at an international seminar on the ageing of the population, Futuribles International, Paris.

Jones, J. (1988b). Retiree health benefits: The generational equity perspective. *Proceedings from the National Conference of Americans for Generational Equity* (p. 7). Washington, DC: Americans for Generational Equity.

Jorgenson, L. P. (1987). *The state and the non-public school, 1825–1925.* Columbia: University of Missouri Press.

Kaestle, C. F. (1983). *Pillars of the republic: Common schools and American society, 1780–1860.* New York: Hill and Wang.

Kaestle, C. F., & Vinovskis, M. A. (1980). *Education and social change in nineteenth-century Massachusetts.* Cambridge: Cambridge University Press.

Kalvemark, A.-S. (1980). *More children of better quality? Aspects of Swedish population policy in the 1930s.* Uppsala: Uppsala University Press.

Kamerman, S., & Kahn, A. (Eds.). (1978). *Family policy: Governments and families in fourteen countries.* New York: Columbia University Press.

Kampf der Generationen: Jung gegen Alt. (1989, July). The struggle of generations: Young against old. *Der Spiegel,* Heft, p. 81.

Katz, M. B. (1968). *The irony of early school reform: Educational innovation in mid-nineteenth-century Massachusetts.* Cambridge, MA: Harvard University Press.

Katz, M. B. (1986). *In the shadow of the poorhouse.* New York: Basic Books.

Keith, J., Fry, C., & Ikels, C. (1990). Community as context for successful aging. In J. Sokolovsky (Ed.), *The cultural context of aging* (pp. 245–261). New York: Bergin and Garvey.

Keller, W. J., ten Cate, A., Handepool, A. J., & van de Stadt, H. (1987). Real income changes of households in the Netherlands, 1977–83. *Review of Income and Wealth, 33*(3), 257–272.

Kelley, W. (in press). Japan's debates about an aging society: The later years in the land of the rising sun. In L. Cohen (Ed.), *Justice across generations: What does it mean?* Washington, D. C.: American Association of Retired Persons.

Kertzer, D. I. (1983). Generations as a sociological problem. *Annual Review of Sociology, 9,* 125–149.

Kilner, J. F. (1984). Who shall be saved? An African answer. *Hastings Center Report, 14,* 18–22.

Kingson, E. R. (1988). Generational equity: An unexpected opportunity to broaden the politics of aging. *Gerontologist, 28,* 765–772.

Kingson, E. R., Hirshorn, B. A., & Cornman, J. M. (1986). *Ties that bind: The interdependence of generations.* Washington, DC: Seven Locks Press.

Klein, R. (1981). *Wounded men, broken promises.* New York: Collier Macmillan.

Koch, A., & Peden, W. (Eds.). (1944). *The life and selected writings of Thomas Jefferson.* New York: Modern Library.

Kotlikoff, L. (1992). *Generational accounting: Knowing who pays, and when, for what we spend.* New York: Free Press.

Kreps, J. (1977). Intergenerational transfers and the bureaucracy. In E. Shanas & M. Sussman (Eds.), *Family bureaucracy and the elderly* (pp. 215–226). Durham, NC: Duke University Press.

Kriegel, A. (1978). Generational difference: The history of an idea. *Daedalus, 107*(4), 23–38.

Lace, O. J. (Ed.). (1965). *Understanding the New Testament.* Cambridge: Cambridge University Press.

Lamm, R. D. (1985). *Megatraumas: America in the year 2000.* Boston: Houghton Mifflin.

Lammers, W. (1983). *Public policy and the aging.* Washington, DC: Congressional Quarterly Press.

Land, H., & Rose, H. (1985). Compulsory altruism or an altruistic society for all? In P. Bean, J. Ferris, & D. Whynes (Eds.), *Defence of welfare* (pp. 74–95). London: Tavistock.

Laslett, P. (1965). *The world we have lost.* London: Methuen.

Laslett, P. (1979). The conversation between generations. In P. Laslett & J. Fishkin (Eds.), *Philosophy, politics and society* (pp. 36–56). New Haven, CT: Yale University Press.

Laslett, P. (in press). Is there a generational contract? In P. Laslett & J. Fishkin (Eds.), *Philosophy, politics and society VI: Relations between age groups and generations.* New Haven, CT: Yale University Press.

Leach, E. (1987). Fishing for men. In R. Alter & F. Kermode (Eds.), *The literary guide to the Bible* (pp. 580–600). Cambridge, MA: Harvard University Press.

Leavitt, J. W. (1984). *Women and health in America.* Madison: University of Wisconsin Press.

Lesthaeghe, R. (1980). On the social control of reproduction. *Population and Development Review, 4,* 527–548.

Lesthaeghe, R. (1983). A century of demographic and cultural change in Western Europe: An explanation of underlying dimensions. *Population and Development Review, 9,* 411–435.

Levin, E., Sinclair, I., & Gorbach, P. (1986). *Families, services and confusion in old age.* London: Allen & Unwin.

LeVine, R. (1980). Adulthood among the Gusii of Kenya. In N. Smelser & E. Erikson (Eds.), *Theories of work and love in adulthood* (pp. 77–104). Cambridge, MA: Harvard University Press.

Levy, F. (1987). *Dollars and dreams: The changing American income distribution.* New York: Russell Sage Foundation.

Levy, F., & Michel, R. C. (1991). *The economic future of American families: Income and wealth trends.* Washington, DC: Urban Institute Press.

Lewis, J., & Meredith, B. (1988). *Daughters who care.* London: Routledge.

Light, L. (1981, November 28). The organized elderly: A powerful lobby. *Congressional Quarterly Weekly Report,* p. 2345.

Lillard, L. A., & Macunovich, D. J. (1989, April). *Why the baby bust cohorts haven't boomed yet: A reconsideration of cohort variables in labor market analyses.* Paper presented at the Annual Meeting of the Population Association of America, Baltimore.

Lin, H., & Hong, Y.-C. (1989, December). *Comparative studies on the old population's economic situations in China's urban and rural areas.* Paper presented at the International Academic Conference on China's Aging Population, Beijing.

Lipset, S. M. (1990). *Continental divide: The values and institutions of the United States and Canada.* New York: Routledge.

Lister, R. (1982). Income maintenance for families with children. In R. Rapoport (Ed.), *Families in Britain* (pp. 432–446). London: Routledge and Kegan Paul.

Liu, W. T., & Yu, E. (1990, February). *The aging of Asian Americans: Problems and issues.* Unpublished manuscript.

Logue, B. J. (1990). Modernization and the status of the frail elderly: Perspectives on continuity and change. *Journal of Cross-Cultural Gerontology, 5,* 345–374.

London, K. A. (1991). Cohabitation, marriage, marital dissolution, and remarriage: United States, 1988. In *Advance Data, 194* (DHHS Publication No. PHS 91–1250). Washington, DC: U.S. Government Printing Office.

Longhurst, B. (1989). *Karl Mannheim and the contemporary sociology of knowledge.* London: Macmillan.

Longman, P. (1982, November). Taking America to the cleaners. *Washington Monthly,* pp. 24–30.

Longman, P. (1985a). Can Social Security really survive? *Medical Economics, 62*(23), 127–128.

Longman, P. (1985b, June). Justice between generations. *Atlantic Monthly,* pp. 73–81.

Longman, P. (1986). Age wars: The coming battle between young and old. *Futurist, 20*(1), 8–11.

Longman, P. (1987a). Great train robbery. *Washington Monthly, 19*(11), 12–14.

Longman, P. (1987b). *Born to pay: The new politics of aging in America.* Boston: Houghton Mifflin.

Longman, P. (1988). Challenge of an aging society. *Futurist, 22*(5), 33–37.

Longman, P. (1989a, August 21). Catastrophic follies. *New Republic,* pp. 16–18.

Longman, P. (1989b). Social Security and the baby boom generation. *Journal of Aging and Social Policy, 1,* 131–153.

Lunneborg, P. W. (1990). *Women changing work.* New York: Bergin & Garvey.

Mace, N. L., & Rabins, P. V. (1981). *The 36-hour day.* Baltimore: Johns Hopkins University Press.

Macunovich, D. J., & Easterlin, R. A. (1990). How parents have coped: The effect of life cycle demographic decisions on the economic status of pre-school age children, 1964–1987. *Population and Development Review, 16,* 299–323.

Maier, P. (1980). *The old revolutionaries.* New York: A. A. Knopf.

Main, J. T. (1974). *Anti-federalists.* New York: W. W. Norton.

Malone, D. (1981). *The sage of Monticello.* Boston: Little, Brown.

Mannheim, K. (1952). The problem of generations. In P. Kecskemeti (Ed. and Trans.), *Essays on the sociology of knowledge* (pp. 276–320). London: Routledge and Kegan Paul. (Original work published 1928)

Mannheim, K. (1956). The problem of intellectuals. In K. Mannheim (Ed.), *Essays on the sociology of culture* (pp. 276–320). London: Routledge & Kegan Paul. (Original work published 1928)

Mare, R. O., & Winship, C. (1985). *Current population series, March.* Uniform Series, Data Files. Madison: University of Wisconsin and Chicago: Northwestern University.

Marmor, T. R., Mashaw, J. L., & Harvey, P. L. (1990). *America's misunderstood welfare state*. New York: Basic Books.

Marshall, V. W. (1979). Age irrelevance or generational conflict: Contrasting images of the future. In *The Young-Old . . . A New North American Phenomenon, Proceedings of the 30th Annual Winter Conference, Couchiching Institute of Public Affairs* (pp. 13–20). Toronto: Couchiching Institute.

Marshall, V. W. (1980). Aging in an aging society: Cohort differences, conflicts and challenges. *Multiculturalism, 4,* 6–13.

Marshall, V. W. (1981). Societal toleration of aging: Sociological theory and social response to population aging. In *Adaptability and Aging I, Proceedings, IXth International Conference on Social Gerontology* (pp. 85–104). Paris: International Centre of Social Gerontology.

Marshall, V. W. (1984). Tendencies in generational research: From the generations to the cohort and back to the generations. In V. Garms-Homolova, E. R. Hoerning, & D. Schaeffer (Eds.), *Intergenerational Relations.* Lewinston, NY, and Toronto: C. J. Togrefe.

Marshall, V., Rosenthal, C., & Daciuk, J. (1987). Older parents expectations for filial support. *Social Justice Research, 1,* 405–424.

Martin, L. (1988). The aging of Asia. *Journal of Gerontology: Social Sciences, 43,* 99–113.

Matthews, D. R. (1983). *The creation of regional dependency.* Toronto: University of Toronto Press.

Matthews, R. K. (1984). *The radical politics of Thomas Jefferson.* Lawrence: University Press of Kansas.

Mattila, J. P. (1978). GI bill benefits and enrollments. *Social Science Quarterly, 59,* 535–545.

McCoy, D. (1989). *The last of the fathers.* New York: Cambridge University Press.

McDaniel, S. A. (1987). Demographic aging as a guiding paradigm in Canada's welfare state. *Canadian Public Policy, 13,* 330–336.

McGilly, F. (1990). *Canada's public social services.* Toronto: McClelland and Stewart.

McGoldrick, M. (1989). Women through the family life cycle. In M. McGoldrick, C. M. Anderson, and F. Walsh (Eds.), *Women in families: A framework for family therapy* (pp. 201–236). New York: W. W. Norton.

McKenzie, R. (1991, March 12). The retreat of the elderly welfare state. *Wall Street Journal,* p. 29.

Mead, L. (1986). *Beyond entitlement: The social obligations of citizenship.* New York: Free Press.

Meeks, W. A. (1983). *The first urban Christians.* New Haven, CT: Yale University Press.

Merrilees, W. J. (1986). Economic determinants of retirement. In R. Mendelsohn (Ed.), *Finance of old age* (pp. 203–222). Canberra: ANU Press.

Merton, R. K. (1968). *Social theory and social structure* (enlarged ed.). New York: Free Press.

Messinger, H., & Powell, B. J. (1987). The implications of Canada's aging society on social expenditures. In V. W. Marshall (Ed.), *Aging in Canada: Social perspectives* (2nd ed., pp. 569–585). Markham: Fitzhenry and Whiteside.

Miller, W. E., & The National Election Studies. (1989). *American national election study, 1988: Pre- and post-election survey.* Ann Arbor, MI: Inter-University Consortium for Political and Social Research.

Minkler, M. (1986). "Generational equity" and the new victim blaming: An emerging public policy issue. *International Journal of Health Services, 16*, 539–551.

Modigliani, F. (1961). Fluctuations in the saving-income ratio: A problem in economic forecasting. In Conference on Research in Income and Wealth, *Studies in Income and Wealth, XI*, pp. 371–443. New York: National Bureau of Economic Research.

Moody, H. R. (1988). *The abundance of life: Human development policies for an aging society.* New York: Columbia University Press.

Moore, S. F. (1978). Old age in a life-time social arena: Some Chagga of Kilimanjaro in 1974. In B. Myerhoff & A. Simic (Eds.), *Life's career—aging* (pp. 23–75). Beverly Hills: Sage.

Moran, G. F., & Vinovskis, M. A. (1986). The great care of godly parents: Early childhood in Puritan New England. *History and research in child development, 50*(4–5), 24–37.

Moroney, R. M. (1976). *The family and the state.* London: Longman.

Mufson, S. (1990, October 15). Older voters drive budget. *Washington Post,* p. A1.

Munnell, A. H. (1982). *The economics of private pensions.* Washington, DC: Brookings Institute.

Murray, C. (1984). *Losing ground: American social policy, 1950–1980.* New York: Basic Books.

Murstein, B., Cerreto, M., & MacDonald, M. (1977). A theory and investigation of the effect of exchange-orientation on marriage and friendship. *Journal of Marriage and the Family, 39*, 543–548.

Myerhoff, B. (1978). *Number our days.* New York: Dutton.

Myles, J. (1983). Conflict, crisis, and the future of old age security. *Milbank Memorial Fund Quarterly, 61*, 462–472.

Myles, J. (1984). *Old age in the welfare state.* Boston: Little Brown.

Myles, J. (1989). *Old age and the welfare state.* Lawrence: University Press of Kansas.

National Advisory Council on Aging. (1989). *1989 and beyond: Challenges of an aging Canadian society.* Ottawa: Author.

National Center for Education Statistics. (1989). *Digest of education statistics: 1989.* Washington, DC: U.S. Government Printing Office.

National Commission on Excellence in Education. (1983). *A nation at risk: The imperative for educational reform.* Washington, DC: U.S. Government Printing Office.

Neugarten, B. L. (1973). Patterns of aging: Past, present, and future. *Social Service Review, 47*, 571–80.

Neugarten, B. L., & Neugarten, D. A. (1986). Changing meanings of age in the aging society. In A. Pifer & L. Bronte (Eds.), *Our aging society* (pp. 33–52). New York: W. W. Norton.

Neustadt, R., & May, E. R. (1987). *Thinking in time.* New York: Free Press.

Neysmith, S. M. (1987a). Organizing for influence: The relationship of structure to impact. *Canadian Journal on Aging, 6*, 105–116.

Neysmith, S. M. (1987b). Social policy implications of an aging society. In V. W. Marshall (Ed.), *Aging in Canada: Social perspectives* (3rd ed., pp. 586–597). Markham: Fitzhenry and Whiteside.

Noddings, N. (1989). *Women and evil.* Berkeley: University of California Press.

Nydegger, C. (1983). Family ties of the aged in cross-cultural perspective. *Gerontologist, 23*, 26–32.

O'Connor, J. (1973). *The fiscal crisis of the state.* New York: St. Martin's Press.

OECD. (annual). *National accounts.* Paris.

OECD. (1988a). *Reforming public pensions.* Paris: OECD.

OECD. (1988b). *Ageing populations—The social policy implications.* Paris: OECD.

Older voters drive budget. (1990, October 15). *The Washington Post.* p. 1.

Ortega y Gasset, J. (1958). *Man and crisis.* New York: W. W. Norton.

Osberg, L. (1984). *Economic inequality in the United States.* Armonk, NY: M. E. Sharpe.

Ozawa, M. N. (Ed.). (1989). *Women's life cycle and economic insecurity: Problems and proposals.* New York: Praeger.

Page, B. (1983). *Who gets what from government?.* Berkeley: University of California Press.

Page, W. F. (1982). Why veterans choose Veterans Administration hospitalization. *Medical Care, 20*, 308–320.

Palmer, J. L., Smeeding, T., & Torrey, B. B. (Eds.). (1988). *The vulnerable.* Washington, DC: Urban Institute Press.

Palmer, M. (1987). The People's Republic of China: Some general observations on family law. *Journal of Family Law, 25*, 48–54.

Pampel, F., Williamson, J., & Stryker, R. (1990). Class context and pension response to demographic structure in advanced industrial democracies. *Social Problems, 37*, 535–550.

Parrish, W. L., & Whyte, M. K. (1978). *Village and family in contemporary China.* Chicago: University of Chicago Press.

Patterson, J. (1981). *America's struggle against poverty, 1900–1980.* Cambridge, MA: Harvard University Press.

Pechman, J. (1985). *Who paid the taxes, 1966–85?.* Washington, DC: Brookings Institute.

Peil, M., Bamisaiye, A., & Ekpenyong, S. (1989). Health and physical support for the elderly in Nigeria. *Journal of Cross-Cultural Gerontology 4*, 89–106.

Pelikan, J. (1971). *The Christian tradition: Vol. 1. The emergence of Catholic tradition.* Chicago: University of Chicago Press.

Perrett, G. (1973). *Days of sadness, years of triumph.* Baltimore: Penguin Books.

Peterson, M. D. (1970). *Thomas Jefferson & the new nation.* New York: Oxford University Press.

Phillipson, C. (1982). *Capitalism and the construction of old age.* London: Macmillan.

Piele, P. K., & Hall, J. S. (1973). *Budget, bonds, and ballots.* Lexington, MA: Lexington Books.

Pierce, N., & Choharis, P. (1982, September 11). The elderly as a political force: 26 million strong and well organized. *National Journal,* pp. 1559–1562.

Pillemer, K. A., & Wolf, R. S. (1986). *Elder abuse: Conflict in the family*. Dover, MA: Auburn House.

Piven, F. F., & Cloward, R. A. (1974). *Poor people's movements and why they fail*. New York: Pantheon.

Ponza, M., Duncan, G. J., Corcoran, M., & Groskind, F. (1988). The guns of autumn? Age differences in support for income transfers to the young and old. *Public Opinion Quarterly, 52*(4), 492–512.

Popenoe, D. (1988). *Disturbing the nest: Family change and decline in modern society*. Hawthorne, NY: Aldine de Gruyter.

Pratt, H. J. (1976). *The gray lobby*. Chicago: University of Chicago Press.

Pratt, H. J. (1987). Aging policy and process in the Canadian federal government. *Canadian Public Administration, 30*, 57–75.

Premo, T. (1989). *Winter friends*. Urbana: University of Illinois Press.

President's Commission on Veterans' Pensions. (1956). *Veterans' benefits in the United States*. Washington, DC: Government Printing Office.

Preston, S. H. (1984a). Children and the elderly: Divergent paths for America's dependents. *Demography, 21*, 435–57.

Preston, S. H. (1984b). Children and the elderly in the United States. *Scientific American, 251*(6), 44–49.

Quadagno, J. (1982). *Aging in early industrial society: Work, family, and social policy in nineteenth-century England*. New York: Academic Press.

Quadagno, J. (1989). Generational equity and the politics of the welfare state. *Politics and Society, 17*, 353–376.

Quadagno, J. (1990). Generational equity and the politics of the welfare state. *Intergenerational Journal of Health Services, 20*, 631–649.

Qureshi, H., & Walker, A. (1989). *The caring relationship*. London: Macmillan.

Radner, D. (1985). Family income, age and size of unit: Selected international comparisons. *Review of Income and Wealth, 31*(2), 103–126.

Rauch, J. (1981). Vietnam veterans are wondering whether they have a friend in the V.A. *National Journal, 13*, 1291–1295.

Rauch, J. (1987, January 17). The politics of joy. *National Journal*, pp. 125–130.

Reday-Mulvey, G. (1990). Work and retirement: Future prospects for the baby-boom generation. *Geneva Papers, 55*, 100–113.

Reid, J. (1985). "Going up" or "going down": The status of old people in an Australian aboriginal society. *Ageing and Society, 5*, 69–95.

Rein, M. (1981). Private provision of welfare. In R. Henderson (Ed.), *The welfare stakes: Strategies for Australian social policy* (pp. 9–39). Melbourne: Institute of Applied Economic and Social Research.

Richards, L. N., Bengtson, V. L., & Miller, R. (1989). The "generation in the middle": Perceptions of adults' intergenerational relationships. In K. Kreppner & R. Lerner (Eds.), *Family systems and life-span development* (pp. 341–366). Hillsdale, NJ: Lawrence Erlbaum.

Riley, J. W., Jr. (1992). Death and dying. In E. F. Borgatta, & M. L. Borgatta (Eds.), *The encyclopedia of sociology* (pp. 413–418). New York: Macmillan.

Riley, M. W. (1983). The family in an aging society: A matrix of latent relationships. *Journal of Family Issues, 4*, 439–454.

Riley, M. W. (1985). Age strata in social systems. In R. H. Binstock & E. Shanas (Eds.), *Handbook of aging and the social sciences* (2nd ed., pp. 369–411). New York: Van Nostrand Reinhold.

Riley, M. W. (1988). The aging society: Problems and prospects. *Proceeding of the American Philosophical Society, 132*(2), 148–153.

Riley, M. W. (1989, November). *Commentary: Aging and intergenerational relations in cross cultural perspective.* Paper presented at the meeting of the Social Science History Association, Washington, DC.

Riley, M. W. (1992). Cohort perspectives. In E. F. Borgatta & M. L. Borgatta (Eds.), *The encyclopedia of sociology.* New York: MacMillan.

Riley, M. W., Foner, A., Moore, M. G., & Rook, B. K. (1968). *Aging and Society,* Vol. I. New York: Russell Sage Foundation.

Riley, M. W., Foner A., & Waring, J. (1988). Sociology of age. In N. Smelser (Ed.), *Handbook of sociology* (pp. 243–290). Newbury Park, CA: Sage.

Riley, M. W., Johnson, M., & Foner, A. (1972). *Aging and society Vol. III: A sociology of age stratification.* New York: Russell Sage Foundation.

Riley, M. W., & Riley, J. W., Jr. (1986). Longevity and social structure. In A. Pifer & L. Bronte (Eds.), *Our aging society* (pp. 53–78). New York: W. W. Norton.

Riley, M. W., & Riley, J. W., Jr. (1991). Viellesse et changement des roles sociaux. *Gerontologie et Societe, 56,* 5–14.

Rosenberg, H. (1990). Complaint discourse, aging, and caregiving among the !Kung San of Botswana. In J. Sokolovsky (Ed.), *The cultural context of aging* (pp. 19–41). New York: Bergin and Garvey.

Rosenthal, C. J. (1985). Kin-keeping in the familial division of labor. *Journal of Marriage and the Family, 45,* 509–521.

Ross, D. R. B. (1969). *Preparing for Ulysses.* New York: Columbia University Press.

Rossi, A. S. (1968). Transition to parenthood. *Journal of Marriage and the Family, 30,* 26–39.

Rossi, A. S., & Rossi, P. H. (1990). *Of human bonding: Parent child-relationships across the life course.* Hawthorne, NY: Aldine de Gruyter.

Rossi, A. S., & Rossi, P. H. (1991). Normative obligations and parent-child help exchange across the life course. In K. Pillemer & K. McCartney (Eds.), *Parent-child relations throughout life* (pp. 201–223). Hillsdale, NJ: Lawrence Erlbaum.

Rossi, P. H., & Nock, S. L. (1982). *Measuring social judgments: The factorial survey approach.* Newbury Park, CA: Sage.

Rowland, C. (1985). *Christian origins.* Minneapolis: Augsburg.

Russell, L. B. (1982). *The baby boom generation and the economy.* Washington, DC: Brookings Institute.

Ryder, N. B. (1968). Cohort analysis. In D. L. Sills (Ed.), *International Encyclopedia of the Social Sciences, Vol. 5* (pp. 546–550). New York: Macmillan and Free Press.

Ryder, N. B. (1990). What is going to happen to American fertility? *Population and Development Review, 16,* 433–454.

Salmon, R. G. (1987). State/local fiscal support of public elementary and secondary education: A look backward and prospects for the future. *Journal of Education Finance, 12*(4), 549–560.

Samuelson, R. (1981, October 3). Benefit programs for the elderly: Off limits to federal budget cutters? *National Journal*, pp. 1757–1762.

Sankar, A. (1989). Gerontological research in China: The role of anthropological inquiry. *Journal of Cross Cultural Gerontology, 4*, 199–224.

Sapolsky, H. M. (1977). America's socialized medicine. *Public Policy, 25*, 359–382.

Saunders, P. (1987). *Growth in Australian social security expenditures, 1959/60 to 1985/6*. Canberra: Department of Social Security.

Schattschneider, E. E. (1960). *The semisovereign people*. New York: Holt, Rinehart and Winston.

Schlesinger, A. M., Jr. (1986). *The cycles of American history*. Boston: Houghton Mifflin.

Schneider, D. M. (1980). *American kinship* (2nd ed.). Chicago: Chicago University Press.

Schneider E. B., & Krupp, S. (1965). An illustration of the use of analytical theory in sociology: The application of the economic theory of choice to non-economic variables. *American Journal of Sociology, 70*, 695–703.

Seccombe, K. (1991). Assessing the costs and benefits of children: Gender comparisons among childfree husbands and wives. *Journal of Marriage and the Family, 53*, 191–202.

Seward, S. (1986). More and younger? *Policy Options, 7*, 16–19.

Shahrani, M. N. (1981). Growing in respect: Aging among the Kirghiz of Afghanistan. In P. Amoss & S. Harrell (Eds.), *Other ways of growing old* (pp. 175–191). Stanford: Stanford University Press.

Shanas, E. (1979). Social myth as hypothesis: The case of the family relations of old people. *Gerontologist, 19*, 3–9.

Shanas, E., & Sussman, M. (Eds.). (1977). *Family bureaucracy and the elderly*. Durham, NC: Duke University Press.

Shils, E. (1968). Karl Mannheim. *International Encyclopedia of Social Sciences*, Vol. 9. New York: Macmillan.

Shiratori, R. (1985). The experience of the welfare state in Japan and its problems. In S. Eisenstadt & O. Ahimeir (Eds.), *The welfare state and its aftermath* (pp. 200–223). London: Croom Helm.

Shirley, I. (1990). New Zealand: The advance of the new right. In I. Taylor (Ed.), *The social effects of free market policies: An international text* (pp. 351–390). London: Harvester Wheatsheaf.

Shomaker, D. (1990). Health care, cultural expectations and frail elderly Navajo grandmothers. *Journal of Cross-Cultural Gerontology, 5*, 21–34.

Siegel, J., & Taeuber, C. M. (1986). Demographic dimensions of an aging population. In A. Pifer & L. Bronte (Eds.), *Our aging society* (pp. 79–110). New York: Norton.

Siegel, J., & Taeuber, C. M. (1991). Demographic perspectives on the long-lived society.

Silverman, P. (1987). Comparative studies. In P. Silverman (Ed.), *The elderly as modern pioneers* (pp. 312–344). Bloomington: Indiana University Press.

Simic, A. (1978). Winners and losers: Aging Yugoslavs in a changing world. In B. Myerhoff & A. Simic (Eds.), *Life's career—aging* (pp. 77–103). Beverly Hills: Sage.

Simmons, L. (1945). *The role of the aged in primitive society.* New Haven: Yale University Press.

Simonton, D. R. (1984). Generational time-series analysis: A paradigm for studying sociocultural change. In K. J. Gergen & M. M. Gergen (Eds.), *Historical social psychology.* London: Erlbaum.

Skolnick, A. S., & Skolnick J. H. (1989). *Family in transition* (6th ed.). Glenview, IL: Scott, Foresman.

Smolensky, E., Danziger, S., & Gottschalk, P. (1988). The declining significance of age in the United States: Trends in the well-being of children and the elderly since 1939. In J. Palmer, T. Smeeding, & B. Torrey (Eds.), *The vulnerable* (pp. 29–54). Washington, DC: Urban Institute Press.

Soldo, B. (1981). America's elderly in the 1980s. *Population Bulletin, 35*(4).

Soltow, L., & Stevens, E. (1981). *The rise of literacy and the common school in the United States: A socioeconomic analysis to 1870.* Chicago: University of Chicago Press.

Spengler, J. (1979). *France faces depopulation, Postlude edition, 1936–76.* Durham, NC: Duke University Press.

Spitzer, A. B. (1973). The historical problem of generations. *American Historical Review, 78,* 1353–1385.

Stack, C. B. (1974). *All our kin: Strategies for survival in a black community.* New York: Harper & Row.

Statistics Canada. (1989). *Income distribution by size in Canada* (Cat. 13–207). Ottawa: Ministry of Supply and Services Canada.

Stone, R., Cafferata, G. L., & Sangl, J. (1987). Caregivers of the frail elderly: A national profile. *Gerontologist, 27,* 616–62.

Stouffer, S. A., Suchman, E. A., DeVinney, L. C., Star, S. A., & Williams, R. M. (1949). *Studies in social psychology in World War II. Volume I: The American soldier: Adjustment during wartime life.* Princeton, NJ: Princeton University Press.

Strauss, W., & Howe, N. (1991). *Generations: The history of America's future, 1584–2069.* New York: Morrow.

Sweet, J. A. (1989). *Differentials in the approval of cohabitation* (Working Paper No. 8). Madison: University of Wisconsin, National Survey of Families and Households.

Sweet, J. A., & Bumpass, L. L. (1987). *American families and households.* New York: Russell Sage Foundation.

Taeuber, C. M. (1990). Diversity: The dramatic reality. In S. Bass, E. Kutza, & F. Torres-Gil (Eds.), *Diversity in aging: Challenges facing planners and policymakers in the 1990s* (pp. 1–46). Glenview, IL: Scott, Foresman.

Task Force on Retirement Income Policy. (1979). *The retirement income system in Canada: Problems and alternative policies for reform,* Vol. 1. Ottawa: Government of Canada.

Teitelbaum, M., & Winter, J. (1985). *The fear of depopulation.* Orlando, FL: Academic Press.

Thatcher, M. (1981, January). *Facing the new challenge.* Paper presented to the Womens Royal Voluntary Service, National Conference, London.

Therborn, G., & Roebroek, J. (1986). The irreversible welfare state: Its recent maturation, its encounter with the economic crisis, and its future prospects. *International Journal of Health Services, 16,* 319–338.

Thomas, K. (1976). Age and authority in early modern England. *Proceedings of the British Academy, 62,* 205–248.

Thomson, D. (1988, October). *The welfare state and generation conflict.* Paper presented at the Conference on Work, Retirement, and Intergenerational Equity, St. Johns College, Cambridge.

Thomson, D. (1989). The welfare state and generation conflict: Winners and losers. In P. Johnson, C. Conrad, & D. Thomson (Eds.), *Workers versus pensioners: Intergenerational justice in an ageing world* (pp. 33–56). Manchester: Manchester University Press.

Thomson, D. (1991). *Selfish generations? The ageing of New Zealand's welfare state.* Wellington: Bridget Williams Books.

Thomson, D. (in press). Generations, justice and the future of collective action. In P. Laslett & J. Fishkin (Eds.), *Philosophy, politics and society: Vol. VI. Relations between age groups and generations.* New Haven, CT: Yale University Press.

Tibbitts, C. (Ed.). (1960). *Handbook of social gerontology.* Chicago: University of Chicago Press.

Tindale, J. A., & Marshall, V. W. (1980). A generational-conflict perspective for gerontology. In V. W. Marshall (Ed.), *Aging in Canada: Social perspectives* (pp. 43–50). Don Mills: Fitzhenry and Whiteside.

Tinsley, E. J. (1965). *The gospel according to Luke.* Cambridge: Cambridge University Press.

Togonu-Bickersteth, F. (1989). Conflicts over caregiving: A discussion of filial obligations among adult Nigerian children. *Journal of Cross-Cultural Gerontology, 4,* 35–48.

Tonkinson, R. (1978). *The Mardudjara aborigines.* New York: Holt, Rinehart, and Winston.

Torres-Gil, F. M. (1981). We need a new domestic agenda. *Generations, Winter,* 10–13.

Torres-Gil, F. M. (1984). Pre-retirement issues that affect minorities. In H. Dennis (Ed.), *Retirement preparation* (pp. 109–128). Lexington, MA: D. C. Heath.

Torres-Gil, F. (1989). The politics of catastrophic and long-term care coverage. *Journal of Aging and Social Policy, 1*(1/2), 61–86.

Torres-Gil, F. (1990). Seniors react to the Medicare Catastrophic Bill: Equity or selfishness? *Journal of Aging and Social Policy, 2,* 1–8.

Torrey, B., & Taeuber, C. (1986). The importance of asset income amongst the elderly. *Review of Income and Wealth, 32*(4), 443–450.

Treas, J. (1979). Socialist organization and economic development in China: Latent consequences for the aged. *Gerontologist, 19,* 34–43.

Tsui, M. (1989). Changes in Chinese urban family structure. *Journal of Marriage and the Family, 51*(3), 737–747.

Tucker, C. (1990, October 10). U.S. coddles elderly but ignores plight of children. *Atlanta Constitution,* Section A, p. 9.

Uhlenberg, P. R. (1980). Death in the family. *Journal of Family History, 5,* 313–320.

Uhlenberg, P. R. (1990). *Implications of increasing divorce for the elderly.* Paper presented at the United Nations International Conference on Aging Population in the Context of the Family, Kitakyushu, Japan.

Uhlenberg, P. R., & Cooney, T. M. (1990a). Family size and mother-child relations in late life. *Gerontologist, 30,* 618–625.

Uhlenberg, P. R., & Cooney, T. M. (1990b). *Support from parents over the life course: The adult child's perspective.* Paper presented at the 1990 Meeting of the American Sociological Association, Washington, D.C.

Uhlenberg, P. R., Cooney, T. M., & Boyd, R. L. (1990). Divorce for women after midlife. *Journal of Gerontology, 45,* S3-S11.

Ulrich, L. T. (1990). *A midwife's tale—The life of Martha Ballard: Based on her diary, 1785–1812.* New York: Alfred Knopf.

United Nations. (1956). *The ageing of populations and its economic and social implications.* New York: Author.

U.S. Bureau of the Census. (1981). *Statistical abstract of the United States: 1981.* Washington, DC: U.S. Government Printing Office.

U.S. Bureau of the Census. (1986). *Projections of the Hispanic population: 1983–2080* (Current Population Reports, Series P-25, No. 995). Washington, DC: U.S. Government Printing Office.

U.S. Bureau of the Census. (1989a). *Marital status and living arrangements: March 1989* (Current Population Reports, Series P-20, No. 445). Washington, DC: U.S. Government Printing Office.

U.S. Bureau of the Census. (1989b). *Voting and registration in the Election of November, 1988* (Current Population Reports, Series P-2O, No. 435). Washington, DC: U.S. Government Printing Office.

U.S. Bureau of the Census. (1990a). *Money income and poverty status in the United States: 1989* (Current Population Reports, Series P-60, No. 168). Washington, DC: U.S. Government Printing Office.

U.S. Bureau of the Census. (1990b). *Statistical abstract of the United States: 1990.* Washington, DC: U.S. Government Printing Office.

U.S. Committee on Veterans' Affairs. (1981). *Legacies of Vietnam: Comparative adjustment of veterans and their peers* (97th Cong., H. R. Document 14).

U.S. Committee on Veterans' Affairs. (1987). *Status and concerns of women veterans* (100th Cong., H. R. Document 100–106).

U.S. Congressional Budget Office. (1988). *Trends in family income: 1970–1986.* Washington, DC: U.S. Government Printing Office.

U.S. Department of Health, Education, & Welfare. (1979). *The family in changing times* (DHEW Publication No. ADM 79–897). Washington, DC: U.S. Government Printing Office.

U.S. House of Representatives, Select Committee on Aging. (1986). *Investing in America's families: The common bond of generations* (Report No. H141–43). Washington, DC: U.S. Government Printing Office.

U.S. Senate. (1988). *Aging America: Trends and projections*. Washington, DC: Department of Health and Human Services.

U.S. Senate Special Committee on Aging. (1987–88). *Aging America*. Washington, DC: U.S. Department of Health and Human Services.

Vayda, E., & Deber, R. (1984). The Canadian health care system: An overview. *Social Science and Medicine, 18*, 191–197.

Villers Foundation. (1987). *On the other side of easy street: Myths and facts about the economics of old age*. Washington, DC: The Villers Foundation.

Vinovskis, M. A. (1985). *The origins of public high schools: An examination of the Beverly High School controversy*. Madison: University of Wisconsin Press.

Vinovskis, M. A. (1987a). Family and schooling in colonial and nineteenth-century America. *Journal of Family History, 12*(1–3), 19–37.

Vinovskis, M. A. (1987b). The unraveling of the family wage since World War II: Some demographic, economic, and cultural considerations. In B. J. Christensen (Ed.), *The family wage: Work, gender, and children in the modern economy*. Rockford, IL: Rockford Institute.

Vogel, J., Andersson, L-G., Davidsson, U., & Häll, L. (1988). *Inequality in Sweden: Trends and current situation, 1975- 85*. Stockholm: Statistics Sweden.

Wadensjo, E. (1990). *Early exit from the labour force in Sweden*. Stockholm: Institute for Social Research.

Walker, A. (1981). Towards a political economy of old age. *Ageing and Society, 1*(1), 73–94.

Walker, A. (1986a). Dependency and interdependency in old age: Theoretical perspectives and policy alternatives. In C. Phillipson, M. Bernard, & P. Strong (Eds.), *Dependency and interdependency in old age: Theoretical perspectives and policy alternatives* (pp. 30–45). London: Croom Helm.

Walker, A. (1986b). The politics of Ageing in Britain. In C. Phillipson, M. Bernard, & P. Strong (eds.), *Dependency and interdependency in old age: Theoretical perspectives and policy alternatives* (pp. 30–45). London: Croom Helm.

Walker, A. (1986c). The social creation of poverty and dependency in old age. *Journal of Social Policy, 9*, 40–49.

Walker, A. (1986d). Social policy and elderly people in Great Britain: The construction of dependent social and economic status in old age. In A. Guillemard (Ed.), *Old age and the welfare state* (pp. 143–167). Beverly Hills: Sage.

Walker, A. (1987). Enlarging the caring capacity of the community: Informal support networks and the welfare state. *International Journal of Health Services, 17*, 369–386.

Walker, A. (1990a). The economic "burden" of ageing and the prospect of intergenerational conflict. *Ageing and Society, 10*(4), 377–396.

Walker, A. (1990b). Les politiques de retraites dans la Communante Europeénne. *Revue Francaise Des Affaires Sociales, 44*(3), 113–126.

Walker, A. (1990c). The strategy of inequality: Poverty and income distribution in Britain 1979–89. In I. Taylor (Ed.), *The social effects of free market policies: An international text* (pp. 29–48). London: Harvester Wheatsheaf.

Walker, A. (1991a). Thatcherism and the new politics of old age. In J. Myles & J. Quadagno (Eds.), *States, labor markets and the future of old age policy*. Philadelphia: Temple University Press.

Walker, A. (1991b). The relationship between the family and the state in the care of older people. *Canadian Journal on Aging, 10*(2), 94–112.

Wall, R. (1984). Residential isolation of the elderly: A comparison over time. *Ageing and Society, 4,* 483–503.

Wall, R. (1990, April). *Inter-generational relations in the European past*. Paper presented to the Annual Conference of the British Sociological Association.

Watkins, S. C., Menken J. A., & Bongaarts, J. (1987). Demographic foundations of family change. *American Sociological Review, 52,* 346–358.

Weber, M. (1952). *The Protestant ethic and the spirit of Capitalism* (T. Parsons, Trans.). New York: Charles Scribner's Sons. (Original work published 1920)

Weitzman, L. (1985). *The divorce revolution*. New York: Free Press.

Williams, N. (1990). The Mexican American family: Tradition and change. In L. T. Reynolds (Ed.), *The Reynolds Series in Sociology*. Dix Hills, NY: General Hall.

Williamson, J. B., Evans, L., & Powell, L. A. (1982). *The politics of aging: Power and policy*. Springfield, IL: Charles C. Thomas.

Wilson, R. R. (1977). *Genealogy and history in the biblical world*. New Haven, CT: Yale University Press.

Wolfson, M. (1986). Stasis and change in income inequality in Canada, 1965–83. *Review of Income and Wealth, 32*(4), 337–370.

Zarit, S. H., Anthony, C. R., & Boutselis, M. (1987). Interventions with caregivers of dementia patients: Comparison of two approaches. *Psychology and Aging, 2,* 225–232.

Zimmer, L. (1987). "Who will bury me?": The plight of childless elderly among the Gende. *Journal of Cross-Cultural Gerontology, 2,* 61–77.

Biographical Sketches of the Contributors

W. Andrew Achenbaum teaches history at the University of Michigan, Ann Arbor and is Deputy Director of its Institute of Gerontology. His research focuses on the history of the elderly in the United States. He currently is completing a book on the history of gerontology. Among his numerous publications are *Images of Old Age in America, 1790 to the Present* and *Social Security: Visions and Revisions*.

Vern L. Bengtson is AARP/University Professor of Gerontology and Sociology at the University of Southern California, and Past President of the Gerontological Society of America. His publications include *The Social Psychology of Aging, Youth, Generations, and Social Change, Grandparenthood, The Measurement of Intergenerational Relations, Emergent Theories of Aging,* and *The Course of Later Life*.

Fay Lomax Cook is Associate Professor of Human Development and Social Policy and Associate Director of the Center for Urban Affairs and Policy Research at Northwestern University. She is the author or co-author of three books including, most recently, *Support for the American Welfare State: The Views of Congress and the Public* and of numerous articles and book chapters on aging and social policy, agenda setting, and public opinion. She is a member of the National Academy of Social Insurance and serves on the North American Program Committee for the 1993 International Congress of Gerontology.

Eileen M. Crimmins is Professor of Gerontology and Sociology at the University of Southern California where she is Director of Training in the Demography of Aging. Her research focuses on trends in health among the older population. This research has been supported by the National Institutes on Aging. Recently, she has undertaken a project supported by the Milbank Memorial Fund that examines the interaction of health change, residential mobility, and change in social support among older Americans.

Richard A. Easterlin is Professor of Economics at the University of Southern California and author of *Birth and Fortune: The Impact of Numbers on Personal Welfare.* He is a former president of the Population Association of America and the Economic History Association.

Nancy Foner is Professor of Anthropology at the State University of New York, Purchase. She is the author of *Status and Power in Rural Jamaica: A Study of Educational and Political Change, Jamaica Farewell: Jamaican Migrants in London,* and *Ages in Conflict: A Cross-Cultural Perspective on Inequality Between Old and Young,* and editor of *New Immigrants in New York.* Her forthcoming book, *The Caregiving*

Dilemma: Work in an American Nursing Home, is based on recent research in a New York nursing home.

Diane J. Macunovich is Assistant Professor of Economics at Williams College and a Research Associate at the RAND Corporation. She is currently the Andrew W. Mellon Visiting Scholar at the Population Reference Bureau. Her research is concerned with birth cohort size effects on fertility and in the labor market.

Joanne Gard Marshall is Associate Professor in the Faculty of Library and Information Science at the University of Toronto where she teaches courses in Online Information Retrieval and Health Science Information Resources. Professor Marshall also holds cross appointments in the Department of Health Administration and the Centre for Health Promotion at the University. Her research interests include the adoption and use of information services.

Victor W. Marshall is Director of the Centre for Studies of Aging and Professor of Behavioral Science at the University of Toronto. He also serves as Network Director of CARNET: The Canadian Aging Research Network. His current research interests focus on work and aging, long-term-care issues, health promotion, and theoretical developments in the sociology of aging.

Bernice L. Neugarten is the Rothschild Distinguished Scholar at the Center on Aging, Health and Society and Chapin Hall Center for Children, the University of Chicago. She is also Professor Emeritus, Department of Behavioral Sciences there. She has published widely in the areas of adult development and aging, the sociology of age, and social policy. She has received both the Brookdale Award and the Sandoz International Prize for her research in gerontology.

Jill Quadagno is Professor of Sociology at Florida State University where she holds the Mildred and Claude Pepper Chair in Social Gerontology. Her most recent books include *The Transformation of Old Age Security: Class and Politics in the American Welfare State* and the edited volume *States, Labor Markets and the Future of Old Age Policy.*

John W. Riley, Jr., is a Consulting Sociologist, living in Maryland and Maine. He has taught at Marietta, Wellesley, Harvard, and Rutgers; served with the Psychological Warfare Division in World War II and Korea; and "retired" from The Equitable as Senior Vice President. He has held many professional offices: President of the American Association for Public Opinion Research, Sociological Research Association, and District of Columbia Sociological Society. Author of numerous books and articles, he frequently publishes on age-related issues with his wife, Matilda White Riley.

Matilda White Riley is Senior Social Scientist, National Institutes on Aging (NIA)/ National Institutes of Health; formerly Associate Director at NIA for

Social and Behavioral Research; Professor Emerita at Rutgers University and Bowdoin College; and past President of the American Sociological Association (ASA). Among her recent honors are: Meritorious Rank Award from the President of the United States, the Distinguished Career Award for the Practice of Sociology (ASA), and the Kent Award (Gerontological Society of America). Among her many publications are the three-volume *Aging and Society* and (with John W. Riley, Jr.) *The Quality of Aging: Strategies for Intervention.*

Alice S. Rossi is Harriet Martineau Professor Emeritus of Sociology at the University of Massachusetts (Amherst). She is co-author (with Peter H. Rossi) of *Of Human Bonding: Parent-Child Relations Across the Life Course,* editor of *Gender and the Life Course,* co-editor of *Parenting Across the Life Span: Biosocial Dimensions,* and author of numerous journal articles on gender, adult development, family and kinship, and the status of women. She is currently a member of a MacArthur Foundation research network on mid-life development, editing a volume on sexuality across the life course, and writing a monograph on menstruation and menopause.

David W. Thomson, Senior Lecturer in History, Massey University, New Zealand, has a Ph.D. from Cambridge University. He has been a member of the Aging Unit, Cambridge Group for the History of Population and Social Structure, since 1985. He is the author of numerous papers on old age in 19th and 20th century societies, and most recently of *Selfish Generations? The Ageing of New Zealand's Welfare State.*

Fernando M. Torres-Gil is Professor of Social Welfare at the University of California, Los Angeles and Adjunct Professor of Gerontology at the University of Southern California. His research interests are in the areas of social policy, politics of aging, minority aging, health care, and long-term care. Among his scholarly publications is a recent book on *The New Aging: Politics and Change in America.*

Judith Treas is Professor and Chair of Sociology at the University of California, Irvine. The author of numerous chapters and articles on families and aging, she is now engaged in a study of 1980–1990 changes in the older population of the United States.

Maris A. Vinovskis is Professor of History and a Research Scientist at the Institute for Social Research at the University of Michigan. He has recently co-authored (with Gerald Moran) *Religion, Family, and the Life Course: Explorations in the Social History of Early America.* Currently he is on leave from the University of Michigan and serves as the Research Advisor to the Assistant Secretary, U.S. Department of Education.

Alan Walker is Professor of Social Policy and Chairperson of the Department of Sociological Studies at the University of Sheffield, England. He has been researching and writing in the field of social gerontology for some twenty years and is closely associated with the Political Economy of Ageing paradigm. His principal research interests are aging and social policy, intergenerational relations, family and social care, pensions and the living standards of other people, the politics of aging, and the employment of older workers. His books include *Ageing and Social Policy* and *The Caring Relationship*.

Wei Wang is a graduate student in sociology at the University of Southern California and is engaged in research on older people in China.

Index

AAB (American Association of
Boomers), 247
Academia, 123–126
AGE (Americans for Generational
Equity)
founding of, 120, 138, 247
generational equity and, 12
intergenerational equity and,
120, 136–137, 138, 139
policymakers and, 137, 247
political influence of, 100
Age cohorts
in conflict, 99
definition of, 10
dichotomization of social world
and, 162
economic status and
average economic status
trends, 73–74
children and earners per
household, 79
data on, 71–72
earning trends, 72–73
income distribution trends,
78
living arrangements, 74–78
educational funding and
children in family, 56, 60–61
education, 57, 59
educational facility, 61
gender, 57
income, 59
multiple classification
analysis (MCA) on, 56–57,
60, 61
political party, 59–60

population size of
community, 60
problem of, 45–46
race, 57
region of residence, 60
survey on, 53–55
kin connections and
age stratification system,
174–176
change, 178–180
structure, 176–178
normative obligations in
parent-child relationships
and, 203–205
social program funding and,
62
Age consciousness, 251
Aged (*See* Elderly; Generational
relations)
Age-gapped intergenerational
structure, 16
Age group conflicts
economic status and, 82–83
factors influencing, 8, 99
future prospects for, 19–20,
21–22
increase in, 217
interest group politics and,
247–248
at macrosocial level of social
structure, 7, 12–13
at microsocial level of social
structure, 7, 13–19
modern state and
beneficiaries, 230–235
taxpayers, 222–227

303